KB033795

# A Summer to Die

LOIS LOWRY

ISBN 979-11-91343-89-2   14740

Longtail Books

# 1

It was Molly who drew the line.

She did it with **chalk**—a fat piece of white chalk left over from when we lived in town, had **sidewalks**, and used to play hopscotch,★ back when we both were younger. That piece of chalk had been around for a long time. She **fished** it out of a little **clay** dish that I had made in last year's **pottery** class, where it was **lying** with a piece of **string** and a few paper clips and a battery that we weren't quite sure was

---

★ hopscotch 땅따먹기. 어린이 놀이의 하나로 바닥에 그려진 놀이판을 뛰어넘으면서 노는 놀이.

dead.

She took the chalk and drew a line right on the **rug**. Good thing it wasn't a **fuzzy** rug or it never would have worked; but it was an old, **worn**, **leftover** rug from the dining room of our other house: very **flat**, and the chalk made a perfect white line across the blue—and then, while I watched in **amazement** (because it was unlike Molly, to be so angry), she kept right on drawing the line up the wall, across the wallpaper with its blue flowers. She stood on her desk and drew the line up to the **ceiling**, and then she went back to the other side of the room and stood on her bed and drew the line right up to the ceiling on that wall, too. Very **neat**ly. Good thing it was Molly who drew it; if I had tried, it would have been a **mess**, a **wavy** line and off center. But Molly is very neat.

Then she put the chalk back in the dish, sat down on her bed, and picked up her book. But before she started to read again, she looked over at me (I was still standing there amazed, not believing that she had drawn the line at all) and said, "There. Now be as much of a **slob** as you want, only keep your mess on your side. *This* side is *mine.*"

When we lived in town we had our own rooms, Molly and I. It didn't really make us better friends, but it gave us a chance to **ignore** each other more.

Funny thing about sisters. Well, about us, anyway;

Dad says it's unacademic to generalize. Molly is prettier than I am, but I'm smarter than Molly. I want with my whole being to *be* something someday; I like to think that someday, when I'm grown up, people everywhere will know who I am, because I will have accomplished something important—I don't even know for sure yet what I want it to be, just that it will be something that makes people say my name, Meg Chalmers, with respect. When I told Molly that once, she said that what *she* wants is to have a different name when she grows up, to be Molly Something Else, to be Mrs. Somebody, and to have her children, lots of them, call her "Mother," with respect, and that's all she cares about. She's content, waiting for that; I'm restless, and so impatient. She's sure, absolutely sure, that what she's waiting for will happen, just the way she wants it to; and I'm so uncertain, so fearful my dreams will end up forgotten somewhere, someday, like a piece of string and a paper clip lying in a dish.

Being both determined and unsure at the same time is what makes me the way I am, I think: hasty, impetuous, sometimes angry over nothing, often miserable about everything. Being so well sorted out in her own goals, and so assured of everything happening the way she wants and expects it to, is what makes Molly the way she is: calm, easygoing, self-confident, downright smug.

Sometimes it seems as if, when our parents created us, it took them two tries, two daughters, to get all the qualities of one whole, well-**put**-together person. More often, though, when I think about it, I feel as if they got those qualities on their first try, and I **represent** the leftovers. That's not a good way to feel about yourself, especially when you know, down in the part of you where the **ambition** is, where the dreams are, where the **logic** lies, that it's not true.

The hardest part about living in the same room with someone is that it's hard to keep anything hidden. I don't mean the **unmatched**, dirty socks or the fourteen **crumple**d papers with tries at an unsuccessful **poem** on them, although those are the things that upset Molly, that made her draw the line. I mean the parts of yourself that are private: the tears you want to **shed** sometimes for no reason, the thoughts you want to think in a **solitary** place, the words you want to say aloud to hear how they sound, but only to yourself. It's important to have a place to close a door on those things, the way I did in town.

The house in town is still there, and it's still our house, but there are other people living in it now, which does something terrible to my stomach when I think about it too much. My room had red-and-white-checked wallpaper; there is a place in one corner, by a window, where I played three games of tick-tack-toe* on the wallpaper with a Magic

Marker.✳ Cats' games,✳ all of them. I played against myself, so it didn't matter much, but it's funny, how you want to win anyway.

The university clock in its high **brick** tower was just across the street from the house; at night, when I was supposed to be sleeping, I could hear it **strike** each hour, the **chime**s coming clear and well **defined** as **silhouettes** from the **ivied** circle of the numbered **face** in the dark. That's one of the things I miss most, living out here in the country, out here **in the middle of nowhere**. I like quiet. And it sure is quiet here. But there are times when I lie awake at night and all I can hear is Molly breathing in the bed next to mine; cars **seldom** go past on this road, and no clocks strike, nothing **measure**s the moments. There is just this quiet, and it seems lonely.

The quiet is why we came. The university has given my dad just this year to finish his book. He worked on it for a while in the old house, shut in his **study**; but even though he was officially on leave from teaching, the students kept **stop**ping by. "I just thought I'd **drop in** for a minute to see Dr. Chalmers," they'd say, standing on the **porch**, looking

---

★ tick-tack-toe 삼목 놀이. 두 명이 번갈아가며 O와 X를 3×3 판에 써서 먼저 같은 글자가 가로, 세로, 혹은 대각선 상에 놓이게 하면 승리하는 놀이.
✳ Magic Marker (상표명) 매직펜.
✳ Cats' games tic-tac-toe 게임에서 승부를 내지 못하고 비겼을 때 이를 cat's game이라고 부르고 게임판에 커다랗게 알파벳 'C'를 적어둔다.

embarrassed. My mother would say, "Dr. Chalmers can't be **disturb**ed," and then my father's voice would call from upstairs, "Let them in, Lydia, I want to stop for coffee anyway."

So my mother would bring them in, and they would stay for hours, having coffee, talking to Dad, and then he would **invite** them for dinner, and Mother would add some **noodle**s to the casserole*, wash another **head of lettuce** for the salad, or quickly **peel** a few more **carrot**s for the **stew**. We would take hours eating, because everyone talked so much, and my father would open a bottle of wine. Sometimes it would be late at night before they left. I would be in bed by then, listening to the clock chime across the street as they said good-bye on the porch, **linger**ing to ask questions, to **exhaust** an **argument**, to laugh at another of my father's **anecdote**s. Then I would hear my parents come upstairs to bed, and I would hear my father say, "Lydia, I am *never* going to finish this book."

The title of the book is *The **Dialectic Synthesis** of **Irony***. When Dad announced that, very proud of it, at dinner one night, Mom asked, "Can you say that three times fast?" Molly and I tried, and couldn't, and it **broke** us **up**. Dad looked very **stern**, and said, "It is going to be a very

---

★ Casserole 식탁에 올리는 뚜껑 있는 찜냄비.

8

important book"; Molly said, "What is?" and he tried to say the title again, couldn't, and it broke him up, too.

He tried to explain to me once what the title means, but he gave up. Molly said *she* understood it very well. But Molly is **full of bull** sometimes.

It was at breakfast the Saturday morning before Thanksgiving* that Mom and Dad told us we were leaving the house in town. I had **figure**d that something was going on, because my mother had been on the phone all week, and my mother is not the type of woman who talks on the phone very much.

"We've found a house," Mom said, pouring more coffee for herself and Dad, "out in the country so that your father can have some peace and quiet. It's a lovely house, girls, built in 1840, with a big **fireplace** in the kitchen. It's on a **dirt road**, and surrounded by one hundred sixty acres* of woods and fields. When summer comes we'll be able to put in a vegetable garden—"

*Summer.* I guess Molly and I had been thinking the same thing, that she was talking about a month or so, maybe till after Christmas vacation. But *summer*. It was only November. We sat there like **idiot**s, with our mouths

---

★ Thanksgiving 추수감사절. 우리나라 추석에 해당하는 명절로, 첫 수확을 하느님께 바쳐 감사를 표한다는 의미를 담고 있다. 11월 넷째주 목요일로 이날에는 보통 칠면조(turkey) 요리를 해먹는다.
⚹ acre 에이커. 면적의 단위로 약 4046.8m², 또는 약 1,224평.

open. I had been *born* while we lived in the house in town, thirteen years before, and now they were talking about leaving it behind. I couldn't think of anything to say, which is not unusual for me. But Molly always thinks of things to say.

"What about school?" she asked.

"You'll go by bus, to the Macwahoc Valley **Consolidated** School.* It's a good school, and it's only about a twenty-minute bus ride."

"Can you say that three times fast?" asked Dad, **grin**ning. "Macwahoc Valley Consolidated School?" We didn't even try.

Consolidated school. I didn't even know what that meant. To be honest, it sounded to me as if the school needed a **laxative**. Anyway, school wasn't my main **concern**. I was thinking about my Thursday afternoon art class, which was just about to get into oils* after **umpteen** weeks on **watercolor**s, and my Saturday morning photography class, where my photograph of the clock tower at sunset had just been selected Best of the Week, **beating out** the eight others in the class, which were all taken by boys.

But I didn't even ask about my classes, about what

---

★ consolidated school 통합 학교. 이웃한 학군이 공동으로 세워 여러 학군의 학생들이 같이 다니는 학교.

＊ oils 유화물감. oil colors의 줄임말.

would happen to them when we moved to the country. Because I knew.

"Dad," **groan**ed Molly. "I've just made *cheerleader*."

Boy,* was that the wrong thing to say to my father.

He's proud of Molly, because she's pretty and all that, even though he always seems somewhat surprised by her, that **all of a sudden** since she turned fifteen, she has boyfriends and **stuff**. **Every now and then** he looks at her and shakes his head in a kind of **astonish**ment, and pride. But he has this thing about **priorities**, and when Molly said that, he set down his coffee cup very hard and looked at her with a **frown**.

"Cheerleading," he said, "does not have top priority."

And that was that. It was all decided, and there wasn't anything to argue or **fuss** about. It was too busy a time, anyway. We almost **skipped** Thanksgiving, except that there were students who couldn't go home for the vacation, and so five of them spent that Thursday with us, and Mom cooked a turkey. But most of the day we packed. The students helped to put books into boxes, and some of them helped Mom, packing dishes and kitchen things. I did all my packing alone that week. I cried when I **fitted** my new, unused box of oil paints—a gift for my thirteenth

---

★ boy 아, 이런, 맙소사, 놀람 등을 나타내는 감탄사로 우리가 흔히 알고 있는 '소년'이라는 의미가 아니니 주의하자.

birthday the month before—into a box, and I cried again when I packed my camera. But at least those things, the things I cared about most, were going with me. Molly had to give her blue and white cheerleading **outfit** to one of the **substitute** cheerleaders, a girl named Lisa Halstead, who **pretend**ed to be sad and **sympathetic**, but you could tell it was **phony**; she couldn't wait to get home and try on that **pleat**ed skirt.

And all of that was only last month. It seems like a hundred years ago.

Strange, how the age of a house makes a difference. That shouldn't surprise me, because certainly the age of a person makes a big difference, like with Molly and me. Molly is fifteen, which means that she puts on eyeshadow when Mom doesn't catch her at it, and she spends hours in front of the mirror **arranging** her hair different ways; she stands **sideways** there, too, to see what her figure looks like, and she talks on the phone every evening to friends, mostly about boys. It took her about two days to make friends in the new school, two days after that to have boyfriends, and the next week she was chosen as a substitute cheerleader.

Me, I'm only two years younger, and that seems to make such a difference, though I haven't **figured** out why. It's not only **physical**, although that's part of it. If I stand sideways in front of a mirror—which I don't **bother** doing—I **might**

**as well** be standing backwards, for all the difference it makes. And I couldn't begin to put on eyeshadow even if I wanted to, because I can't see without my glasses. Those are the physical things; the real difference seems to be that I don't care about those things. Will I, two years from now? Or do I care now, and pretend I don't, even to myself? I can't figure it out.

As for friends? Well, the first day at the consolidated school, when the first teacher said, "Margaret Chalmers" and I told him, "Would you call me Meg, please," a boy on the side of the classroom called out, "Nutmeg!*" Now, three weeks later, there are 323 people in the Macwahoc Valley Consolidated School who call me Nutmeg Chalmers. You know the old saying about with friends like that, who needs **enemies**?

But I was talking about the age of houses. As my mother had said, this house was built in 1840. That makes it almost one hundred and forty years old. Our house in town was fifty years old. The difference is that the house in town was big, with a million **closet**s and **stairway**s and windows and an **attic**, all sorts of places for **privacy** and escape: places where you could **curl up** with a book and no one would know you were there for hours. Places that were

---

★ Nutmeg 육두구. 보통 말려서 향신료로 쓰는 식물이다.

just mine, like the little alcove★ at the top of the attic stairs, where I **tack**ed my photographs and watercolors on the wall to make my own private gallery, and no one **bug**ged me about the **thumbtack** holes in the wall.

It's important, I think, to have places like that in your life, secrets that you share only by choice. I said that to Molly once, and she didn't understand; she said she would like to share everything. It's why she likes cheerleading, she said: because she can throw out her arms and a whole crowd of people **respond**s to her.

Here, in the country, the house is very small. Dad explained that it was built this way because it was so hard to keep it warm way back then. The ceilings are low; the windows are small; the **staircase** is like a tiny tunnel. Nothing seems to fit right. The floors **slant**, and there are wide spaces between the **pine** boards. If you close a door, it falls open again all on its own, when you're not looking. It doesn't matter much, the doors not closing, because there's no place for privacy anyway. Why bother to close the door to your room when it's not even your own room?

When we got here, I ran inside the empty house while the others were all still standing in the yard, trying to help the **moving van** get turned around in the **snowy driveway**.

---

★ alcove 알코브. 방 한쪽에 설치한 오목하게 들어간(凹) 장소. 침대, 책상, 서가 등을 놓고 원래 방과 독립적 소공간으로서 사용한다.

I went up the little flight of stairs,* looked around, and saw the three bedrooms: two big ones, and the tiny one in the middle, just off the narrow hall. In that room the ceiling was slanted almost down to the floor, and there was one window that looked out over the woods behind the house, and the wallpaper was yellow, very **fade**d and old but still yellow, with a tiny green leaf here and there in the pattern. There was just room for my bed and my desk and my **bookcase** and the few other things that would make it really mine. I stood for a long time by that one window, looking out at the woods. Across a field to the left of the house, I could see another house far away; it was empty, the outside unpainted, and the windows, some of them broken, black like dark eyes. The **rectangle** of the window in the little room was like the **frame** of a painting, and I stood there thinking how I would wake up each morning there, looking out, and each day it would change to a new kind of picture. The snow would get deeper; the wind would blow those last few leaves from the trees; there would be **icicle**s hanging from the edge of the **roof**; and then, in spring, things would **melt**, and change, and turn green. There would be rabbits in the field in the early morning.

---

★ flight of stairs 한 줄로 이어진 계단. 여기서 'flight'는 일반적으로 사용하는 '여행, 비행, 항공편'이 아니라 '층과 층 사이의 계단들, 층계'라는 의미이다. 'a flight of stairs'가 덩어리로 한 단어처럼 사용되니 알아두도록 하자.

Wild flowers. Maybe someone would come to live in that **abandon**ed house, and light would come from those dark windows at night, across the **meadow**.

Finally I went downstairs. My mother was in the empty living room, figuring out how to fit in the big **couch** from the other house. Dad and Molly were still outside, **sprinkling** salt on the driveway so that the moving men wouldn't **slip** on the snow.

"Mom," I said, "the little room is mine, isn't it?"

She stopped to think for a minute, remembering the upstairs of the new house. Then she put her arm around me and said, "Meg, the little room is for Dad's study. That's where he'll finish the book. You and Molly will share the big bedroom at the end of the hall, the one with the pretty blue-**flowered** wallpaper."

Mom always tries to make things right with **gesture**s: hugs, quick kisses blown across a room, **wave**s, winks, smiles. Sometimes it helps.

I went back upstairs, to the big room that wasn't going to be all mine. From the windows I could still see the woods, and part of the empty house across the field, but the view was partly **block**ed by the big gray falling-down **barn** that was **attach**ed to our house on the side. It wasn't the same. I'm pretty good at making the best of things, but it wasn't the same.

Now, just a month later, just two days before Christmas, the house looks lived in. It's warm, and full of the sound of fires in the fireplaces, the sound of Dad's **typewriter** upstairs, and full of winter smells like wet boots drying, and **cinnamon**, because my mother is making **pumpkin** pies and gingerbread.* But now Molly, who wants more than anything to throw out her arms and share, has drawn that line, because I can't be like those crowds who smile at her, and share back.

---

★ gingerbread 생강(ginger)이 들어간 빵(bread)이나 쿠키. 크리스마스 음식 중 하나다.

## 2

Good things are happening here. That surprises me a little. When we came, I thought it would be a place where I would just have to **stick it out**, where I would be lonely for a year. Where nothing would ever happen at all.

Now good things are happening to all of us. Well, it's hard to tell with my mother; she's the kind of person who always enjoys everything anyway. Molly and Mom are a lot **alike**. They get so **enthusiastic** and excited that you think something wonderful has happened; then, when you stop to think about it, nothing has really happened at all. Every morning, for example, Mom puts fresh **birdseed** in the bird **feeder** outside the kitchen window. Two minutes later the first bird **stops by** for breakfast, and Mom jumps up, says "Shhh" and goes to look, and you forget that 400 birds were there the day before. Or a plant in the kitchen gets a new leaf and she almost sends out birth **announcement**s. So it always seems as if good things are happening to Mom.

Dad is more like me; he waits for the truly good things, as if getting excited about the little ones might keep the big ones from coming. But the book is going well for Dad, and he says it was coming here that did it.

He goes into the little room each morning, closes the door, and sets a **brick** against it so that it won't fall open while he's working. He's still there when Molly and I get home from school at four, and Mom says he doesn't come out all day, except **every now and then** when he appears in the kitchen and pours himself a cup of coffee without saying a word, and goes back upstairs. Like a **sleepwalker**, Mom says. We can hear the **typewriter** going full speed; every now and then we hear him **rip up** or **crumple** a piece of paper, and then roll a fresh one into the typewriter and start **clatter**ing away again. He talks to himself, too— we can hear him **mutter**ing behind the door—but talking to himself is a good sign. When he's silent, it means things aren't going well, but he's been talking to himself behind

20

the door to the little room ever since we came here.

Last night he came to dinner looking very **preoccupied**, but smiling to himself now and then. Molly and I were talking about school, and Mom was telling us how she had decided to make a patchwork quilt★ while we're living in the country, using **scrap**s of **material** from all the clothes Molly and I wore when we were little. We started remembering our old dresses—we don't even *wear* dresses anymore; I don't think I've worn anything but jeans for two years. Molly said, "Remember that **yucky** dress I used to have that had butterflies on it? The one I wore at my sixth birthday party?" I didn't remember it, but Mom did; she laughed, and said, "Molly, that was a *beautiful* dress. Those butterflies were hand-**embroider**ed! It's going into a special place on the quilt!"

Dad hadn't heard a word, but he'd been sitting there with a half-smile on his face. **All of a sudden** he said, "Lydia, I really **have a grip on** Coleridge!*" and he jumped up from his chair, leaving half a piece of apple pie, and went back to the **study**, taking the stairs two at a time. We could hear the typewriter start up again.

Mom looked after him with that special **fond** look she

---

★ patchwork quilt 조각 누비이불. patchwork로 만든 quilt. patchwork는 조각난 천을 이어 붙여 1장의 천을 만드는 수예로 한국의 조각보와 비슷하다. quilt는 두 겹의 천 사이에 솜을 넣고 줄이 지게 바느질하여 만든 이불이나 쿠션, 혹은 그렇게 만드는 기법을 지칭한다.

＊ Coleridge 콜리지(Samuel Taylor Coleridge). 영국의 시인이자 비평가.

gives to things that are slightly foolish and very **lovable**. She smiles, and her eyes look as if they can see back into her memory, into all the things that have gone into making a person what they are. With Dad, I think she looks back to when she knew him as a student, when he must have been serious and **forgetful** and very kind, the way he still is, but young, which he isn't anymore. With me, I know her memories go back to all sorts of **frustration**s and **confusion**s, because I was never an "easy" child; I remember that I questioned and argued and **rage**d. But her look, for me, is still that same **caring** look that **goes beyond** all that. As for Molly? I've seen her look at Molly that way, too, and it's a more **complicated** thing; I think when Mom looks at Molly, her memories go back farther, to her own self as a girl, because they are so alike, and it must be a **puzzling** thing to see yourself growing up again. It must be like looking through the wrong end of a **telescope**—seeing yourself young, far away, on your own; the distance is too great for the **watcher**, really, to do anything more than watch, and remember, and smile.

Molly has a boyfriend. Boys have *always* liked Molly. When she was little, boys in the **neighborhood** used to come to repair her bike; they **loan**ed her their skate keys,*

---

★ skate key 스케이트날을 조이거나 푸는데 사용하는 일종의 드라이버.

brought her home when she **skin**ned her knees and waited, anxious, while she got a Band-Aid;* they shared their trick-or-treat candy* with Molly at Halloween.* When I was down to the **dreg**s in my paper bag, two weeks later, down to eating the **wrinkle**d apples in the bottom, Molly always had Mounds bars* left, gifts from the boys on the **block**.

How could boys *not* like a girl who looks the way she does? I've **gotten used to** Molly's looks because I've lived with her for thirteen years. But every now and then I **glance** at her and see her as if she were a stranger. One night recently she was sitting in front of the fire doing her homework, and I looked over because I wanted to ask her a question about negative numbers.* The light from the fire was on her face, all gold, and her blond hair was falling down across her **forehead** and in **wave**s around her cheeks and onto her shoulders. For a second she looked just like a picture on a Christmas card we had gotten from friends in Boston; it was almost **eerie**. I **held my breath** when I looked at her for that moment, because she looked so beautiful. Then she saw me watching her, and **stuck her**

---

★ Band-Aid 반창고. 일회용 반창고의 대표적인 상표명이기도 하다.
✳ trick-or-treat candy 할로윈에 아이들이 집집마다 다니며 '과자(treat)를 주지않으면 장난 (trick)을 치겠다'고 말하며 받는 사탕과 과자.
✱ Halloween 10월 31일 밤에 행하는 서양의 연례 행사로, 오늘날에는 미국 어린이들의 축제로 유명하다. 밤이 되면 분장한 어린이들이 집집마다 다니며 과자를 얻어 간다.
✶ Mounds bar 허쉬(Hershey's) 초콜릿에서 만드는 초콜릿 바.
★ negative number [수학] 음수(陰數).

**tongue out**, so that she was just Molly again, and familiar.

Boys, I think, probably see that part of her all the time, the beautiful part. And now suddenly this one boy, Tierney McGoldrick, who plays on the basketball team and is also president of the junior class,* is **hang**ing **around** her every minute in school. They're always together, and he lets her wear his school jacket with a big MV for Macwahoc Valley on the back. Of course, because we live out here in the middle of the woods, so far from everything, they can't actually date. Tierney's not old enough to drive, even if he wanted to drive all the way from where he lives; half the distance is a **dirt road** that's usually covered with snow. But he calls her up every single night. Molly takes the phone into the **pantry**, so that the long cord is **stretch**ed all across the kitchen, and my mother and I have to step over it while we're putting the dinner dishes away. Mom thinks it's quite funny. But then Mom has **curly** hair too, and was probably just as beautiful as Molly once. Maybe it's because I have straight **stringy** hair and glasses that the whole thing makes me feel a little sad.

So Dad has a grip on Coleridge, whatever that means, and Molly has a grip on Tierney McGoldrick. Me, I can't actually say I have a grip on anything, but good things have

---

★ junior 고등학교의 2학년생.

been happening to me here, too.

I have a new friend.

Just after New Year's, before school vacation ended, I went out for a walk. It was a walk I'd been **meaning to** take ever since we moved to the house, but things had been so busy, first with school and fixing up the house, then Christmas, then **settling down** after Christmas—I don't know, the time just never seemed right for it. I guess I like to think that it was **fate** that sent me out for this **particular** walk on this particular day. Fate, and the fact that the sun finally came out after weeks of grayness and snow.

I took my camera—the first time I'd taken my camera out since we came to the country—and went, all **bundled up** in my down jacket* and wearing heavy boots, down the dirt road beyond our house. I walked toward the **abandon**ed house that I could see across the fields from the upstairs window.

The snow kept me from getting close to it. The house is a long distance back from the road and of course the **driveway**, really a narrow road in its own right, hadn't been **plow**ed. But I stood, **stamp**ing my feet to keep warm, and looked at it for a long time. It reminds me of a very honest and kind **blind** man. That sounds **silly**. But it looks

---

★ down jacket 오리털을 속에 넣어 누빈 재킷.

honest to me because it's so **square** and straight. It's a very old house—I know that because of the way it's built, with a center **chimney** and all the other things I've learned about from living in *our* old house—but its corners are all square like a man holding his shoulders straight. Nothing **sags** on it at all. It's a **shabby** house, though, with no paint, so that the old boards are all **weather**ed to gray. I guess that's why it seems kind, because it doesn't mind being poor and paintless; it even seems to be proud of it. Blind because it doesn't look back at me. The windows are empty and dark. Not **scary**. Just waiting, and thinking about something.

I took a couple of photographs of the house from the road and walked on. I know the dirt road ends a mile beyond our house, but I had never gone to the end. The school bus turns around in our driveway, and no other cars ever come down this road except for one **beat-up** truck now and then.

That same truck was parked at the end of the road, beside a tiny, **weatherbeaten** house that looked like a distant, poorer **cousin** of the one I'd passed\*. An **elderly** cousin, **frail** but very proud. There was smoke coming out of the chimney, and curtains in the two little windows on

---

★ 지금 이 집은 방금 지나온 집보다(the one I'd passed) 더 낡은 모습을 하고 있어서, 먼(distant) 친척 쯤 되는 더 가난한(poorer) 사촌(cousin) 같아 보였다고 재미있게 표현하고 있다. 'poor cousin'은 '앞서 언급한 것과 비슷하지만 더 열악한 것'을 지칭할 때 종종 사용된다.

26

either side of the door. A dog in the yard, who **thump**ed his tail against a **snowbank** when he saw me coming. And beside the truck—no, actually in the truck, or at least with his head inside it, under the **hood**, was a man.

"Hi," I called. It would have been silly to turn around and start walking home without saying anything, even though I've promised my parents all my life that I would never talk to strange men.

He lifted out his head, a gray head, with a bright red **woolen** cap on it, smiled—a nice smile—and said, "Miss Chalmers. I'm glad you've come to visit."

"Meg," I said **automatic**ally. I was puzzled. How did he know who I was? Our name isn't even on the mailbox.

"For Margaret?" he asked, coming over and shaking my hand, or at least my **mitten**, leaving a **smear** of **grease** on it. "Forgive me. My hands are very dirty. My battery dies in this cold weather."

"How did you know?"

"How did I know Meg for Margaret? Because Margaret was my wife's name; therefore, one of my favorite names, of course. And I called her Meg at times, though no one else did."

"They call me Nutmeg at school. I bet no one ever called your wife Nutmeg."

He laughed. He had beautiful blue eyes, and his face

moved into a new pattern of wrinkles when he laughed. "No," he admitted, "they didn't. But she wouldn't have minded. Nutmeg was one of her favorite **spice**s. She wouldn't have made an apple pie without it."

"What I meant, though, when I said, 'How did you know?' was how did you know my name was Chalmers?"

He **wipe**d his hands on a **greasy rag** that was hanging from the door handle of the truck. "My dear, I **apologize**. I have not even introduced myself. My name is Will Banks. And it's much too cold to stand out here. Your **toe**s must be **numb**, even in those boots. Come inside, and I'll make us each a cup of tea. And I'll tell you how I know your name."

I briefly **envision**ed myself telling my mother, "So then I went in his house," and I briefly envisioned my mother saying, "You went in his *house?*"

He saw me **hesitate**, and smiled. "Meg," he said, "I'm seventy years old. **Thoroughly harmless**, even to a beautiful young girl like you. Come on in and keep me **company** for a bit, and get warm."

I laughed, because he knew what I was thinking, and very few people ever know what I'm thinking. Then I went in his house.

What a surprise. It was a tiny house, and very old, and looked on the outside as if it might fall down any minute.

For that matter, his truck was also very old, and looked as if *it* might fall down any minute. And Mr. Banks himself was old, although he didn't appear to be **fall**ing **apart**.

But inside, the house was beautiful. Everything was perfect, as if it were a house I'd imagined, or dreamed up with a set of paints. There were only two rooms on the first floor. On one side of the little front hall was the living room: the walls were painted white, and there was an **oriental rug** on the floor, all **shade**s of blues and reds. A big **fireplace**, with a painting that was a real painting, not a print, hanging over the **mantel**. A pewter **pitcher**⃰ standing on a **polish**ed table. A large **chest** of **drawer**s with bright brass handles⃰. A wing chair⃰ that was all done in needlepoint⃰—all done by hand, I could tell, because my mother does needlepoint sometimes. Sunlight was pouring in the little windows, through the white curtains, making patterns on the rug and chairs.

On the other side of the hall was the kitchen. That's where Mr. Banks and I went, after he had shown me the living room. A wood **stove** was burning in the kitchen, and

---

⭐ pewter pitcher 은회색 빛깔을 띠는 백랍 주전자. 백랍(pewter)은 주석과 납의 합금이다.
⃰ brass handles 놋쇠(황동) 손잡이. 놋쇠(brass)는 구리와 아연을 섞은 합금으로 노란색 빛깔을 띤다.
⃰ wing chair 안락의자의 일종으로 등받이 양쪽에 기대는 부분이 날개같이 높게 올라와 달려있다.
⃰ needlepoint 캔버스천에 바늘로 수를 놓는 자수법.

a copper **kettle**\* sat on top of it, steaming. A round **pine** table was **laid** with **woven** blue mats, and in the center of it a blue and white bowl held three apples like a still life.\* Everything was **scrub**bed and shiny and in the right place.

It made me think of a song that we sang in **kindergarten**, when we sat at our desks and folded our hands. "We're all in our places with bright shiny faces," we used to sing. I could hear the words in my mind, the little voices of all those five-year-olds, and it was a good memory; Mr. Banks' house was like that, a house warm with memories, of things in their places, and smiling.

He took my jacket and hung it up with his, and poured tea into two thick **pottery** mugs. We sat at the table, in pine chairs that **gleam**ed almost yellow from a **combination** of old wood, polish, and sunlight.

"Is yours the little room at the top of the stairs?" he asked me.

How did he know about the little room? "No," I explained. "I wanted it to be. It's so perfect. You can see the other house across the field, you know"—he nodded; he knew "—but my father needed that room. He's writing a book. So my sister and I have the big room together."

"The little room was mine," he said, "when I was a

---

★ copper kettle 적갈색 빛깔이 도는 구리(copper) 주전자(kettle).
\* still life 정물화.

small boy. Sometime when your father isn't working there, go in and look in the **closet**. On the closet floor you'll find my name **carve**d, if no one's **refinish**ed the floor. My mother **spank**ed me for doing it. I was eight years old at the time, and I'd been shut in my room for being **rude** to my older sister."

"You lived in my house?" I asked in surprise.

He laughed again. "My dear Meg," he said, "*you* live in *my* house.

"My grandfather built that house. Actually, he built the one across the field, first. Then he built the other one, where you live. In those days families stuck together, of course, and he built the second house for his sister, who never married. Later he gave it to his oldest son—my father—and my sister and I were both born there.

"It became my house when I married Margaret. I took her there to live when she was a **bride**, eighteen years old. My sister had married and moved to Boston.* She's dead now. My parents, of course, are **gone**. And Margaret and I never had children. So there's no one left but me. Well, that's not entirely true—there's my sister's son, but that's another story.

"Anyway, there's no one left here on the land but me.

---

★ Boston 보스턴. 미국 Massachusetts 주의 중심 도시.

There were times, when I was young, when Margaret was with me, when I was **tempt**ed to leave, to take a job in a city, to make a lot of money, but—" He lit his **pipe**, was quiet for a minute, looking into the past.

"Well, it was my grandfather's land, and my father's, before it was mine. Not many people understand that today, what that means. But I *know* this land. I know every rock, every tree. I couldn't leave them behind.

"This house used to be the **hired man**'s **cottage**. I've fixed it up some, and it's a good little house. But the other two houses are still mine. When the taxes went up, I just couldn't afford to keep them going. I moved here after Margaret died, and I've **rent**ed the family houses whenever I come across someone who has reason to want to live in this **wilderness**.

"When I heard your parents were looking for a place, I offered the little house to them. It's a perfect place for a writer—the **solitude stimulate**s imagination, I think.

"Other people come now and then, thinking it might be a cheap place to live, but I won't rent to just anyone. That's why the big house is empty now—the right family hasn't come along."

"Do you get lonely here?"

He finished his tea and set the cup down on the table. "No. I've been here all my life. I miss my Margaret, of course. But I have Tip"—the dog looked up at his name, and thumped his tail against the floor—"and I do some **carpentry** in the village now and then, when people need me. I have books. That's all I need, really.

"Of course," he smiled, "it's nice to have a new friend, like you."

"Mr. Banks?"

"Oh please, please. Call me Will, the way all my friends do."

"Will, then. Would you mind if I took your picture?"

"My dear," he said, **straighten**ing his shoulders and buttoning the top button of his **plaid** shirt. "I would be **honor**ed."

The light was coming in through the kitchen window onto his face: soft light now; it had become late afternoon, when all the **harsh** shadows are gone. He sat right there, smoked his pipe, and talked, and I finished the whole roll of film, just shooting quickly as he **gestured** and smiled. All those times when I feel **awkward** and **inept**—all those times are **made up for** when I have my camera, when I can look through the viewfinder★ and feel that I can control the focus and the light and the **composition**, when I can capture what I see, in a way that no one else is seeing it. I

---

★ viewfinder 뷰파인더. 사진사가 사진을 찍기 위해 혹은 촛점을 맞추기 위해 들여다 보는 사진가의 장치.

felt that way while I was taking Will's picture.

I **unload**ed the **exposed** film and carried it home in my pocket like a secret. When I looked back from the road, Will was by his truck again, waving to me; Tip was back by his snowbank, thumping his tail.

And deep, way deep inside me somewhere was something else that kept me warm on the walk home, even though the sun was going down and the wind was coming over the piles of snow on either side of the road, blowing **sting**ing powder into my eyes. It was the fact that Will Banks had called me beautiful.

# 3

February is the worst month, in New England.* I think so, anyway. My mother doesn't agree with me. Mom says April is, because everything turns to mud in April; the snow **melt**s, and things that were **buried** all winter—dog **mess**es, lost **mitten**s, beer bottles **toss**ed from cars— all reappear, still partly **frozen** into icy mixtures that are half the gray remains of old snow and half the brown beginnings of mud. Lots of the mud, of course, ends up on

★ New England 메인, 뉴햄프셔, 버몬트, 매사추세츠, 로드아일랜드, 코네티컷의 6개 주를 포함하는 미국 북동부 지역을 지칭하는 말.

the kitchen floor, which is why my mother hates April.

My father, even though he always **recite**s a **poem** that begins "April is the **cruel**est month" to my mother when she's **scrub**bing the kitchen floor in the spring, agrees with me that it's February that's worst. Snow, which was fun in December, is just boring, dirty, and **downright** cold in February. And the same sky that was blue in January is just nothing but white a month later—so white that sometimes you can't tell where the sky ends and the land begins. And it's cold, **bitter** cold, the kind of cold where you just can't go outside. I haven't been to see Will, because it's too cold to walk a mile up the road. I haven't taken any pictures, because it's too cold to take off my mittens and **operate** the camera.

And Dad can't write. He goes in the little room and sits, every day, but the typewriter is quiet. It's almost noisy, the quietness, we are all so aware of it. He told me that he sits and looks out the window at all the whiteness and can't **get a grip on** anything. I understand that; if I were able to go out with my camera in the cold, the film wouldn't be able to **grip** the edges and corners of things because everything has **blend**ed so into the colorless, **stark** mass of February. For Dad, everything has blended into a mass without any edges in his mind, and he can't write.

I showed him the closet floor, where *William* is **carved** into the pine.

"Will Banks is a **fascinating** man," Dad said, **lean**ing back in his **scruffy** leather chair in front of the typewriter. He was having a cup of coffee, and I had tea. It was the first time I had visited him in the little room, and he seemed glad to have **company**. "You know, he's well educated, and he's a **master cabinetmaker**. He could have earned a **fortune** in Boston, or New York, but he wouldn't leave this land. People around here think he's a little crazy. But I don't know, I don't know."

"He's not crazy, Dad. He's nice. But it's too bad he has to live in that **teeny** house, when he owns both these bigger ones that were his family's."

"Well, he's happy there, Meg, and you can't argue with happiness. Problem is, there's a **nephew** in Boston who's going to make trouble for Will, I'm afraid."

"What do you mean? How can anyone make trouble for an old man who isn't **bother**ing anybody?"

"I'm not sure. I wish I knew more about law. Seems the nephew is the only relative he has. Will owns all this land, and the houses—they were left to him—but when he dies, they'll go to this nephew, his sister's son. It's valuable **property**. They may not look like much to you, Meg, but these houses are real **antique**s, the kind of things that a lot of people from big cities would like to buy. The nephew, apparently, would like to have Will **declared** what the law calls '**incompetent**'—which just means crazy. If he could do that, he'd have control over the property. He'd like to sell it to some people who want to build **cottage**s for tourists, and to turn the big house into an **inn**."

I stood up and looked out the window, across the field, to where the empty house was standing gray against the whiteness, with its **brick chimney** tall and straight against the sharp line of the **roof**. I imagined cute little blue **shutter**s on the windows, and a sign over the door that said "All Major Credit Cards Accepted." I **envision**ed a **parking lot**, filled with cars and campers from different states.

"They can't do that, Dad," I said. Then it turned into a question. "Can they?"

My father **shrug**ged. "I didn't think so. But last week the nephew called me, and asked if it were true, what he had heard, that the people in the village call Will '**Loony** Willie.'"

"'*Loony Willie*'? What did you say to him?"

"I told him I'd never heard anything so **ridiculous** in my life, and to stop bothering me, because I was busy writing a book that was going to change the whole history of **literature**."

That **broke** us both **up**. The book that was going to change the whole history of literature was **lying** in **stack**s all over my father's desk, on the floor, in at least a hundred

**crumple**d sheets of typing paper in the big wastebasket, and in two pages that he had made into paper airplanes and **sail**ed across the room. We laughed and laughed.

When I was able to stop laughing, I remembered something that I had wanted to tell my father. "You know, last month, when I visited Will, I took his picture."

"Mmmmm?"

"He was sitting in his kitchen, smoking his **pipe** and looking out the window, and talking. I shot a whole roll. And you know, Dad, his eyes are so bright, and his face is so alive, so full of memories and thoughts. He's interested in everything. I thought of that when you said Loony Willie."

"Could I see the pictures?"

I felt a little **silly**. "Well, I haven't been able to **develop** them yet, Dad. I can't use the darkroom★ at school because I have to catch the early bus to get home. It's just that I *remember* his face looking like that when I photographed him."

My father sat up straight in his chair very suddenly. "Meg," he said, "I have a *great* idea!" He sounded like a little boy. Once Mom told Molly and me that she didn't mind not having sons, because often Dad is like a little boy,

---

★ darkroom 암실. 사진 감광재료의 취급, 필름의 현상 · 확대 등의 처리를 하는 작업실.

and now I could see exactly what she meant. He looked as if he were ten years old, on a Saturday morning, with an exciting and probably impossible project in mind.

"Let's build a darkroom!" he said.

I could hardly believe it. "*Here?*" I asked.

"Why not? Now look, I don't know anything about photography. You'll be the **expert consultant**. But I *do* know how to build. And I need a little vacation from writing. Could I do it in a week?"

"Sure, I think so."

"What would you need?"

"A space, first of all."

"How about that little **storeroom** in the **passageway** between the house and the **barn**? That's big enough, isn't it?"

"Sure. But it's too cold, Dad."

"Aha. You're not thinking, Consultant. We need a **heater**." He turned to his desk, found a fresh sheet of paper, and wrote, "1. Heater." My father loves to make lists. "What next?"

"Let's see. There are already **shelves** in there. But I'd need a counter top* of some sort." He wrote that down.

"And special lights. They're called safelights. You know, so you won't **expose** the photographic paper accidentally."

---

★ counter top 주방용 조리대, 작업대.

"No problem. There's electricity out there. What else? You'll need lots of **equipment**, won't you? If you're going to have a darkroom, it **might as well** be the best darkroom around."

I **sigh**ed. I could already tell what the problem was going to be. But, as I said, my father loves making lists. **What the heck.** I started telling him everything a darkroom would need: an enlarger,* a timer, **trays**, **chemicals**, paper, developing tanks,* special **thermometers**, **filters**, a focuser.* The list grew very long and he started on a second sheet of paper. It was kind of fun, listing it, even though I knew it was just a dream. It was a dream I'd had for a long time, one that I'd never told anyone.

"Where can you get this kind of **stuff**?" he asked. I went to my room, picked out one of my photography magazines, and brought it back. We looked through the ads in the back pages: New York. California. Boston.

"Boston," he said **triumphant**ly. "**Terrific**. I have to go down there to see my publisher anyway; might as well do it this week." He wrote down the name and address of the company. "Now. How much is all of this going to cost?"

I started to laugh, even though I didn't really feel like

---

★ **enlarger** 사진 확대기. 사진 필름의 상을 확대(enlarge)하고 투영하여 인화지에 새기는 기계.
✳ **developing tank** 필름을 현상(develop)할 때 사용하는 빛이 통하지 않는 용기.
✳ **focuser** 암실에서 사진의 촛점(focus)을 맞추는 기계.

laughing. It was so **typical** of my father, that he didn't think of the **obvious** problem till last. We looked through the Boston company's price list, wrote the prices on my father's paper, and finally added them up. **His face fell**. Good thing I'd realized **all along** it was a dream; that made it less disappointing. Poor Dad; he'd thought it was real, and it took him by surprise that it wasn't.

We both kept smiling very hard, because neither of us wanted the other to be sad.

"Listen, Meg," he said slowly, folding the list up and putting it on a corner of his desk. "Sometimes when I'm sitting here working on the book, I come to a problem that seems **insurmountable**. When that happens, I just let it go for a while. I keep it in the back of my mind, but I don't *agonize* over it. Do you know what I mean?"

I nodded. I'm pretty good at not agonizing.

"So far," he explained, "all of those problems have **resolved** themselves. **Out of nowhere**, all of a sudden, the **solution**s appear. Now here's what I want you to do." He **tap**ped the folded darkroom list with his finger. "I want you to put this out of your mind for a while, but keep it somewhere in the back where your **subconscious** will be working on it."

"Okay," I agreed.

"And before long, the solution will come. I'm absolutely

sure of it. Probably soon, too, because *both* of our subconscious will be working."

I laughed. He was so sure, and I didn't believe it for a minute. "All right," I promised.

"Or would that be 'subconsciese'? The **plural**, I mean?"

"Dad," I said, picking up our empty cups to take them to the kitchen, "*you're* the English professor."

Mom was in the kitchen, sitting by the fireplace **stitch**ing on her quilt. She was so excited about that quilt, and it *was* pretty, what she had done so far. But Molly and I **cringe**d when we looked at it too closely, I suppose because it was full of memories; **let's face it**, some memories **are better off** forgotten, especially when you haven't lived far enough beyond them yet. There was the dress with the butterflies, which Molly always hated, right near the center. Near it was a blue-and-white-**striped** piece that I didn't want to be reminded of. It was the dress that I wore to my fifth birthday party, the day when I **threw up** all over the table, just after the cake was served. There was the pink with little white flowers, that I wore to Sunday School on Easter* when I was supposed to say a poem to a **roomful** of people, forgot every word of it, and cried instead, when I was maybe six. There was the blue **plaid** that Molly wore

---

★ Easter 부활절. 예수 그리스도의 부활을 기념하는 축일.

her first day in junior high,* when she didn't realize that every other girl would be wearing jeans. And there was a piece of my old Brownie uniform;* I hated Brownies, always spent my **due**s on candy before I got there, and was **scold**ed every week.

"What's that white piece with the **embroidery**?" I asked Mom. She really liked it when Molly and I took an interest in the quilt.

She turned the quilt around and held it toward the window so that she could see the piece I meant. Then her face got all **nostalgic**. "Oh," she said **affectionate**ly. "That's Molly's first bra."

"*What?*"

I hadn't even noticed Molly until she **burst out** with "*What?*" She was lying on a **couch** in the corner. (Old houses are **neat**, in many ways. How many houses have a couch in the kitchen?) Actually, it didn't surprise me that she was there. Molly's had the **flu** all of February, and she's kind of like a **fixture**, or a piece of furniture herself now, lying there with a box of Kleenex.*

In a way, it's fun having Molly sick, because she's home

---

★ junior high 중학교.

＊ Brownie uniform 걸스카웃의 유니폼. 걸스카웃은 나이에 따라 여러 단계로 나뉘는데 Brownie는 7~10세에 해당하는 단계이다. 다양한 활동을 하는데 그 중엔 이후 언급된 것처럼 캔디를 파는 활동도 있다.

＊ Kleenex 미국의 대표적인 휴지 상표.

44

all the time, instead of off with her friends after school and on weekends. We've been doing things we hadn't done since we were little, like playing Monopoly.★ It's fun to play with Molly, silly games like that, because she doesn't take them seriously. I build hotels all over everything, even on stupid old Baltic Avenue, and when she throws the **dice** and realizes she's going to land where I have hotels, she starts **giggling**. She moves her piece along, closer and closer, and laughs harder and harder till she gets there, and then sits him down, **thump**, by the hotel, and just starts counting out all her money. "You got me," she says. "I'm absolutely **wiped out**!" Then she hands over all her money, laughing, and says right away, "Let's play again."

I'm a terrible loser. I go around **mutter**ing "It isn't fair" after I lose. I thought about it once, about what makes the difference, when I was feeling stupid and childish because I had cried after I lost a game of gin rummy,※ and said, "You **cheat**ed!" to Molly, even though I knew she hadn't. I think it's because Molly has always won at important things, or the things that are important to her, like making cheerleader, and having the best-looking boyfriend; so the little things, like Monopoly games, don't matter to her.

---

★ Monopoly 한국의 부루마블 게임과 유사한 보드게임의 일종. 부동산을 사고 팔며 재산을 증식하며 가장 많은 돈을 가진 사람이 승자가 된다.
※ gin rummy 진 러미. 가지고 있는 패의 합계가 10점 혹은 그 이하일 때 서로 가진 패를 보여서 승부를 내는 카드놀이.

Maybe someday, if I succeed at something, I'll stop saying "It isn't fair" about everything else.

It's also a **nuisance**, Molly being sick. She's **grouchy**, which isn't like her, because she's missing school—which means missing Tierney McGoldrick, even though he calls every day—and because she worries about how she looks. She can't be feeling *too* bad, because she spends a lot of time in front of the mirror in our room, trying to fix her hair which has gotten kind of **scroungy** looking, and putting rouge* on her face, because it's so **pale**.

Sometimes, when Molly is **messing around** with a hairbrush and bobby pins,* making herself even more beautiful, which isn't necessary, I kind of wish that she would notice *my* hair and offer to do something about *it*. I can't quite get up the **nerve** to ask her to. I'm almost positive she wouldn't laugh at me, but I can't bring myself to take the chance.

"Molly, don't get up," sighed Mom, because Molly was about to **charge** across the room to **examine** the piece of her bra. "Your nose will start up again."

Molly's flu consists mainly of **nosebleed**s. Mom says that's because she's an **adolescent**; Mom says that about almost everything. The doctor from the village says it's

---

★ rouge 루즈, 립스틱.
＊ bobby pin 머리를 고정시키는 헤어핀의 일종.

because of the cold weather, which damages the **nasal membranes**.* Whichever it is, it's downright **messy**. Even though her side of our room is still **nasty** neat, the rug is **spatter**ed with Molly's **dumb** nosebleeds, which to my mind is a good deal more **disgusting** than anything I leave lying around on my side.

It was time for dinner anyway. Mom put the quilt away, which ended the **argument** they were about to have about the bra, and served pork chops* and applesauce* at the kitchen table. I had to move my salad plate over to the side to make room for Molly's box of Kleenex. Dad didn't say anything, even though he likes a **tidy**-looking table at dinner, because we've had a couple of unpleasant meals when Molly *didn't* bring her Kleenex.

It was a quiet meal, with Molly eating very carefully because of her nose, and Dad and I both a little **preoccupied** because it isn't all that easy to **tuck** something into your subconscious and keep it back there. Mom kept starting conversations that ended because nobody joined them. Finally she put down her fork, sighed, and said, "You know, much as I love this place, even in winter, I'll be glad

---

★ membrane [생물] 세포막.
＊ pork chop 돼지 갈비살 요리. 돼지 갈비에 소스를 발라 구워낸 요리.
＊ applesauce 사과 소스. 따로 먹기도 하고, 햄이나 돼지고기 등 주 요리와 같이 나오기도 한다.

when summer comes. You'll be feeling better about the book, Charles, because it'll be almost finished, and you girls can go to camp and you won't be so bored—"

"Camp," I said suddenly. "*Camp*." My mother **stare**d at me. Molly and I have gone to the same camp every summer since I was eight and she was ten.

"*Camp*," said my father suddenly, looking at me with a **grin** starting.

"How much does camp cost?" I asked my mother.

She **groan**ed **good-natured**ly. "Plenty," she said. "But don't worry about that all of a sudden. Your father and I have always felt it was important enough that we've kept the money put aside each month. You girls will be able to go to camp."

"Mom," I said slowly, "do I *have* to go to camp?"

She was **amaze**d. I've won the Best Camper Award for two years running for my age group. "Of course you don't have to go to camp, Meg. But I thought—"

"Lydia," announced my father. "I'm going to Boston tomorrow. I have to see my publisher, and I'm going to do some shopping. Meg and I are building a darkroom in the storeroom by the barn, if Will Banks doesn't mind. I'll call him tonight, Meg."

My mother was sitting there with a piece of **lettuce** on the end of her fork, shaking her head. She started to

48

laugh. "This family is absolutely **nuts**," she said. "I haven't the slightest idea what anyone is talking about. Molly, your nose."

Molly **grab**bed a piece of Kleenex and **clutch**ed her nose. From behind her Kleenex she said **haughtily**, "*I* don'd know what anyone is talking about either. Bud *I'm* going to camp, whether Meg does or nod."★

Then she giggled. Even Molly realized how silly she looked and sounded, talking from behind a **wad** of tissues. "Thad is," she added, "if by dose ever stobs **bleed**ing."

★ 코를 막고 이야기하느라 t와 p 발음 등을 제대로 하지 못하고 있다.

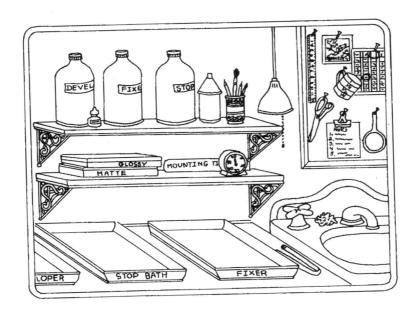

# 4

**All of a sudden** I know how Dad feels when he completes a chapter of the book. Or Mom, when one of her plants suddenly **blossom**s, or she finishes a new section of the quilt, and goes around with a smile on her face all day, even when no one's looking. I know how Molly must have felt when Tierney McGoldrick asked her to **go steady**, which is what happened two weeks ago. She came home wearing his tiny gold basketball on a chain around her neck, and was so **giggly** and cheerful and **bounce**d around so much that Mom finally had to tell her to calm down so that her newly normal nose wouldn't have a **relapse**.

Molly's nose had finally stopped **blee**ding at the beginning of March, which is about the same time that the sun came out after a month of gray cold; Dr. Putnam in the village said that **prove**d what he had thought, that the bad weather was causing her **nosebleed**s. Molly said she didn't care *what* caused them, she was just glad they were over, glad she could go back to school. Dad said he was sorry he hadn't bought **stock** in the Kleenex company.

I've hardly seen the sun at all because I've been in my darkroom. My darkroom! It's finished; it's all finished, and perfect. My father did it, just the way he said he would, and everything is just the way I dreamed of it. There is *nothing* that my father can't do.

The first pictures I **develop**ed were the ones of Will Banks. I'd had that roll of film **tuck**ed away in a **drawer** under my knee socks for almost two months. I was **scared stiff** when I developed it—scared that I had forgotten how, that I would do something wrong. But when I took the **strip** of negatives* out of the tank and held it to the light, there were two pictures of the old house across the field, and then thirty-four pictures of Will, looking at me in thirty-four different ways. I felt like a **genius**, like an artist.

---

★ negative 네거티브 필름. 음화. 사진으로 인화가 가능하게 현상된 필름. 아직 피사체와는 명암 관계가 반대인 상태로 사진 인화지에 확대 인화하면 우리가 알고 있는 사진이 된다.

When the negatives were dry, I printed them all on one sheet. It's hard to see, from the negatives, exactly how a print will look, so I **crossed my fingers** again when I developed the contact sheet* that would show me the real pictures for the first time. I stood there over the **tray** of developer and watched in the **dim** red light as the sheet changed from white to gray, and then saw the grays change to blacks and the **shade**s become the faces of Will; after two minutes, there he was, looking up at me from the tray, thirty-four of him, still tiny, but complete.

When it was ready I took it, still **drip**ping wet, into the kitchen and **laid** it on the counter beside the sink. Mom was there, **peel**ing potatoes, and she looked over, first curiously, and then as if she were really surprised.

"That's Will Banks!" she said.

"Of *course* it's Will Banks," I told her, grinning.

"Isn't he beautiful?"

She and I looked for a long time at all the tiny prints on the paper. There he was, lighting his pipe, and then smoking it, looking at me, half laughing. Then he **lean**ed back in his chair—I had blown the focus on that one a little, when he leaned back, out of the range of focus. I should have realized that. But then there he was, sitting up

---

*contact sheet 밀착 인화지. 현상을 하기 전에 필름 크기대로 작게 인화하는 것을 밀착 인화라고 한다.

straight, back in sharp focus again, looking at me with his eyes bright with interest; I remembered that he had been asking me questions about the camera, how I **determine**d what settings to use. Toward the end of the roll, his eyes were looking past me and far off, as if he were thinking about something in the distance. He had been telling me about a camera that he had once, that he still had, if he could find it in the **attic** of the little house. He had bought it in Germany, he said, after the Second World War,* when he was **station**ed there with the army. That surprised me.

"You were in the *army?*" I had asked him. The only people I knew who were in the army were boys who had **flunk**ed out of the university and didn't know what to do with themselves. Sometimes they would come back to see Dad in the house in town, with funny haircuts.

Will had laughed. "I was an **officer**," he said. "Would you believe it? People *saluted* me!" He put a **stern** look on his face and made a **rigid** salute. It was there, in the pictures.

Then he had laughed again, and **puff**ed on his pipe. "In those days we all joined the army. It seemed important, then. For me, the best part was coming home. It was in summer, when I came home, and Margaret had made ten

---

★ Second World War 제2차 세계대전.

blueberry pies, to **celebrate**. We ate blueberry pie for three days and then we **were sick of** blueberry pie and there were still six left over. I think she gave them away."

He had closed his eyes, remembering, still smiling. It was the last picture on the sheet. His eyes were closed, and the smoke from his pipe was a thin white line beside his head and circling across the top of the photograph.

I marked six of the tiny prints with a marking pen: my six favorites, each one a little different. Then I went back into the darkroom and spent the rest of the day **enlarging** those. I made two sets of them, so that I could give one of each to Will. I wondered if he'd be pleased. They were good pictures; I knew that, and both my parents had said so, too, and they never lie to me. But it must be a funny feeling, I think, to see your own face like that, caught by someone else, with all your feelings showing in it.

I took my own set of Will's pictures up to my room and taped them to the wall very neatly, with three above and three below. I've been trying to keep my half of the room neater ever since Molly drew the **chalk** line; every time my things start piling up and getting **messy**, Molly draws it over again, just to let me know it's still there.

She was on her bed, drawing pictures in her school notebook, when I went in and put the pictures on the wall.

"Mom'll kill you if you **tear** the wallpaper," she said,

**glancing** over at me.

"I know it." We both knew it wasn't true. My mother hardly ever gets mad. She **scold**s us sometimes, but the thought of Mom killing somebody is **ridiculous**. She doesn't even **step on** ants.

"Hey," said Molly suddenly, sitting up and looking over at the wall. "Those are really *good.*"

I looked over to see if she was joking, and she wasn't. She was looking at Will's pictures with interest, and I could tell that she meant it, that she thought they were good.

"I like that one there, where he's looking off in the distance and smiling," she decided, pointing to one in the bottom row.

"He was talking about his wife," I remembered, looking at the photograph with her.

Molly sat there for a minute, thinking. She looked pretty again, now that she was feeling better. Her hair had gotten its curl back. "Wouldn't it be great," she said slowly, "to be married to someone who felt that way about you, so that he smiled like that whenever he thought of you?"

I hadn't ever really thought about it **in such personal terms**. To be honest, I find the whole idea of marriage **intense**ly boring. But right at that moment I knew what Molly meant, and I could feel how important it was to her. "Tierney looks that way at you all the time," I told her.

56

"Really?"

"Sure. Sometimes when you don't even know he's looking at you. I saw him in **assembly** last Friday, looking over at you. Remember, you were sitting with the cheerleaders? He was watching you, and that's the way he looked, almost like Will is looking in the picture."

"*Really?*" Molly **curl**ed **up** on her bed and grinned. "I'm glad you told me that, Meg. Sometimes I don't know what's going on in Tierney's head at all. Sometimes it seems as if basketball is all he cares about."

"Well, he's only sixteen, Molly." All of a sudden I realized that I sounded like Mom, and I **giggle**d. So did Molly.

"Hey, look, Meg," she said, handing her notebook to me. "You're such a good artist, and I can't draw at all. Can you help me make these look better?"

She'd been drawing **brides**. Good old Molly. She's been drawing brides since she was five. Her drawing ability hadn't **improve**d much in ten years, either, to tell the truth. But suddenly the idea of her drawing brides was kind of **scary**.

I took the ball-point pen. "Look," I told her.

"Your **proportions** are all off. The arms are too short, even though you've tried to hide it with all those big **bouquet**s of flowers. Just **keep in mind** that a woman's arms reach down to the middle of her **thigh**s when she's standing up. Her **elbow**s should reach her **waist**—look, your drawings all have elbows up by the **bosom**; that's why they look wrong. The necks are too long, too, but that's probably all right, because it makes them look **glamorous**. Fashion designers usually draw necks too long. If you look at the ads* in Sunday's *New York Times*, you'll see—Molly?"

"What?"

"You're not thinking about getting *married?*"

Molly got **huffy** and took back her drawings. "Of course I'm thinking about getting married. Not now, stupid. But someday. Don't you think about it?"

I shook my head. "No, I guess I don't. I think about being a writer, or an artist, or a photographer. But I always think about myself alone, not with someone else. Do you think there's something wrong with me?" I meant the question seriously, but it was a hard question to ask, so I **crossed my eyes** and **made a face** when I asked it, and laughed.

"No," she said **thoughtfully, ignoring** my face-making, which was nice of her. "We're just different, I guess." She tucked the drawings into her notebook and put them on her desk very neatly, in line with her schoolbooks.

---

★ ads 광고(advertisement)의 구어.

"Like you're pretty, and I'm not," I pointed out.

What a **dumb** thing to say.

But I'll give Molly credit. She didn't try to **pretend** that it wasn't true. "You'll be pretty, Meg, when you get a little older," she said. "And I'm not sure it makes that much difference anyway, especially for you. Look at all the talent you have. And brains. I'm so *stupid* What do I have, really, except curls and long **eyelash**es?"

I **ruin** everything. I should have known that she meant it **sincere**ly. Molly is never **intentional**ly **snide**. But she doesn't realize how it feels, for someone with **stringy** hair and astigmatism★ to hear something like that. How could she? I can't imagine how it would feel to be beautiful; how could Molly know how it feels *not* to be?

And I **blew up**, as usual. I **struck a phony** model's **pose** in front of the mirror and said **sarcastic**ally, "Oh, poor me, what do I have except curls and long eyelashes?"

She looked surprised, and hurt. Then **embarrassed**, and angry. Finally, because she didn't know what else to do, she picked up a pile of her school papers and threw them at me: a **typical** Molly **gesture**; even in anger, she does things that can't possibly hurt. The papers flew all over, and landed on my bed and the floor. She stood there a moment

---

★astigmatism 난시. 눈이 초점을 맞추지 못해 시력에 문제가 있는 상태.

looking at the mess, and then said, "There, now you should feel right at home, with stuff all over so it looks like a **pigpen**." And she **storm**ed out of the room, **slam**ming the door, which was useless, because it fell open again.

I left the papers where they were, and Molly and I didn't talk to each other when we went to bed that night. Neither of us is very good at **apologizing**. Molly just waits a while after a fight, and then she smiles. Me, I wait until the other person smiles first. I always seem to be the first one in and the last one out of an argument. But that night neither of us was ready to **call it quits**, and Molly didn't even smile when I climbed into bed very carefully so that all her **exercise**s in past participles* stayed where she'd thrown them, and I went to sleep underneath the pile.

I don't know what time it was when something woke me up. I wasn't sure what it was, but something was happening that made me afraid; I had that feeling along the edge of my back, that cold feeling you get when things aren't right. And it wasn't a dream. I sat up in bed and looked around in the dark, shaking off whatever was left of sleep, and the feeling was still there, that something was very wrong. The French papers **slid** to the floor; I could hear the sound of them **flutter**ing off the bed.

---

★ past participle 과거분사.

60

Quietly I got up and went to the window. The first day of spring wasn't very far away, but dates like that don't mean much in New England; it was still very cold, and there was snow, still, in the fields. I could see the whiteness of it as I looked out the window. Beyond the corner of the **barn**, far across, beyond the pine trees, there was a light in the window of the empty house. I looked up to find the moon, to see if it could be **reflec**ting in one window, but there was no moon. The sky was cloudy and dark. But the light was there, a bright **rectangle** in one corner of the old house, and it was reflected in another rectangle on the snow.

"Molly," I whispered. Stupid to whisper, if you want to wake someone up.

But she answered, as if she were already awake. Her voice was strange. **Frighten**ed, and **puzzled**. "Meg," she said, in an **odd** voice, as if she were captured by something, as if she couldn't move. "Call Mom and Dad quick."

**Ordinarily** I argue with Molly if she tells me to do something, just on general **principle**s. But everything felt wrong. She wasn't just telling me; she was ordering me, and she was very scared. I ran from the room, through the darkness, through the shadows in the hall, and woke my parents.

"Something's wrong," I told them. "Something's wrong with Molly."

Usually, when you turn a light on in the night, everything that you're afraid of goes away. At least that's what I thought once, when I was younger. Now I know it isn't true. When my father turned on the light in my bedroom, everything was there, it was so much there, and so bright, so **horrible**, that I turned and hid my face against the wall. And in the corner of the wall, with my face **buried**, my eyes closed tight and tears starting, I could still see it.

Molly was covered with blood. Her **pillow**, her hair, her face were all wet with it. Her eyes were open, frightened, and her hands were at her face, trying to stop it, trying to hold it back, but it was still coming, pouring from her nose onto the sheet and blanket in moving **streams**, and **spattering** on the wall behind her bed.

I could hear my parents moving very fast. I heard my mother go to the hall **linen** closet, and I knew she was getting towels. I could hear my father's low voice, talking to Molly very calmly, telling her everything was all right. My mother went to the phone in their bedroom, and I could hear her dial and talk. Then she moved down the stairs, and outside I heard the car start. "It's okay, it's okay," I heard my father say again and again, **reassuring** Molly in his steady voice. I could hear Molly **choke** and **whimper**.

Mom came back in the house and up the stairs, and

came to where I was still standing with my back to the room. "Meg," she said, and I turned around. My father was in the **doorway** of the bedroom, with Molly in his arms like a small child. There were towels, already **drench**ed with blood, around her face and head; they had wrapped her in the blanket from her bed, and the blood was moving on it slowly. My father was still talking to her, telling her it was all right, it was all right, it was all right.

"Meg," said my mother again. I nodded. "We have to take Molly to the hospital. Don't be scared. It's just another of those nosebleeds, but it's a bad one, as you can see. We have to hurry. Do you want to come with us?"

My father was moving down the stairs, carrying Molly. I shook my head. "I'll stay here," I said. My voice was shaking, and I felt as if I were going to be sick.

"Are you sure?" asked my mother. "We may be gone for quite a while. Do you want me to call Will and ask him to come up and stay with you?"

I shook my head again and my voice got a little better. "I'll be okay," I told her.

I could tell she wasn't sure, but my father was already in the car waiting for her. "Really, Mom, I'll be fine. Go on; I'll stay here."

She hugged me. "Meg, try not to worry. She'll be okay."

I nodded and walked with her to the stairs, and then

she went down, and they were gone. I could hear the car driving very fast away from the house.

The only light on in the house was in my room, mine and Molly's, and I couldn't go back there. I walked to the doorway without looking inside, reached in and turned off the switch so that the whole house was dark. But the beginning of morning was coming; outside there was a very **faint** light in the sky. I took a blanket from my parents' bed, wrapped it around me, and went into my father's study, the little room that I had wanted to be mine. I curled up in his big comfortable chair, tucked the blue blanket around my **bare** feet, looked out the window, and began to cry.

If I hadn't fought with Molly this afternoon, none of this would have happened, I thought **miserably**, and knew that it wasn't true. If I had just said "I'm sorry" before we went to bed, it wouldn't have happened, I thought, and knew that that wasn't true, either. If we hadn't come here to live. If I'd kept my side of the room neater.

None of that makes any sense, I told myself.

The fields were slowly beginning to turn pink as the first **streak**s of sun came from behind the hills and colored the snow. It **startle**d me that morning was coming; it seemed too soon. For the first time since I had heard Molly's frightened voice in our dark bedroom, I remembered the light in the old house. Had I really seen it? Now everything seemed **unreal**, as if it had all been a **nightmare**. On the far side of the pink fields the gray house was very dark against the **gradua**lly lightening sky, and its windows were silent and black, like the eyes of **guardian**s.

But I knew that back in the blue-**flowered** bedroom the blood was still there, that it had not been a dream. I was alone in the house; my parents were gone, with Molly, with Molly's hair **sticky** from blood, and the **stain spread**ing on the blanket around her. Those moments when I had stood shaking and **terrified**, with my eyes tightly closed against the corner of the wall, moments which may have been hours—I couldn't tell anymore—had really happened. I had seen the light in the window across the fields, as well. I remembered standing and watching its **reflection** on the snow, and I knew it was real, too, though it didn't seem important anymore. I closed my eyes and fell asleep in my father's chair.

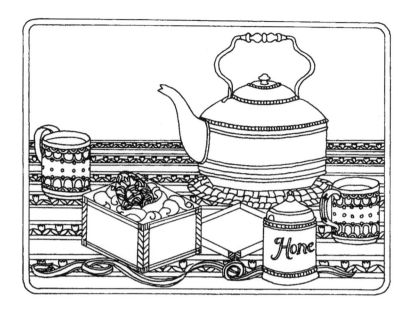

# 5

I made two Easter eggs,★ one for Will and one for Molly. Not just plain old **hard-boiled** eggs that you **dye** with those **vinegar**-smelling colors that never come out looking the way you hoped they would. Molly and I used to do that when we were little—dozens of them, and then we wouldn't eat them, and they turned **rotten**.

No, these were special, and there were only two of them. I blew the insides out of two white eggs, so that only

★ **Easter eggs** 부활절 달걀. 부활절(Easter)에는 예수 그리스도의 부활을 기념해서 생명의 탄생을 의미하는 달걀에 정성스런 그림을 그려 서로 교환한다.

the shells were left, very **fragile** and light. Then I spent hours in my room, painting them.

Molly's was yellow, partly I guess because it reminded me of her blond hair, and partly because my parents told me that her hospital room was **depress**ingly gray-colored, and I thought that yellow would cheer it up a bit. Then, over the **pale** yellow egg, I used my tiniest brush and painted narrow, curving lines in gold, and between the lines, **miniature** blue flowers with gold and white centers. It took a long time, because the **eggshell** was so **delicate** and the painting so small and **intricate**; but it was worth it: when it was finished, the egg was truly beautiful. I **varnish**ed it to make it shiny and **permanent**, and when it was dry, I packed it in **cotton** in a box to protect it, and Mom took it with her when she drove to Portland* to visit Molly. It worked, too; I mean it did make the room more cheerful, Mom said.

Molly was lots better, and coming home the next week. In the beginning she had been very sick. They had, first thing, given her blood **transfusion**s; then, when she was feeling better, they decided to do a lot of tests to find out what was wrong, so that her nose wouldn't **bleed** anymore. They even had **specialist**s see her.

---

★ Portland 미국 Maine주의 항구 도시.

You'd *think* that with medical science as **advanced** as it's supposed to be, that they could **figure out** what the trouble was and fix her up pretty quickly. I mean, *nosebleeds!* What's the big deal about that? It's not as if she had a mysterious **tropical disease**, or something.

But first, Mom said, after they put all that new blood into her, they started taking blood out, to test it. Then they did tests on the inside of her *bones.* Then they x-rayed her. Then, when they thought they knew what was causing the nosebleeds, they started **fool**ing **around** with all different kinds of medicines, to see what would work best. One day Mom and Dad went in, and when they came home, they told me that special medicine had been **inject**ed into Molly's **spine**. That gave me the **creep**s. It made me mad, too, because it seemed to me that they were just **experiment**ing on her, for pete's sake.* By that time they knew what the trouble was—her blood didn't **clot** right—so they just should have given her whatever medicine would fix that and sent her home. But no, instead they started fooling around, trying different things, keeping her there longer.

And my parents were very strange about the whole thing. They were just like the doctors; they didn't even

---

★ for pete's sake 제발 좀!, 도대체!, 진짜로! 화가 나거나 정말적인 일 혹은 이해할 수 없는 일이 일어날 때 감정을 표현하기 위해 외치는 말. for god[heaven, goodness]'s sake이라고 하기도 한다.

think of Molly as a person anymore. They talked about her as if she were a **clinical specimen**. They came home from the hospital and talked very coldly about different drugs with long names: whether this one was better than that one. They talked about **reaction**s, **side effect**s, **contraindication**s; it was hard to believe they were talking about Molly.

I kept my mouth shut as long as I could. But then one night at dinner, the only thing they talked about was something called cyclophosphamide.* There I was, sitting there with them, and I wanted to talk about other things: my darkroom, my Easter eggs that I was working so hard on, what I was going to do during spring vacation from school. *Anything.* Anything, that is, except cyclophosphamide, which I didn't know anything about and couldn't **pronounce**.

"Stop it!" I said angrily. "Stop talking about it! If you want to talk about Molly, then talk about *Molly*, not her stupid medicine! You haven't even sent in her camp **application**, Mom. It's still on your desk!"

They both looked as if I had thrown something at them. But it worked. I don't think I heard the word "cyclophosphamide" again, and for a while they talked of other things, and life was somewhat normal. And

---

★cyclophosphamide 시클로포스파미드. 임파선종 · 백혈병 치료제 이름이다.

70

now Molly will be home soon, all better—and no more nosebleeds—and after all that business with the **fancy drugs**, it turned out that what she ended up with is **pills**. When she comes home, she'll have to take pills for a while. Big deal. They could have found that out when she got there, and sent her home sooner.

But since they didn't, I made the Easter egg for Molly, to cheer her up, and I made another one for Will. Will's egg was blue, and special in a different way. I thought and thought about how to paint it, and finally I looked up **spices** in the **encyclopedia**, and found a picture of nutmeg. I painted tiny nutmeg **blossoms** all over his eggshell, **intertwined** so that they formed a **complicated** pattern of orange, brown, and green over the blue background. I varnished and packed it, and on Easter Sunday I took the box with his egg, and the **envelope** with his pictures, and walked down the road to his house.

I hadn't seen Will since Molly got sick. Things were just too complicated at first. My parents spent a lot of time at the hospital, and I had to do most of the cooking. Then, when she was getting better, my father had to work doubly hard on the book because he hadn't been able to **concentrate** on it when she was so sick. I realized that I hadn't been concentrating on my schoolwork, either, for the same reason, so I had a lot of **catch**ing **up** to do too.

But finally things were calming down. It was school vacation, Molly was getting better, and even the mud outside had dried up a little. At night it would still **freeze**, and in fact I noticed, as I walked past, that there were tire tracks frozen into the **driveway** of the big house across the field.

That was another reason I wanted to see Will. After that first awful night, when I had seen the light in the window, other things had been happening at the house. Nothing seemed as mysterious as that light in the middle of the night; still, I was curious. There was a car at the house **occasional**ly, and the driveway had been cleared of the last spring-**muddied** bits of snow. Sometimes when the day was very quiet I could hear the sound of **saws** and hammers coming from the house. Once I had seen the **figure** of a man on the roof, working. It certainly looked as if someone were getting ready to **move in**. I asked my father if the **nephew** had gotten **permission** to turn the house into an **inn**, but Dad said he hadn't heard anything about it; on the other hand, Dad pointed out, he'd been so **distracted** and so busy that he probably wouldn't have noticed if **spaceship**s had landed in the field.

Will was under the **hood** of his truck again. I should have taken my camera with me. If there is one way in which I will always remember Will, it is under the hood of that old truck.

"Is it your battery again, Will?" I called as I **approach**ed him.

He **straighten**ed up and grinned. "Meg! I was hoping someone would **drop in** for tea. In fact, I have the **kettle** on. I'm so glad **fate** sent you instead of Clarice Callaway. She's been **hint**ing for years that she'll come to call someday, and I live in **perpetual** fear of seeing her heading down this road with her Sunday hat on and a **fistful** of **overdue** library **slip**s to deliver."

I giggled. Clarice Callaway is the village librarian. She's eighty-two years old, and I'm not giving away any secrets when I say that, because she tells everyone that herself as soon as they're introduced to her. She's also the president of the **Historical Preservation** Society, and my father says that's a real **exercise** in **irony**, because Clarice herself is the best-**preserved** historical **monument** for miles around. Also, she **has a crush on** Will. He told me that whenever he goes to the library, she disappears into the ladies' room, and then comes out again with bright pink rouge on her cheeks, so that she looks like a French doll his sister had when she was a child.

He **sigh**ed and **wipe**d his hands on a **rag**. "It's the **radiator** this time. In the winter it's the battery, and when spring comes it's the radiator. The tires go **flat** in summer.

Sometimes I think I'll buy a new truck, but then I figure I'd have to learn to deal with a whole new set of **disaster**s. At least now I *know* that every April the radiator hoses will break and the engine will overheat. Better to know what your **enemy** is before you **confront** him; right, Meg?"

"Right," I agreed, even though I wasn't at all sure I wanted to be confronted by enemies or disasters, whether I knew them or not.

"Come inside," Will said. "I have a surprise for you."

But my surprise was first. After Will had poured tea for both of us, I opened the big envelope and took out the pictures. I laid the six of them on the kitchen table and watched as Will picked them up one at a time. He didn't laugh or **blush** or say "Oh, I look *terrible*" the way kids do when they see pictures of themselves. I knew he wouldn't. He picked up each one and studied it, smiling at some, looking **thoughtful**ly at others. Finally he chose the same one that was my favorite: the one where his eyes were closed, and the smoke from his pipe was a thin line along the side and the top of the photograph. He took it to the window and looked at it in better light.

"Meg," he said at last, "all of these are very, very good. You know that already, I'm sure. This is the best one, I think, because of the **composition**, and also because you hit on just the right **combination** of **shutter** speed and

**aperture** setting. You see how the lines in the face are perfectly sharp—you must have a pretty good lens on that little camera of yours—but you slowed it just enough so that the line of smoke has a slight **blur** to it, as it should. Smoke has an **ephemeral** quality, and you caught that, but you didn't **sacrifice** the **clarity** of the face. It's a *fine* photograph."

Why did I want to cry when he finished talking? I don't even know what ephemeral means. But something inside me **well**ed **up** like hot fudge sauce*—sweet, and warm, and so rich that you can't **bear** to have very much. It was because someone who was a real friend was having the exact same feelings I was having, about something that was more important to me than anything else. I bet there are people who go through a whole life and never experience that. I sat there with my hand around the warm mug of tea, and smiled at Will.

"Meg," he said suddenly, **gulp**ing his own tea. "I'll make a deal with you!"

I laughed. People say that to me at school, and it means that they want to copy my algebra* homework, and in return I get the Hostess Twinkie* from their lunch.

---

★ fudge sauce 퍼지 소스. 설탕, 버터, 우유, 초콜릿으로 만든 끈적끈적한 과자.
⁑ algebra 대수학. 숫자 대신 문자를 사용하여 수의 관계 및 계산 법칙을 배우는 과목.
⁂ Hostess Twinkie 미국 Hostess에서 만드는 간식 케이크이름. 가운데에 크림이 든 노란색의 작은 케이크이다.

"Remember I told you that I had bought a camera in Germany?"

I nodded.

"It's a fine camera," Will said. "The best made, and of course something like that doesn't **diminish** with age. I don't know why I haven't used it in so long, except that I lost my **enthusiasm** for a lot of things when Margaret died. And that," he said **gruffly**, "is the last thing she would have wanted.

"But I'm going to get it out of the **attic**. The camera, and four lenses, and a set of **filters** that go with it. I want you to use it."

The hot fudge started up again. My own camera has just one lens, which can't be removed. I've read about using other kinds of lenses and filters, but I've never had a chance to try.

"I don't know what to say," I told him, and it was true. "What could I possibly do in return?"

"Oh, don't worry about *that!*" laughed Will. "I said I'd make a deal with you. I'm not going to let you off easily, either. In return, I want you to teach me to use the darkroom. Let me borrow your little camera while you're using mine, and we'll set up a regular schedule for lessons. I'll warn you that it's been a long time since I've **undertake**n to learn anything new. But my **eyesight** is good, and my hands are steady, still."

"But, Will," I **wail**ed. "I'm only thirteen years old! I've never taught anybody anything!"

Will looked at me very sternly. "My dear Meg," he said, "Mozart wrote his first composition★ when he was five. Age is a meaningless **commodity** in most **instance**s. Don't **underrate** yourself. Now is it a deal?"

I sat there for a moment, looking at my empty mug. Then I shook his hand. He was right; his hands were firm and strong and steady. "It's a deal, Will," I said.

I remembered the Easter egg. In a way it seemed almost silly, now, but I brought out the little box and gave it to him. He held the egg up **grave**ly and **examine**d the design; his eyes lit up with **recognition**.

"*Myristica fragrans*,✳" he pronounced **solemn**ly. "Nutmeg. Am I right?"

I grinned at him and nodded. "I don't know about the mistica, or whatever you said, but it's nutmeg. You're right."

He put the egg into a **shallow** pewter bowl,✱ and took it to the living room. After he had put the bowl on a small **pine** table by the window, both of us stood in the room and looked at it. The blue of the egg was the same **muted** blue

---

★ composition 작곡. 원래 '구성'을 뜻하지만 음악에서는 일정한 질서에 따라 음을 조립하여 음악작품을 구성하는 '작곡'을 composition이라고 부른다.

✳ Myristica fragrans 육두구(nutmeg)의 학명.

✱ pewter bowl 은회색 빛깔을 띠는 백랍 그릇. 백랍(pewter)은 주석과 납의 합금이다.

as the **oriental rug**; the rust and green **shade**s seemed to **reflect** the colors of the old wood and the hanging, **well-tended** plants. It was perfect there; Will didn't even have to say so. We just looked at it together as the April sunlight from the window fell onto the bowl and the fragile **oval** shell, **outline**d their shadows on the **polish**ed table, and then **brighten**ed a **rectangle** on the pattern of the carpet.

"Now, **scoot**," said Will. "I have to deal with my radiator."

I was just at the end of his muddy driveway, and his head was back under the hood of the truck, when I remembered. I turned and called to him.

"Will? I forgot to ask you about the big house!" He brought his head out and groaned. "And I forgot to tell you my surprise!"

So I went back for a minute. I sat on the front steps and scratched Tip beside his ear, while Will pulled the radiator hoses off—"rotten old things," he said to them. "Why do you do this to me every spring?"—and told me about the house. My question, it turned out, was the same as his surprise.

"I was right here last month," he said, "with my head under the hood, as usual. The battery then, of course. And a car drove up with a young couple in it. They asked if I knew anything about that house.

"In the past year, at least ten people have asked me about the house, but they've always been the wrong people. Don't ask me how I know that. It's just something I can feel. And when this young couple—Ben and Maria, their names are— got out of their car, I could tell they were the right ones.

"Ben helped me clean the leads to the battery, and Maria went in the kitchen and made tea for the three of us. By the time Ben and I had washed our hands and finished our tea, I had **rent**ed the house to them. When you know it's the right people, it's as easy as that.

"They don't have much money. He's a student still, at Harvard, and he said he was looking for a quiet place for the summer, to write his **thesis**."

I groaned. Next thing you knew, this whole valley would be noisy from the sound of **typewriter**s. Will laughed; he'd had the same thought.

"But in return for the summer in the house, they're going to fix the place up. He's been working weekends ever since I told them they could have the house. The roof needs work; the **wiring** needs work; the **plumbing** needs work. Well, you know what it's like when you get old with no one to take care of you!"

We laughed together. I could tell already that I would like Ben and Maria, because Will did.

"And Maria's going to put in a garden when the ground

thaws," he continued. "They'll be moving in officially quite soon, I think. And I've told them about you. They're looking forward to having you stop in, Meg."

Then Will looked a little **sheepish**, the first time I'd ever seen him look that way. "But I forgot to ask them something," he **confess**ed.

"What?"

He looked in several other directions before he answered. He was embarrassed. Finally he explained, "I forgot to ask them if they're married."

I **burst out** laughing. "Oh, Will," I said, "do you think it matters?"

He looked as if it hadn't **occurr**ed to him that it might not matter. "Well," he said finally, "I can tell you that it would have mattered to *Margaret*. But, well, I guess maybe you're right, Meg. I guess it doesn't really matter to me."

Then he wiped his hands on his rag and grinned. "It might matter to their child, though. From the looks of it, there's going to be a baby coming this summer."

A baby. That was a strange thing to think about. I'm not overly **fond** of babies. Molly **adore**s them. She says she's going to have at least six someday herself, even though I keep telling her that's **environmental**ly **absurd**.

I told Molly about it on the phone that night, and she was **thrill**ed at the thought of having a baby in the house across the field. Her voice sounded good, stronger than it has since she got sick. I've talked to her on the phone a lot, and sometimes she's sounded tired and depressed. But now she's feeling well again, and she's looking forward to coming home.

"It's a **drag**, being here," she said. "Even though there are some good-looking doctors."

That made me laugh. I knew she was feeling normal again if she was noticing the doctors.

I told her how much Will liked his photographs, and that he was going to let me use his German camera.

"Hey, Meg?" she asked. "Do me a favor?"

"Sure." Usually I wouldn't say "sure" without knowing what the favor was; but **what the heck**, she'd been pretty sick.

"Would you take my picture when I get home? I want a really good one, to give Tierney for his birthday this summer."

"Molly, I'll make you look like a movie star," I told her, and she giggled before she **hung up**.

# 6

Will Banks is learning to use the darkroom, and he's fantastic. Ben and Maria have moved into the house, and they're **terrific**. Molly is home, and she's being **thorough**ly **unbearable**.

Well, as they say, two out of three isn't bad.

I suppose you can't really **blame** Molly for being a pain. She was **awful**ly sick; no one knows that better than I do. I don't think the sight of her **lying** there in all that blood will ever go out of my mind.

But **apparently** she **got used to** being the center

of attention in the hospital. Who wouldn't, with all those **specialist**s around? Still, here she is at home, and **supposedly** well—or why would they have **discharge**d her from the hospital?—and she acts as if everyone should still **be at her beck and call**. And my parents **put up with** it; that's the **amazing** thing.

"Could I have a **tuna fish** sandwich?" asked Molly at lunchtime, the day after she came home. She was lying on the **couch** in the kitchen, in a pose like Playmate of the Month,* except that she was wearing jeans and a sweatshirt.*

"Do you want **lettuce**?" my mother asked her, **scurry**ing to get the bread and mayonnaise. For pete's sake. Do you want lettuce. Two months ago she would have said, "Make it yourself, **madam**." That's what she would *still* say, to me.

And after all that, Molly didn't even eat the sandwich. She came to the table, ate two **bites**, and then **drift**ed back to the couch and said she wasn't hungry after all.

"Are you sure you're feeling all right, dear?" asked Mom.

"Quit **bug**ging me, will you?" said Molly, and she **storm**ed off to our room, **slam**med the door (which fell open again; Molly will never learn that the door to our

---

★ Playmate of the Month 미국 성인잡지 Playboy에서 선정하는 '이 달의 모델'.
※ sweatshirt 흔히 '추리닝'이라고 부르는 트레이닝복의 상의. 땀 흘릴 때(sweat)입는 상의 (shirt).

room is totally useless in a **tantrum**) and took a **nap** for the rest of the afternoon.

Molly never used to be like that. *I* used to be like that, sometimes, and I hated myself when I was. Now Molly is that way, and I find myself hating her, or at least hating what has happened to her to make her different.

My parents don't say a word. That's different, too. In the past, when one of us was **grouchy**, my mother always said and did things that were both understanding and funny, so that we would start to laugh and whatever was making us **irritable** would just disappear in a comfortable way. Or Dad would be very **stern**. He says he doesn't have time to waste on **rude**ness. "**Shape up**," he would say. And we would shape up, because he didn't leave any choice.

But now Mom doesn't **chuckle** and **tease** when Molly is awful. Dad doesn't **lay down the law**. Instead, Mom gets worried and **confuse**d, which makes things worse. Dad gets **tense** and silent and goes off to his **study** without saying anything. It's as if an upsetting stranger has moved in with us, and no one knows what to do about it.

Part of why Molly is being so **obnoxious**, I think, is because she doesn't look very good, and it was always so important to Molly to look pretty. But she lost weight while she was in the hospital (because the food was so **dreadful**, she says), so that now her face is thinner than it used to be.

And more pale. The paleness, I guess, is because she had to have the blood **transfusion**s, and it probably takes the red blood **cell**s a while to build up again.

Worst of all, for Molly, her hair is **falling out**. That's because of the **pills** she has to take, my parents said. One of the **side effect**s is that your hair falls out! I told her that there might be medicines with *worse* side effects, like making your nose fall off, but no one thought that was very funny. My mother told her that when she is able to stop taking the medicine, after a while, her hair will grow back thicker and curlier than it was before, but when Mom said that, Molly just said, "Great," very **sarcastic**ally and kept staring at her comb full of blond **strand**s. Then Mom said that if it got worse, they would buy her a **wig**, and Molly said, "Oh, *gross!*" and **stomp**ed off to our bedroom.

So things are kind of difficult at our house now.

Molly can't go back to school until she gains a little weight and gets her color back. She says she won't go back to school *anyway* if her hair keeps falling out. Mom and Dad don't say much about school. They're **depress**ed about the whole thing, I can tell.

It will just take time. If we're all patient and wait, everything will be the same as it used to be, I know.

Will Banks is very kind to Molly. He comes to the house three evenings a week to work in the darkroom, and he always brings something for her: a library book to read, or a candy bar, some little thing like that. One night he brought a **handful** of pussy willows* that he had found behind his house: the first ones of spring, and Molly was **thrill**ed. It was the first time I'd seen her really happy about something for a long time.

"Oh, Will," she said softly, "they're beautiful." She held them against her cheek and **rubb**ed the softness like a **kitten**. We were sitting in the kitchen, and I took a small vase and ran some water into it.

"No water, Meg," said Will. "If you put pussy willows in water, they'll **blossom** and then die. Just put them in the vase alone, and they'll stay beautiful forever."

There's so much I don't know. I gave Molly the vase, without water, and she **arrange**d the pussy willows in it; she took them up to our room and put them on the table beside her bed. That night, after we were in bed and Molly was already asleep, I looked over, and the moonlight was across the table and across Molly; behind her, on the wall, was the shadow of pussy willows.

It's not surprising that Will knows so much about so many things, because he has an **incredible** memory. When we began working together in the darkroom, I showed

---

★ pussy willow [식물] 갯버들. 어두운 자주색 꽃이 피며 어린 가지는 노란 빛이 도는 녹색으로 털이 나있다.

him, first, the basic **procedure**s for **develop**ing film. I only showed him once. Then he did it himself, developing a roll that he had shot of his truck and his dog, using his own camera to make sure it was working properly before he gave it to me. He remembered everything: the **temperature**s, the **proportion**s of **chemical**s, the timing right down to the second. His negatives were perfect. The pictures weren't great, because, as he said, he'd been "just **fool**ing **around**, wanting to get the feel of the camera again," but they were **technical**ly perfect, developed exactly right.

And he's **immense**ly curious. When I could see that he'd learned to develop film properly, I wanted to go on to the next step: printing the pictures. But Will said, "Wait. What would happen if, when I was developing the film, I purposely made the chemicals too warm? What would happen if I **agitate**d them less? Or more? And what if I had underexposed the film, Meg, when I took the pictures? Couldn't I **compensate** for that when I developed the film, maybe by **prolong**ing the developing time?"

I thought for a minute. Those things had never **occur**red to me, and they should have. Of *course* you could compensate.

"I never tried," I said, thinking. "But I bet you could. There must be a book that tells how. Let me—"

He **interrupt**ed me. He's also **impatient**, I've found, and very **independent**. "Oh, the **heck** with books, Meg. Let's figure it out for ourselves. Let's **experiment**. Someone must have figured it out once, in order to write a book. Why can't we do the same thing?"

So we did. That was a Monday night, and on Tuesday and Wednesday, each of us shot several rolls of film, purposely underexposing and overexposing them. On Wednesday night we developed them, each one a different way. We changed the temperatures on some, the developing time on some, the amount of **agitation** on some. And we did it! We figured out exactly how to compensate for all sorts of things, how to build up **contrast**, how to **reduce** it. We felt like a couple of miracle workers.

When we came out of the darkroom after three hours, Mom was in the kitchen, working on her quilt. She looked up and laughed. "You two sounded like a couple of crazy people in there," she said, "shouting at each other."

I giggled. We *had* been shouting. "Don't leave it in the developer so long, you **moron**!" I had shouted at Will. "You'll **ruin** it!"

"I'm *trying* to ruin it!" Will had **bellow**ed back. "So I can figure out how to do it perfectly! How can you learn anything if you won't take risks?"

And *I* was supposed to be teaching *him*.

"Lydia," Will explained to Mom that night, sitting

down to have a cup of tea before he went home, "**genius disregards** the **boundaries** of **propriety**. Genius is **permit**ted to shout if shouting is **productive**."

Mom laughed again and **snipped** off the **thread** as she completed a red-and-white-**striped square** from a sunsuit* I wore when I was three years old. She likes Will. "Well," she said, "I've been living with creative genius long enough that I should know that by now. Charles has been known to shout at his **typewriter**, if you can believe that."

Will nodded very seriously, chewing on the **stem** of his **pipe**. "Oh my, yes. It would be necessary to shout at one's typewriter now and then, I would think. **Machinery** needs that kind of **discipline occasional**ly. Just today I was shouting at my truck **radiator**."

Mom was smiling as she **measured** off a new square in the quilt. It was good to see her relaxed and smiling, the way she used to be, for a change. "How about your homework, Meg?" she asked. "You're not disregarding the boundaries of your homework too, are you?"

I **groan**ed. But I'm keeping up with school, same as always. Suddenly, though, algebra and American history seem pretty **dull** compared to other things that are happening. I'll be glad when the **term** ends next month so

---

★ sunsuit 일광욕 · 물놀이를 할 때 입는 어린이용 옷.

that I can spend more time on photography. Molly will be completely well by then, too, and things will be easier. And I'll be able to see a lot of Ben and Maria.

Will took me to meet them just after they moved in. Molly came, too; I was surprised that she wanted to, because she's been so **miserable** and **self-conscious** about the way she looks that mostly she stays in our room. But when I asked her, she said **what the heck**, there wasn't anything better to do.

The three of us walked across the field on a hot, sunny Saturday afternoon that smelled like new growing things. We could have gone down the road, of course, but it seemed like the sort of day when walking across a field would be a nice thing to do. Wild flowers were just beginning to appear. They always take me by surprise. It seems, each year, as if winter will go on forever, even back in town. Then when you've **resign**ed yourself to a whole lifetime of grayness, suddenly bright **burst**s of yellow and purple and white **spring** up in the fields, and you realize they've been hiding there **all along**, waiting.

Will was carrying a heavy stick that he sometimes uses when he's walking, especially in the **rocky** fields. He pointed here and there with the stick, at the little blossoms in the field and the **shady** border of the woods, as we walked along.

"*Anemonella thalictroides, Cerastium arvense, Cornus canadensis, Oakesia sessilifolia*," he said. Molly and I **glance**d at him, **grin**ned at each other, and didn't say anything.

"*Uvularia perfoliata*," Will went on, pointing with his stick to a light yellow, tiny, bell-shaped flower.

"Can you say that three times fast?" asked Molly, laughing.

"Yes," grinned Will back at her.

Suddenly I decided that he was really **put**ting us **on**. "You're making all that up, Will!" I **hoot**ed. "You big **phony**! You had me fooled for a minute, too!"

He looked down his nose at me in a **haughty** sort of way, but his eyes were **twinkling**.

Then he pushed aside some **underbrush** with his stick, and pointed to a **clump** of small purple flowers. "*Viola pedata*," he said, talking to Molly, **ignoring** me. "So called because the leaves **resemble** the foot of a bird. You believe me, don't you, Molly?"

Molly was laughing. The sun was shining through her thin hair, and for the first time since she'd been sick, there was color in her cheeks. "I don't know for sure, Will," she smiled. "I think I believe you, but the only wild flower I recognize is goldenrod.*"

He nodded. "*Solidago*," he said. "Very common around here, a **remarkable** plant. But we won't see it **bloom** until

92

the end of July. In the **meantime**, you should **investigate** some of these others, Molly. It would keep you busy until you can go back to school, and it would be good for you, being in the fresh air."

Molly **shrugged**. She didn't like being reminded of her problems. We walked on.

Ben and Maria were behind the house, starting a garden. They had a **patch** of ground **dug** up, and Ben was standing in the middle of the turned earth, **chop**ping at the **lump**s with a **hoe**. There was **sweat** all over his **bare** back— he wasn't wearing anything but **faded**, patched jeans— and even though there was a **handkerchief** tied around his head, his hair and **beard** were wet with sweat too. He smiled when he saw us.

"Ah, **savior**s!" he called. "You're coming to **rescue** me from this **slave labor**, right?"

"Wrong," called the girl who was sitting in the grass at the corner of the garden patch. "No rescue! I want to get my **pea**s planted. Hi, Will!"

I **burst out** laughing. Will had told me very casually that there seemed to be a baby coming. That was the **understatement** of the year. Sometimes I forget that Will is seventy years old, and that he's a little **shy** about some

---

★ goldenrod [식물] 미역취. 산과 들에 자생하는 여러해살이풀로 황금색과 같은 진한 노란 색 꽃이 핀다.

things. Maria was so thoroughly **pregnant** that I thought we would do well to start boiling water immediately.

She was sitting with her legs crossed, and her middle was resting on her knees. She was wearing a man's shirt with the **sleeves rip**ped out; her arms were bare and very **tan**, the same as her legs. The shirt was buttoned around her, but just **barely**; the middle button was pulled **sideways** by her stomach, and it was going to pop off very soon. I hoped she had a bigger shirt ready; either that, or that the baby would be born before long. It looked like it was going to be a race between the baby and the button, and I didn't know enough about either **pregnancy** or the art of **mend**ing to be able to **predict** which was going to **detach** itself first.

Maria had one long dark **braid** down her back, and a smile that included all three of us, as well as Ben, who was still leaning on his hoe.

"I'd like you to meet my two friends, Meg and Molly Chalmers," Will said. "Meg is the photographer I've been telling you about. And Molly is the cheerleader, but I'm going to try to turn her into a **botanist**. Girls, this is Ben Brady. And Maria."

Maria reached up to shake our hands, and said, "Maria Abbott." Out of the corner of my eye I could see Will **flinch** slightly. It all went right over Molly's head. She was so interested in the baby.

"When is the baby **due**?" asked Molly. "Do you mind my asking? I just love babies."

From the garden, where he had started to **hack** at a **clod** of earth that **obvious**ly had a rock in the middle of it, Ben looked up and chuckled. He rolled his eyes. "Does she *mind* your asking? Prepare yourself, Molly, for an hour . . . two hours, *three* hours . . . of conversation. That's all she talks about! I remember a time—it wasn't so long ago, either, come to think of it—when Maria and I used to talk about books. Music. The weather. **Politics**. Little things like that. Now we sit down in the evening after supper, and we pour a couple cups of tea, put some Beethoven on the **stereo**, and talk about **diapers**." He groaned, but he was looking at Maria **affectionate**ly.

We were all laughing, even Maria. She threw a handful of **weed**s at him lightly, and said, "Just hoe your row, Daddy. Molly, come in the house with me. I'll show you the **cradle** I've been **refinish**ing."

She **got to her feet awkward**ly, and, standing, said, "Look!" She **smooth**ed the shirt over her middle so we could see how round she was. "It isn't due until July. Can you believe that? It's incredible how big I am, but I'm sure July is right. Do you know how you figure out your due date? It's really easy. You add seven days to the date that your last **period** started, and—"

I started talking quickly to Will, because I could see how **embarrass**ed he was by the conversation. Maria and Molly went in the house, and Ben put down the hoe. He showed Will and me how he had **haul**ed rocks from the field to make a small wall beside the driveway, and the work he'd been doing on the **roof**. We **wander**ed around for a long time, talking about what needed to be done to the old house; Will explained how things had been when he was a child, and Ben thought of how to make them that way again. We stood, finally, by a bare patch of earth beside the kitchen door, and Will described the flowers that had been there once, how his grandmother had emptied her dishwater there, over the flowers, and they had grown bigger and healthier than the other plants.

"Of course!" said Ben. "It probably had little **scraped-**off bits of food, **organic stuff**, in it. She was **mulch**ing the flowers without even realizing it. That's cool; that's really cool. We should try that. I bet we could grow **herb**s there; Maria's dying to have an herb garden. 'Parsley,* sage,* rosemary,* and thyme,*'" he sang, **off-key**.

Will looked somewhat **nonplused** by Ben, Maria, the

---

★ parsley 파슬리. 가지를 그대로 쓰거나 기름에 튀겨서 쓰며, 잘게 썰어서 요리에 뿌리기도 한다.
✳ sage 세이지. 소스 · 카레 · 돼지고기 요리 등에 향신료로 쓴다.
✺ rosemary 로즈메리. 바늘 같은 잎을 가진 허브이다.
✳ thyme 타임. 향신료로 사용된다.

whole thing. But he liked them; I could tell. And he was happy about the house; I could tell that, too.

Maria made iced tea for everyone, and we went inside. The house was **furnish**ed with **odds and ends** of things, most of them with the paint partly removed. Maria was busy refinishing everything. There was an old **spinning wheel**, and she said she was going to learn to spin. The cradle, which was almost finished. A **rocking chair**, partly done, with a pile of **sandpaper** on the seat. Ben's typewriter and books stood on a desk made from an old door balanced on two sawhorses.★ Will sat down in the only real chair, a big comfortable one with its **stuffing** popping out like milkweed✳ from the **pod**s in fall.

"Hope no one has hay fever,✲" laughed Maria as Will sat down. "Every time anyone sits in that chair, feathers and dust fly all over the room. But I'm going to **reupholster** it after the baby's born."

Ben groaned. "She's gone mad, really mad," he teased. "I live in constant fear that some morning I'll wake up

---

★ sawhorse 톱질(saw)을 위한 지지용도로 사용되는 받침대의 일종. 4개의 다리 위에 평평한 판자가 붙어있어 나무를 올려놓고 톱질을 할 수 있다. 그 생김새가 마치 말(horse)의 모양과 같아서 'sawhorse'라고 부른다.
✳ milkweed 금관화. 높이 약 1미터 정도의 여러해살이풀.
✲ hay fever 건초열. 봄에서 여름에 걸쳐서 꽃가루 때문에 일어나는 비염. 가축용 건초(hay)를 만드는 계절에 걸리는 열병(fever)이라는 데서 그 이름이 생겨났다.

and find that she's **sand**ed and **scrub**bed and **peel**ed and painted me in the night!"

Maria leaned over and **examine**d his bare foot. "Come to think of it," she **muse**d, "that's not a bad idea. You could use a little work." Then she leaned her head for a moment against his blue-jeaned leg, and he **rumple**d the top of her hair with his hand.

I didn't say much. I was very happy, being there. The sun had gotten lower in the sky, and as it came through the windows it fell on Maria as she sat there on the floor leaning against Ben, in gold patterns on her shoulders and the thick braid of hair. I was making a photograph in my mind.

But Molly **chatter**ed on and on. It was good to hear her; all the **tense**ness and anger were gone. She and Ben and Maria talked about what the inside of the house needed: hanging plants in the sunny windows; fresh white paint on the old **plaster** walls; just the right kind of curtains. "I'll **weave** them myself!" Maria **exclaim**ed; Ben sighed, smiled, and **stroke**d her head.

On the way home, Molly **lag**ged behind Will and me. She was gathering wild flowers, one of each kind. She said she'd press them, and Will told her he would help her to **identify** each one, that he had a book she could use.

"You know," I said slowly to Will, as we walked back

through the field together, "I wish I were more like Molly. I mean, I wish I knew the right things to say to people. Sometimes I seem to just *sit* there."

"Meg," Will said, and he put his arm around me as we walked, "do you see that section of the woods over there, where the spruce tree* is beside the birches?*"

"Yes," I said, looking where he pointed.

"Not far into the woods, beyond the spruce, at the right time of year, there's a clump of fringed gentians.* Have you ever seen a fringed gentian?"

How do you like that? When I said something really serious, really personal, for pete's sake, to my best friend, he wasn't even listening. He was still thinking about his plants.

"No," I told him, a little sarcastically. "I've never seen a fringed gentian."

"It will be after you've moved back to town," he said. "It won't bloom until the end of September, maybe even October. But I want you to come back, so I can show it to you."

"Okay," I sighed. I didn't care about his old fringed gentian.

"It's important, Meg," Will said. "You promise?"

---

★ spruce tree 가문비나무.

✴ birch 자작나무.

✱ fringed gentian 톱니처럼 째진 꽃잎을 가진 용담. 종 모양의 파란색 꽃이 피는 야생화의 일종이다.

Well, if it was important to him, all right. I would want to come back, anyway, and I didn't mind looking at his flower. Maybe he wanted to photograph it or something.

"I promise, Will," I said.

# 7

Finally Molly has stopped being a **grouch**. It was **gradual**, and I'm not even sure the change is a good one. She hasn't gone back to being the old Molly she was before she was sick. She isn't **giggly**, funny Molly anymore, full of smiles and ideas and **silly enthusiasm**s.

I don't know what she is, now. A stranger, mostly. It's as if she has become part of a different world, one that doesn't include me anymore, or even Mom and Dad. She's quieter, more serious, almost **withdrawn**. When I tell her about things that are happening at school, she listens, and asks questions, but it's as if she doesn't really care much; she's only listening to be **polite**.

Only a few things interest her now. She spends a lot of time with the flowers. In the past, for Molly, flowers were things to run through in a field, to pick, to **bury** your nose in, to arrange in a vase on the table. Now, with Will's help, she's learning about them; she reads the books he's brought to her, and **identifies** the wild flowers she's found in the fields. She **classifies** them, **label**s them, arranges them in order in a book that she's **putting together**. It takes most of her time. She's very careful, and very serious, about her flowers. We don't **dare**, ever, to **tease** her about them.

It's as if she has become, suddenly, old.

The other thing that still interests her is the baby. She visits Maria often, and they talk and talk about the baby. Molly is helping Maria to make clothes for it; they **sew** together, and when she finishes something, Molly **smooth**es it with such care, folds it **neat**ly, and puts it away in the **drawer** they're filling with little things.

Even Ben and Maria seem a little **puzzle**d by the **concern** Molly has for all those tiny **nightgown**s and sweaters. Once I heard Ben say to her, "Hey, Moll. It's *already* going to be the best-dressed kid in the valley. Quit sewing for a while, will you? Come with me to see if we can find some wild strawberries."

102

But Molly just smiled at him and shook her head. "You go ahead, Ben," she said. "Take Meg. I want to finish this. I want everything to be perfect when the baby comes."

Ben groaned. "Molly, don't you *know* what babies are like? It's just going to **pee** on those clothes. Why do they need to be perfect with that kind of future **in store for** them?"

Molly smiled at him and went on **stitch**ing.

And sometimes, for no reason, Molly is like a baby, herself. One night after supper, when it was raining outside, we were sitting in front of the **fireplace**. Mom was working on the quilt, Dad was reading, and Molly and I were just watching the **logs shift** and send sparks into the **chimney** as they burned. We had our **pajamas** on.

Suddenly, very quietly, Molly got up, went over to Dad, and climbed onto his **lap**. He didn't say anything. He just put his book down, put his arms around her, held her, and watched the fire. She put her head on his shoulder like a sleepy two-year-old, and with one hand he **stroke**d the fine, **wispy**, babylike hair she has left.

I could understand, I guess, the change in Molly if she were still sick. But she isn't; she's perfectly well. She is still taking the **pill**s, and every few weeks Mom takes her to Portland to the hospital, for tests, to make sure everything is okay. Soon, the doctors said, she'll be able to stop taking the pills altogether, and then her hair will grow back. She'll win a **beauty contest**, the **specialist** told her, when she has her curls again.

Mom told us that at dinner, after they had come back from the hospital, and Molly just smiled, the casual and **tolerant** kind of smile that most people give to small children who say foolish things. But there was a time when it would have meant something to Molly, to be told she was beautiful.

Well, things change. I just have to learn to **adjust** to what they change to.

One morning early in June, my father came into the kitchen, poured himself a cup of coffee, and sighed. I was just finishing my breakfast and had planned to spend all of Saturday morning in the darkroom. I had photographed Maria by her kitchen window, and Will and I were **experiment**ing with different kinds of paper for the finished prints. I could hardly wait to try printing Maria in different **contrast**s, **texture**s, and tones.

But when Dad pours a cup of coffee, sits down in the kitchen, and sighs, I know I'd better **stick around** because something's up.

"I just got a phone call," he said, "from Clarice Callaway."

"Are your books **overdue**?" I asked. "She's a real **stickler** about overdue books."

He laughed. "No, she and I have **achieved** a pretty good understanding about my overdue books. I wish that's all it were. She started the conversation by saying, 'I don't want to **meddle**, but—' You know what that means."

"It means she wants to meddle. Sometimes she starts with, "I don't **mean to** be **inquisitive**, but—?'"

"Right. And that means she means to be inquisitive. I can see you have Clarice figured out, Meg. Well, this time she's upset about Will renting the house. She says the whole village is **up in arms**—which I assume is a Callaway **exaggeration**—because there are hippies* living in Will's house."

"Hippies? What's that supposed to mean?"

Dad **frowned**. "*I* don't know. Ben has a **beard**, and I guess by Clarice's **definition** that makes him a hippie. But maybe you can **shed** some **light on** the things she brought up. Is it true that Ben and Maria are growing marijuana* behind the house?"

I started to laugh. "Dad, of course not. They've put in **pea**s and strawberries so far. Ben wants to plant **squash**, but he hasn't decided what **varieties** yet. And his tomatoes and beans go in this week."

---

★ hippie 히피. 1966년 미국 샌프란시스코에서 청년층을 주체로 하여 시작된, 탈사회적 행동을 하는 사람들을 일컫는 말.
✲ marijuana 대마초. 대마의 잎과 꽃에서 얻어지는 마약이다.

"Is it true that they walk around **nude?**"

"Good grief,* Dad. No, it isn't true, but even if it were, whose business would it be? They're out **in the middle of nowhere**. One afternoon Maria took off her shirt and lay in the sun. When I came along, she had her shirt off, and she asked me if I minded. I said I didn't, and she left it off for a while. She gets so hot and uncomfortable, because the baby's **due** soon."

"Well, that was another of Clarice's topics. Is it true that they're planning to have that baby by themselves, in the house?"

"Yes. But they've both been reading everything they can find about **deliver**ing **a baby**. Maria's doing all sorts of **exercise**s, and they took a course together in Boston. And Dr. Putnam in the village has agreed to come if they need him."

Dad scratched his head. "No chance that they'll change their minds about that?"

"I don't think so, Dad. It's very important to them. They're really excited about doing it themselves, about having the baby born there in the house, instead of in a hospital. They don't like the **impersonal** qualities of a hospital. But the baby's important to them, too. They're

---

★ good grief 맙소사, 세상에!

doing everything they can to be sure the baby will be safe and healthy."

"Well, I guess I can try to **convince** Clarice of that. So that leaves only one thing. They *are* married, aren't they?"

I **stir**red the last **soggy** Rice Krispies* in the bottom of my bowl. "They love each other. They talk about being old together, sitting in **rocking chair**s on their **porch**, and what it will feel like to kiss each other when they have false teeth and bifocals.*"

"That's not what I asked. Are they married?"

Funny how Rice Krispies stick to a bowl when they're wet. I really had to **pry** them **loose** from the sides of the bowl with my spoon. "I don't think so, Dad. Maria doesn't wear a wedding ring, and her last name is different from Ben's."

My father **winced**. "That's what I was afraid of. I don't quite know how to deal with that one. And Clarice has already called Will's nephew in Boston. Well, maybe you should talk to Ben and Maria about it, Meg. They **might as well** be prepared."

Great. What was I supposed to do, go tell my friends

---

★ Rice Krispies 아침용 시리얼의 일종. 바삭바삭하게 한 쌀로 만드는 켈로그 사의 제품.
✵ false teeth and bifocals 'false teeth'는 글자 그대로 가짜(false) 이빨(teeth), 즉 '틀니'를 의미한다. 보통 틀니는 나이가 들어 이빨이 제 기능을 하지 못할 때 착용한다. 'bifocals'는 먼 곳과 가까운 곳을 모두 볼 수 있게 도와주는 '이중 초점 렌즈'를 뜻하는데, 이런 이중 초점 렌즈 역시 나이가 많이 들어 눈이 물체에 초점을 맞추는 능력이 떨어질 때 착용한다.

who were going to have a baby next month that I thought they ought to get married? What business was it of mine?

Still, my father was right. They ought to know what was going on. I gave up my plans for working in the darkroom that morning. Ben and Maria had asked if they could see some of my photographs, so I took the ones I'd done of Will, and two that I'd just finished of Molly. She hadn't even noticed my taking them; she'd been sitting on the front steps, working on some of her wild flowers. With Will's help, she'd **mount**ed each of the flowers she'd pressed, and labeled them with their Latin names.★ One of the pictures showed Molly holding a blossom of Queen Anne's lace✳ up against the sunlight; both she and the blossom were in **silhouette**. The other photograph was of her **bent** head, with what was left of her **curly** hair falling down over her face as she arranged some tiny flowers on a page.

Ben and Maria were hanging sheets and towels on the **clothesline** behind their house when I got there. They did their wash together every Saturday, using an old **wringer** machine that they'd bought at a **garage** sale.✳ Ben always teased Maria that if she didn't have the baby on time, he

---

★ Latin name 국제적인 표준에 따른 학명. 라틴어로 쓴다.
✳ Queen Anne's lace 야생 당근꽃. 꽃모양이 레이스의 무늬와 유사하여 앤 여왕의 레이스 라는 이름을 가지게 되었다.
✳ garage sale 중고 물품 세일. 이사를 하거나 대청소를 한 후에 자기 집 차고(garage) 앞에서 불필요한 물건을 모아 파는 것.

108

would put her through the wringer and **squeeze** it out; just thinking about it makes my stomach **lurch**, but Maria thought it was funny.

"Hey, Meg!" Ben called cheerfully when he saw me coming. "This time next month, we'll be hanging **diaper**s!"

"You mean *you'll* be hanging diapers," laughed Maria, as she **snap**ped a wet dish towel into the air to get the **wrinkle**s out. "*I'm* going to be lying in bed, being waited on. Having tea brought to me on a **tray**, while I **recover**!"

Knowing Maria, I didn't think she was going to be spending much time in bed recovering. She'd probably be up and around the day after the baby arrived, **sand**ing the floors, building a **bookcase**, making raspberry★ jam. I talked her into letting me help Ben with the rest of the **laundry**, and she went inside to make a pot of tea.

We sat around their little painted kitchen table and shared tea with fresh mint in it. I took out the photographs to show them. They loved the ones of Will, because they love Will. But the two of Molly were better. They thought that, and I could see the difference, too. Partly it was because I have been learning so much from working with Will; partly it was because I was using his German camera now. He had taught me to use the different lenses; I had

★ raspberry 라즈베리, 산딸기.

shot these two of Molly with the 90mm lens, and I'd been able, that way, to do it from a distance, so that she hadn't known I was doing it. The look on her face was **absorb**ed, **preoccupied** with her flowers; the fine lens caught the sharp **outline** of sunlight on her hair and the shadows across her face and hands.

"I asked Molly if she wanted to come with me this morning," I explained, "but she wasn't feeling well. She said to say hi, though, and to see how you're coming with the **cradle**."

Maria grinned with pride and pointed into the living room, where the cradle stood, finished. It **glow**ed with wax; folded over one side was a soft yellow **crochet**ed blanket.

"Meg," asked Ben **hesitant**ly, "what's wrong with Molly?"

I told them about her illness, about the **nosebleed**s, the hospital, the **transfusion**s, and the pills that were making her hair **fall out**. They were both very quiet. Ben reached over and ran his hand gently over the top of my head. "That's **rough**," he said. "That's very rough."

"Well," I explained, "it's not that big a deal And she's lots better. Look." I pointed to one of the photographs. "See how round her face is getting? She's gained ten pounds* since she came home from the hospital."

---

★ pound 파운드. 무게의 단위로 0.453 kg에 해당한다.

Maria poured more tea into our cups. "I'm glad we came here, Ben," she said suddenly, "for Molly. She's so excited about the baby."

That reminded me why I had come to see them. "Ben? Maria?" I said. "You know the little church in the village?"

"Sure," Ben said. "The white **steeple**. It looks like a postcard picture. Why? You going to photograph it?"

"No," I said. "But last Saturday, when I was in town with Mom to buy **groceries**, there was a wedding there. It was really neat. The **bride** came out and threw her **bouquet** from the step. The **bridesmaids** all had light blue dresses on, and—" I **hesitated**. "Well, I don't know. It was just nice."

Ben and Maria were both **making face**s. Ben is quite good at making faces; he **screw**ed his mouth up **sideways** and crossed his eyes. "Weddings," he said. "**Yuck**."

Maria rolled her eyes and agreed with him. "Yuck," she said.

"*Why?*" I asked. "What's wrong with getting married, **darn** it*?"

They both looked surprised. "Nothing's wrong with getting *married*," Ben said. "It's weddings that are so awful. What do you think, Maria, shall we show her?"

Maria grinned and nodded. "Yeah," she said. "She's a

---

★ darn it 에잇, 참! 못마땅하거나 짜증스러울 때 damn을 피하기 위해 쓰는 순화된 표현.

good kid."

Ben went into the living room and took a box out of the **closet**. He brought it back to the kitchen table and set it down. He **leer**ed, fingered his beard, and said in a **diabolical** voice, "Ya wanna see some **feelthy** pictures, lady?" Then he opened the box.

I started to laugh. They weren't bad photographs; in fact, **technical**ly, they were very good photographs, even though I'm not crazy about color.

But they were *awful*. And they were of Ben and Maria's wedding, for pete's sake. They were in a thick white leather album that said *Our Wedding* on the cover in gold letters. And I could see, while I looked at them, what Ben and Maria meant about **yucky** weddings.

There were the **tuxedo**s, and the **tail**s, and the top hats.* There was Maria with her dress pulled up to show a **lacy** blue garter.* There were the huge baskets of flowers beside the **altar** of the church. "Know what happened to those flowers?" Maria asked. "Two hundred dollars' worth of flowers? They got thrown away as soon as the service was over."

There was the wedding cake, about three feet high,*

---

★ top hat 둥글고 높은 원통 형태의 모양을 가진 예식용 남자 모자. 실크 해트 혹은 중산모 라고 부르기도 한다.
✳ garter 가터벨트. 스타킹이 흘러내리는 것을 막아주는 고리 모양의 장치가 달린 속옷.
✳ thee feet high 3피트(약 1미터) 높이. 피트(feet)는 길이의 단위로 30.48센티미터이다.

decorated with birds and flowers and **frosting** ribbons. "Know how much that cake cost?" grinned Ben. "A hundred **bucks**. Know what it tasted like? **Cardboard**."

There were hundreds of people drinking champagne.★ "Know who those people are?" asked Maria. "My parents' friends. Ben's parents' friends. Know what they're doing? Getting drunk, on five hundred dollars' worth of champagne."

And there were Ben and Maria, surrounded by people, flowers, food. They were smiling at the camera, but they both looked as if they didn't mean it much.

"Know who that is?" Ben asked. I nodded.

"That's Ben Brady and Maria Abbott, who wanted to get married in a field full of daisies※ beside a **stream**. Who wanted to have guitar music instead of a five-piece band;※ **homemade** wine instead of champagne," he said. He **slam**med the book closed and put it back in the box.

"Why didn't you?" I asked.

They shrugged. "Oh, sometimes it's just easier to please people," Maria said finally. "Ben's parents wanted a big wedding. My parents wanted a big wedding. We did it for them, I guess."

"Can I ask you a funny question?"

★ champagne 샴페인. 백포도주의 일종으로 마개가 빠질 때 나는 소리와 흰 거품이 특징인 술.
※ daisy 데이지 꽃. 국화과의 식물이다.
※ five-piece band 다섯 개의 악기로 구성된 밴드.

"Sure."

"Why don't you both have the same last name?"

It was Maria who answered me. "You know, Meg, I had the name Abbott all my life. Maria Abbott did things that I was proud of. I won a music award in high school, and I was Maria Abbott. I was **elect**ed to Phi Beta Kappa* in college, something I worked hard for, and I was Maria Abbott. When I realized I wanted to marry Ben, I also realized that I didn't want to stop being Maria Abbott. Ben could understand that. There's no law that says a wife must take her husband's name. So I didn't. Someday you may feel the same way about Meg Chalmers."

Right now I know there's no one I would rather be than Meg Chalmers. It's a funny thing about names, how they become part of someone. I thought suddenly of the little boy Will Banks, years ago, who sat in a room angry and sad, and **carve**d WILLIAM on the closet floor.

"Hey," I said. Funny I hadn't thought to ask before. "The baby. What are you going to name him? Her? It?"

Maria groaned. "Ask any other question, Meg. *Don't* ask what we're going to name him her it. We can't decide. We fight about it all the time. We scream at each other. It's *awful.*"

---

★ **Phi Beta Kappa** 파이 베타 카파회. 미국 대학의 우등생들로 구성된 친목 단체.

Ben said, "I've quit worrying about it. I **figure** the baby is going to arrive and before it does anything else, it's going to shake hands all around and say, 'Hi. I'm———.' That's the only way we're going to know what its name is."

Then he jumped up, **bound**ed through the living room, and opened a door. "But look! This is where it will be born!" I looked through the living room and saw an empty room beyond, very clean, its walls freshly painted white, with a brass bed* alone in the center.

"And this is where it will sleep," said Maria, smiling, touching the cradle with her bare foot, so that it **rock**ed slightly.

"And this is what it'll wear!" said Ben proudly, reaching into the drawer of a partly sanded pine **chest**, and pulling out a tiny blue nightgown. The drawer was filled with little folded things.

"This is what it'll eat!" grinned Maria, **cup**ping her hands around her **breast**s.

"And—" Ben stood still suddenly, in the middle of the living room. "Meg, come. I want to show you something." He took my hand, and I followed him out the back door, picking up my photographs on the way. It was almost lunchtime.

---

★ brass bed 놋쇠(황동) 침대. 침대 틀을 놋쇠(brass)로 만든 침대.

Ben took me past the garden where the peas were **thriving** against the wire trellises,* across the newly cleared space where he'd been pulling up alders,* past the little wooden bird **feeder** that Maria filled with seeds each morning. Behind a **clump** of young pine trees, he had pulled out brush and **expose**d part of a rock wall that had been there, I knew, for more than a hundred years. The sunlight **filter**ed down through the nearby woods into the little **seclude**d space; he had cut the grass there, and it was very soft, very green, very quiet.

He put his arm over my shoulders and said, "This is where we'll bury the baby, if it doesn't live."

I couldn't believe it. I pushed his arm off me and said, "*What?*"

"You know," he said firmly, "sometimes things don't work out the way you want them to. If the baby dies, Maria and I will bury it here."

"It's not going to die! What a **horrible** thing to say!"

"Look, Meg," Ben said, "you can *pretend* that bad things will never happen. But life's a lot easier if you realize and admit that sometimes they do. Of course the baby's probably going to be just fine. But Maria and I talk about

---

★ wire trellis 포도 같은 덩굴 식물들이 자랄 수 있도록 돕는 줄(wire)로 만든 격자 구조물(trellis).

✳ alder [식물] 오리나무. 높이 20m 정도에 달하며 갈색 가지를 가지고 있다. 옛날에 거리를 표시하기 위해 5리마다 심었던 데서 오리나무라는 이름이 붙여졌다.

116

the other possibility, too. **Just in case**; Just in case."

I turned away from him and left him standing there. I was so angry I was shaking. I looked back; his hands were in his pockets, and he was watching me.

I said, "Just in case you're interested, Ben Brady, I think you're an absolutely **rotten** person. That baby doesn't **deserve** you for a father."

Then I walked home, and on the way home I was sorry I had said it, but it was too late to go back.

# 8

Molly is in the hospital again, and it's my fault.

Why can't I learn when to keep my mouth shut? I'd already said something I **regret**ted, to Ben, and hadn't had the **nerve** to go to him and **apologize**. It was just a week later that I **blew it** with Molly.

She was **lying** on her bed, in her **nightgown**, even though it was eleven in the morning. She's gotten so **darn** lazy, and my parents don't even say anything to her about it. That's partly why I was mad at her, **to begin with**, because she was still in her nightgown at eleven in the morning.

She was **grouchy** and mad, too. I'm not sure why. I think mostly it was because school had just ended, before she'd even had a chance to go back. Tierney McGoldrick hardly ever calls her anymore. She doesn't know it, but toward the end of school he started dating a red-haired **senior** girl. At least I was smart enough not to tell Molly *that*.

But there she was, lying on her bed, **grumbling** about how awful she looks. I **am** so **sick of** hearing Molly talk about how she looks. Her face is too fat. Her hair is too thin. To hear her talk, you'd think she was really a **mess**, when the truth is that she's still a **billion** times prettier than I am, which is why I'm sick of listening to her.

I told her to shut up.

She told me to **drop dead**, and before I dropped dead, to pick up my **sneaker**s from her side of the room.

I told her to pick them up herself.

She started to get up, I think to pick up my sneakers and throw them at me, and when she **swung** her legs over the side of the bed, I suddenly saw what they looked like.

"Molly!" I said, forgetting about the sneakers. "What's wrong with your *legs?*"

"What do you *mean*, what's wrong with my legs?" No one had ever **criticize**d Molly's legs before; in fact, even I have to admit that Molly's got nice legs. She held up her nightgown and looked down.

Both of her legs were covered with dark red **spot**s. It looked like a lot of **mosquito bite**s, except that they weren't **swollen**.

"Does it hurt?"

"No," she said slowly, looking **puzzled**. "What could it be? It wasn't there yesterday; I know it wasn't."

"Well, it's there now, and it sure looks **weird**."

She pulled her nightgown down to cover her legs. Then she got into bed and pulled the covers up around her. "Don't tell anyone," she said.

"I will, too. I'm telling Mom." I started out of the room.

"Don't you *dare*," Molly ordered.

I'll be darned* if I'll take orders from Molly. Anyway, I really thought my parents ought to know. I went downstairs and told Mom that there was something wrong with Molly's legs; she jumped up with a **frighten**ed look and went upstairs. I stayed out of it after that, but I listened.

I heard Mom and Molly arguing. I heard my mother get my father from the study. Then more arguing with Molly. I heard my mother go to the upstairs phone, make a call, and go back to Molly.

---

★ I'll be darned (= I am surprised.) 뭔가 놀랍고, 충격적이고, 당황스러울 때 쓰는 표현.

Then Molly crying. **Yell**ing. I had never in my life heard Molly like that before. She was screaming, "No! I won't! I won't!"

Things quieted after a few minutes, and then my father came down. His face was very **drawn**, very tired. "We have to take Molly back to the hospital," he told me **abrupt**ly, and without waiting for me to answer, he went out to start the car.

Mom came downstairs with Molly. She was in her **bathrobe** and slippers, and she was **sob**bing. When they were by the front door, Molly saw me standing all alone in the living room. She turned to me, still crying, and said, "I hate you! I hate you!"

"Molly," I whispered, "please don't."

They were in the car and ready to leave when I heard my mother call to me. I went outside, letting the **screen door bang** behind me, and walked over to the car. "Molly wants to tell you something," Mom said.

Molly was in the back seat, **huddled** in the corner, **rub**bing her eyes with the back of her hand. "Meg," she said, **choking** a little because she was trying to stop crying, "tell Ben and Maria not to have the baby until I get home!"

"Okay," I nodded. "I'll tell them." As if they had any control over it! But I would tell them what Molly said, just

122

because Molly asked me to. At that point I would have done anything in the world for Molly.

I went back upstairs, picked up my sneakers and put them in the closet. I **made** Molly's **bed**. The pussy willows were still there, in their little vase. The photographs of Will were back on the wall, and the two of Molly and her flowers were with them now. The **chalk** mark was still there, faded, but there. It was a nice room, except that an hour before, Molly had been in it, and now she wasn't, and it was my fault.

I went down to the darkroom, gathered up the photographs of Maria I'd been working on, and walked across the field to their house.

Will Banks was there, having lunch with Ben and Maria. They were all sitting outside at the picnic table, eating the **entire crop** of **pea**s. There was a huge bowl of them in the middle of the table, and they were each eating from it with their own spoons, as if it were the most normal sort of lunch in the world.

"Hey, Meg!" Ben **greet**ed me. "How's it going? Have a pea. Have *two* peas!"

He **fed** me two peas from his spoon; they were the **tender**est, sweetest peas I've ever eaten. I sat down on the bench beside Will, and said, "Molly's back in the hospital, and she says please don't have the baby until she comes home. I know that's a **dumb** thing to say," and then I started to cry.

Will Banks put his arms around me and **rock**ed me back and forth as if I were a baby. I cried until his shirt **collar** was wet clear through, saying "It's my fault, it's my fault, it's my fault" **over and over** again. Will said nothing except "There. There.★"

Finally I stopped crying, sat up straight, blew my nose on the **handkerchief** Will gave me, and told them what had happened. No one said very much. They told me, of course, that it wasn't my fault. I knew that already. Ben said, "You know, sometimes it's nice just to have someone to **blame**, even if it has to be yourself, even if it doesn't **make sense**."

We sat there quietly for a minute, and then I asked if I could borrow Maria's spoon. She **wipe**d it on her napkin and gave it to me, and I ate all the peas that were left in the big bowl. There were *pounds* of peas, and I ate them all. I have never been so hungry in my life.

The three of them watched in **amaze**ment while I ate all those peas. When I was finished, Maria started to **giggle**. Then we all started to laugh, and laughed until we were **exhaust**ed.

---

★ there, there 위로·격려·동정·단념 등을 나타낼 때 하는 말. 그래그래, 오냐오냐.

It is so good to have friends who understand how there is a time for crying and a time for laughing, and that sometimes the two are very close together.

I took out the photographs of Maria. Will had seen them, of course, because we'd worked on them together. He is as able in the darkroom now as I am, but our interests are different. He is **fascinated** by the **technical aspect**s of photography: by the chemicals, and the inner workings of cameras. I don't care so much about those things. I care about the expressions on people's faces, the way the light falls onto them, and the way the shadows are in soft patterns and **contrast**.

We looked at the pictures together, and talked about them. Ben was much like Will, interested in the problems of **exposure** and film latitude;* Maria was like me: she liked seeing how the shadows curved around the fullness of the baby inside her, how her hands rested on the roundness of her middle, how her eyes were both **serene** and excited at the same time.

"Meg," she said, "Ben and I were talking about something the other night, and we want you to think it over and talk about it with your parents. If you want to, and if they don't mind, we'd like you to photograph the birth of

---

★ film latitude [사진] 노출 허용도.

the baby."

I was **floor**ed. "**Golly**," I said slowly, "I don't know. It never **occurr**ed to me. I mean, I don't want to **intrude**."

But they were both shaking their heads. "No," Ben said. "It wouldn't be an **intrusion**. We wouldn't want just anyone there, and of course you'd have to be careful to stay out of the way and not to touch anything **sterile**. But you're special, Meg; you're close to us. Someday Maria and I would like to be able to look back at that moment. We'd like the baby, someday, to be able to see it, too. You're the one who can do it, if you want to."

I wanted to, **desperate**ly. But I had to be honest with them, also. "I've never seen a baby being born," I said. "I don't even know much about it."

"Neither have we!" Maria laughed. "But we'll prepare you for that part. Ben will show you our books, and explain everything **in advance** so that you'll know exactly what to expect when the time comes. Only, Ben," she added to him, "I think you'd better do it *soon*, because I don't know how much longer we have. The calendar says two weeks, but there are times when I wonder if it might be sooner."

I promised to talk to my parents, and Ben said he would, too. Suddenly I thought of something. "What if it's born at night?" I asked. "There won't be enough light. I could use a flash, I suppose, but—"

Ben held up one hand. "Don't worry!" he said. He cupped his hands into a megaphone and held them against Maria's stomach. Then he spoke to the baby through his hands: "Now hear this, kid. You are under instructions to wait until Molly comes home. Then come, but do it in daylight, you hear?

"That'll do it," Ben said. "Maria and I are determined to have an obedient child."

Before I left, I took Ben aside and spoke to him alone. "I'm sorry, Ben, for what I said that day."

He squeezed my shoulders. "That's okay, Meg. We all say things we're sorry for. But do you understand now what I was talking about that day?"

I shook my head and answered him seriously, honestly. "No. I think you're wrong, to anticipate bad things. And I don't understand why you even want to think about something like that. But I'm still sorry for what I said."

"Well," Ben said, "we're friends, anyway. Hang in there, Meg." And he shook my hand.

Will walked me home across the field. He was very quiet. Halfway home, he said, "Meg, you're very young. Do you think it's a good idea, really, being there when that child is born?"

"Why not?"

"It might be very frightening. Birth isn't an easy thing,

you know."

"I know that." I **dislodge**d a small rock with one **toe** and kicked it through a clump of tall grass. "For pete's sake, Will, how can I learn if I don't take risks? You're the one who taught me that!"

Will stopped short and thought for a minute. "You're absolutely right, Meg. Absolutely right." He looked a little **sheepish**.

I looked around the field. "Will, what happened to all those little yellow flowers that were here last month?"

"Gone until next June," he told me. "They've all been **replace**d by July's flowers. Molly's goldenrod will be in **bloom** before long."

"I *liked* those little yellow ones," I said **grumpily**.

"'Margaret, are you **grieving** over Goldengrove **unleaving?**'" Will asked.

"What?" I was puzzled. He never called me Margaret; what was he talking about?

He smiled. "It's a **poem** by Hopkins.★ Your father would know. 'It is the **blight** man was born for, It is Margaret you **mourn** for,'" he went on.

"Not me," I told him **arrogant**ly. "I *never* mourn for myself."

---

★ Hopkins 홉킨스(Gerard Manley Hopkins). 영국의 시인이자 성직자.

"We all do, Meg," Will said. "We all do."

That was three weeks ago. July is almost over. Molly isn't home yet. The baby hasn't been born, so I suppose it's following Ben's instructions and waiting for her. I've studied the books on **deliver**ing **babies** with Maria and Ben, and I'm ready to do the photographs. My parents don't mind. When I asked them, they said "Sure" without even discussing it. They're very **preoccupied**. I know why, finally.

It was a few nights ago, after supper. My dad was smoking his **pipe** at the kitchen table. The dishes were done; Mom was **sew**ing on the quilt, which is almost finished. I was just **hang**ing **around**, talking too much, trying to **make up for** the quiet that had been **consuming** our house. I even turned the radio on; there was some rock music playing.

"Hey, Dad, dance with me!" I said, pulling at his arm. It was something silly we used to do sometimes, back in town. My dad is a *terrible* dancer, but sometimes he used to dance with Molly and me in the kitchen; it used to **break** my mother **up**.

He finally put down his pipe and got up and started dancing. Poor Dad; he hadn't gotten any better since the last time we did it, and I think I have, a little. But he's pretty **uninhibited**, and he tried. It was dark outside; we had eaten late. Mom turned on the light, and I could see on the kitchen walls some of the drawings of wild flowers that Molly had been doing, that she had hung here and there. Dad and I danced and danced until he was **sweat**ing and laughing. Mom was laughing, too.

Then the music changed, to a slow piece. Dad breathed a great **sigh** of **relief** and said, "Ah, my **tempo**. May I have the pleasure, my dear?" He **held out** his arms to me and I **curl**ed **up** inside them. We **waltz**ed slowly around the kitchen like people in an old movie until the music ended. We stood facing each other at the end, and I said suddenly, "I wish Molly was here."

My mother made a small noise, and when I looked over at her, she was crying. I looked back at Dad in **bewilder**ment, and there were tears on his face, too, the first time I had ever seen my father cry.

I reached out my arms to him, and we both held out our arms to Mom. She moved into them, and as the music started again, another slow, **melancholy** song from some past summer I couldn't remember, the three of us danced together. The wild flowers on the wall moved in a gradual **blur** through our circling and through my own tears. I held my arms tight around the two of them as we moved around in a kind of rhythm that kept us close, in an **enclosure** made of ourselves that kept the rest of the world away, as we danced and **wept** at the same time. I knew then what they hadn't wanted to tell me, and they knew that I knew, that Molly wouldn't be coming home again, that Molly was going to die.

# 9

I dream of Molly again and again.

Sometimes they are short, sunshine-filled dreams, in which she and I are running side by side in a field filled with goldenrod. She's the old Molly, the Molly I knew all my life, the Molly with long blond curls and her light laugh. The Molly who runs with strong **tan** legs and **bare** feet. She runs faster than I can, in my dream, looks back at me, laughing, and I call to her, "Wait! Wait for me, Molly!"

She **hold**s **out** her hand to me, and calls, with her hair blowing around her, **streak**ed with sun, "Come on, Meg!

You can **catch up** if you try!"

I wake up; the room is dark, and her bed is empty beside mine. I think of her somewhere in a hospital I have never seen, and wonder if she is dreaming the same dream.

Sometimes they are darker dreams of the same field. I am the one, in this darker dream, who has run faster; I have reached some **misty destination**, a dark and empty house, where I stand waiting for her, watching her from a window as she runs. But the flowers in the field have begun to turn brown, as if summer is ending too soon, and Molly is **stumbling**; it is she who is calling to me, "Meg, wait! Wait! I can't make it, Meg!" And there is no way I can help her.

I wake from this dream, too, in a dark and empty room from which the sound of her breathing in the next bed has gone.

I have a **nightmare** in which a baby is born, but is old, already, at birth. The baby looks at us, those of us who are there, with **aged** and tired eyes, and we realize with horror that his life is ending at the very moment of its beginning. "Why? Why?" we ask, and the baby doesn't answer. Molly is there, and she is angry at our asking; she **shrugs** coldly and turns away from us. Only she knows the answer, and she won't share it with us, although we **plead** with her.

I wake **terrified** that it is real.

I told my father of the dreams. When I was a very little

girl and had nightmares, it was always my father who came to my room when I cried out. He used to turn on the light and hold me; he showed me that the dreams weren't true.

Now he can't. We sat on the front steps in the evening, and I blew the gray **fuzz** of dying dandelions★ into the pink **breeze** as the sun was setting. The fears that come into my room in the night seemed far away, but Dad said, "Your dreams come out of what is real, you know. It helps, some, to think about what they mean. That you and Molly are going to be **separate**d, even though you don't want to be. That you want to know why, why life sometimes ends too soon, but no one can answer that."

I **crush**ed the **stem** of a dandelion in my hand. "It doesn't help, understanding why I have nightmares. How can it help? It can't make Molly better.

"It isn't fair!" I said, the way I said it so often when I was a little girl.

"Of course it isn't fair," Dad said. "But it happens. It happens, and we have to accept that."

"And it wasn't fair that you and Mom didn't tell me!" I said, looking for someone to **blame** for something. "You knew **all along**, didn't you? You knew from the very beginning!"

---

★ dandelion 민들레.

He shook his head. "Meg, the doctors told us that there was a chance she would be all right. They have these medicines that they try. There is always a chance something will work. There was no way that Mom and I could tell you when there was a chance."

"Then isn't there *still* a chance?"

He shook his head slowly. "Meg, we can hope for it. We *do* hope for it. But the doctors say there isn't, now. The medicines aren't working for Molly now."

"Well, I don't believe them."

He put his arm around me and watched the sun setting.

Then he said, in his **quoting** voice, "'We are such stuff as dreams are made on, and our little life is rounded with a sleep.' That's Shakespeare,★ Meg."

I was **furious**. "What did *he* know? He never knew Molly. And why *Molly?* Dad, *I'm* the one who always got into trouble! I'm the one who **threw up** on my own birthday cake, who broke the window in **kindergarten**, who stole candy from the **grocery** store. Molly never did anything bad!"

"Meg," he said. "Meg. Don't."

"I don't care," I said angrily. "Someone has got to<sup>＊</sup> explain to me *why*."

---

★ Shakespeare 셰익스피어(William Shakespeare). 영국이 낳은 세계 최고 시인 겸 극작가.
＊ has[have] got to (= have to) …하지 않으면 안 된다, …해야 한다.

136

"It's a **disease**, Meg," he said in a tired voice. "A **horrible, rotten** disease. It just happens. There *isn't* any why."

"What's it called?" Better to know what your **enemy** is before you **confront** it, Will had told me once.

Dad sighed. "It's called 'acute myelogenous leukemia.*'"

"Can you say that three times fast?" I asked him **bitter**ly.

"Meg," said Dad, putting his arms around me and holding me so tight that his voice was **muffled**, "I can't even say it once. It **breaks my heart**."

Mom and Dad go back and forth to the hospital in Portland. They don't take me. I am too young, according to the hospital rules, to visit, but I don't think that's the reason. I think they don't want me to have to see Molly dying.

I don't argue with them. All the times I've argued with them in the past: to be allowed to see a certain movie, to drink a glass of wine with dinner, to sit in the back of one of Dad's classes at the university, listening. "I'm old enough! I'm old enough!" I remember saying. Now I don't argue, because they know and I know I'm old enough; but I'm **scared**. The dreams and the emptiness at home are enough; it takes all the courage I have to deal with those. I'm afraid

---

★ acute myelogenous leukemia 급성 골수성 백혈병.

to see my own sister, and **grateful** that they don't ask me to come.

When she's at home, my mother stitches on the quilt and talks about the past. Every **square** that she fits into place reminds her of something. She remembers Molly learning to walk, wearing the **pale** blue **overall**s that are now part of the pattern of the quilt.

"She used to **fall down on her bottom**, again and again," my mother smiled. "She always jumped back up laughing. Dad and I used to think sometimes that she fell **on purpose**, because it was funny. Molly was always looking for things to laugh at when she was a baby."

"What about me? Do you remember *me* learning to walk?"

"Of course I do," Mom said. She turned the quilt around until she found the piece she was looking for, a **flowered** pattern of blue and green. "This was a little dress. It was summer, and you weren't yet a year old. You were so **impatient** to do the things that Molly could do. I remember watching you in the back yard that summer. You were very serious and **solemn**, pulling yourself to your feet, trying to walk across the grass alone.

"You'd fall, and never take time to cry, or laugh, either. Your **forehead** would wrinkle up as you **figured out** how to do it right, and tried again."

"I'm like Dad."

She smiled. "Yes, you are, Meg."

"And Molly is more like you. I always thought that was an easier way to be."

Mom sighed and thought about it for a minute. "Well," she said, "it's easier for the little things, to be able to laugh at them. It makes life seem pretty simple, and a lot of fun.

"But you know, Meg," Mom said, **smooth**ing the quilt with her fingers, "when the big, difficult things come, people like Molly and me aren't ready for them. We're so **accustom**ed to laughing. It's harder for us when the time comes that we can't laugh."

I realized that it was the first time I had ever seen my mother not able to shrug things off with a quick smile and an easy **solution**. And I knew that, hard as it was for me, with my **helpless**ness, my anger, and the dreams that came like **faceless prowler**s into my sleep and filled me with fear, it was worse for Mom.

"Dad and I are here, Mom," I said **uncertain**ly, "if that helps."

"Oh, Meg," she said, and hugged me. "I don't know what I'd do without you and Dad."

# 10

It was five in the morning when Ben called on the third of August. Mom was in Portland, staying with friends who live near the hospital where Molly was; she and Dad were **taking turns** being there. It was Dad who got me up when Ben called.

I **threw on** my jeans and a sweater and **sneaker**s, **grab**bed the camera in a big hurry, and headed across the field. It was going to be a beautiful day. The sun was coming up, very red, so that even the yellow goldenrod looked pink. The baby had **obey**ed Ben's **instruction** and **elected** to come in daylight. It would be a, well, a semi-**obedient**★ baby; it wouldn't wait any longer for Molly to come home. Maybe it understood the realities of things better than the rest of us.

When I knocked at their door, Ben called for me to come on in. "I can't open it!" he called. "I'm **sterile**!

"I mean, I'm **sterile**d. Or something," he explained when I went inside and met him in the living room. He was wearing a long, white, **wrinkle**d shirt backwards, and holding his hands up carefully so that he wouldn't touch anything.

"We blew the timing, I guess," he said, looking **apologetic**. "Or the book was wrong. Everything's happening faster than it was supposed to. Remember in the book, Meg, about the first stage of **labor**, which lasts a long time? I figured that was when we'd all be **hang**ing **around**, planning what we'd do next!

"I don't know what happened. Maria just woke up about an hour ago and said she felt funny. And now, I don't know, I feel as if we ran a **stoplight** and ought to go back and do it again the way we were supposed to.

"I mean, I think it's going to be born right away! And I've forgotten everything the book said. I'm running around

---

★ semi 형용사나 명사 앞에 쓰여 '어느 정도는', '절반의'라는 의미를 만든다. 따라서 semi-obedient는 '절반 정도는 순종적인'.

holding my sterile hands in the air, afraid to turn the pages of the book to find out what it said about the second stage. *Maria's* fine. But I feel so stupid, Meg!" He stood there, looking **helpless**.

I could **sympathize** with how he felt, because suddenly I felt **panicky**, and forgot how the camera worked.

"Is that Meg?" called Maria. She sounded **astonishing**ly healthy for someone who was about to have a baby any minute. Ben went back in the room where she was, and motioned for me to follow.

She was on the bed, with her head **prop**ped up on a **pillow**. It didn't bother me that she was **naked**. We had talked about things like that enough, the three of us.

It **bother**ed me a little that she was so cheerful. I thought something must be wrong; it wasn't supposed to be easy, having a baby. But Maria looked happy and full of energy. It was only Ben and I who were pale and **scared**.

I lifted my camera and photographed Maria smiling. The instant I had the camera in my hands, things felt comfortable. The light was good; the settings **fell into place** as I **manipulate**d them; everything was okay.

Ben had a **stethoscope**, and he listened through Maria's **abdomen** to the baby. I could see that he experienced the same thing; when he picked up the simple **instrument**, he felt in control of things again. It was the helplessness that scared us both. "Listen!" Ben said, and handed the stethoscope to me.

I put the camera down. I listened where he told me to and could make out the **rapid**, strong heartbeat of the baby. It was full of energy and life; I smiled, hearing it, and nodded in response to Maria's questioning eyes.

Then, as I watched, she closed her eyes and began to breathe rapidly. I photographed her again, and turned the camera toward Ben. He was **lean**ing over, watching carefully. I photographed the **intent**ness of his face as he waited and watched, not touching her; she **bent** her knees and **arch**ed her back slightly. There was no sound in the room but her breathing, and I could see the **strain** move through her whole body.

"Look," Ben whispered to me. I moved to the foot of the bed, and could see, as the **passage** widened, **taut**, almost shaking with the action of the laboring **muscle**s, the top of the baby's head. I could see its dark hair.

Then it disappeared, **withdraw**ing like a **mitten**ed **fist** pulled back into a **sleeve**. Maria relaxed, opened her eyes, and sighed. Ben moved up near her head and talked quietly to her. "Everything's fine," he said gently. "I can see the head. It'll be soon, very soon." He smiled at her, and I photographed their heads together, and realized they had forgotten I was there.

Maria closed her eyes again and drew a deep, loud breath. Ben moved quickly again to the foot of the bed; I stood back and watched. Then I remembered the camera, moved farther from the bed, and photographed her whole body as she lay **poise**d, gathering herself, her **chin** up, mouth open and **gasp**ing, waiting. Suddenly she **groan**ed and lifted her whole body from the bed.

"**Take it easy**, take it easy," Ben was **murmur**ing. He leaned forward and touched the baby's head carefully, guiding it as it moved from her body. I came closer and photographed his strong hands holding the tiny head like the shell of an egg. The face was toward me, **flat** and motionless, its features nothing more than lines like a **hastily** drawn **cartoon**: the straight line of a motionless mouth, two **slit**s of **swollen**, tightly closed eyes, and the tiny, **squash**ed curve of a nose. Maria relaxed again. Ben stood very still, his hands still gently around the head, and the small, **flatten**ed face was as **immobile** as the painted face of a plastic toy.

"Once more," he told Maria. I don't think she heard him at all; her whole being was **clench**ed tight, and then she gasped as the rest of the little body **slid** toward Ben.

And still the only sound was Maria breathing. I was shooting pictures but I didn't even hear the click of the **shutter**, just the long, quiet, **exhaust**ed breaths.

Then, the cry of the child. Ben was holding it there in his two hands, **rub**bing it between them. He rubbed its narrow, **grayish** back; finally, the **incredibly** small arms and legs moved a little, like a sleeper **startled** from a dream, and it **wail**ed briefly. Maria smiled at the sound and lifted her head to see. Ben **grin**ned at her and said, "It's a boy. I told you it would be a boy."

He lay the baby on her stomach, waited a moment, and then tied the cord\* in two places and cut carefully between them. The baby was free of Maria now, but it **squirm**ed against her as if it wanted to stay close. Its face, in those few moments, had changed from **bluish**-gray to pink, and like a **sponge dip**ped in water, a shape had grown from the flatness of it. The tiny nose had risen into a soft and perfect curve; the thin line of mouth had become a moving, searching thing, and a **tongue** came from between the lips, tasting the air; the eyes opened and closed, **blink**ing and **squint**ing; the forehead drew up into wrinkles as the head turned against Maria's skin. She reached down with one hand, touched it gently, and smiled. Then she closed her eyes and rested again.

"Meg?" Ben handed me a soft white towel from the pile of things he had on a table beside him. "Take the baby for a

---

★ cord (=umbilical cord) 탯줄.

few minutes, would you, while I finish up here?"

I put my camera on the floor in the corner, wrapped the towel around the baby, and lifted it away from Maria. It was so tiny, so light. I pushed the towel away from the little face, and held it down so Maria could see. She smiled at me, murmured, "Thank you," and I took the baby into the living room.

I held him for a moment in the open front doorway of the house. The sun was golden now, and the **dew** was already **evaporating** from the tall grass and flowers in the field. The birds were awake. "Listen," I whispered to the baby, "the birds are singing to you." But he was asleep, his fingers relaxed and warm against my chest.

I sat in the **rocking chair** and moved slowly back and forth, trying with the soft, steady rhythm of the chair to **make up for** the **abrupt** and **agonizing** journey he had just had. I thought of the **overwhelm**ing force that had **grip**ped Maria's whole **being** at his birth, and the startled, almost painful way that he had moved as he felt his way to life outside her body. I was shaken more than I had **anticipated** by the **awesome**ness of the **transition**.

With one hand I took a corner of the towel and **wiped** his face, which was still **stain**ed from his **delivery**. As the towel touched him, he gave a surprised **jerk** and opened both eyes; his fingers **flutter**ed. Then he fell asleep again, breathing softly. The corners of his mouth moved briefly into what seemed to be a **momentary** smile, and he made a little sound with his lips as he slept.

"Ben?" I called softly.

"Yes? Everything okay? **I'm** almost **through**."

"Everything's fine. He says to tell you he's happy."

Ben came out of the room where Maria was, wiping his hands on a towel. He leaned over me, looked down at the baby, and grinned. "He says he's happy? I *told* you he'd tell us his name."

I gave the baby to Ben, went in the bedroom to get my camera, and kissed Maria on the cheek. She was covered with a blanket, and sleeping. I left the three of them there by themselves, and went back home to where my father was waiting.

And they did name him Happy. Happy William Abbott-Brady. When Will Banks heard that, he **was a little taken aback** at first. "Happy William?" he asked in surprise. "What kind of name is *that?*" Then he thought for a moment. "Well, there's a flower called *Sweet* William.*
*Dianthus barbatus,*＊ actually. So I suppose there's no reason why a boy can't be named Happy William. **So long as** he **live**s **up to** it, of course."

---

★ Sweet William [식물] 수염패랭이꽃.
＊ Dianthus barbatus 수염패랭이꽃의 학명.

Suddenly I wanted to be the one to tell Molly.

I had been afraid to see Molly, and now I wasn't. There isn't any way to explain that. The only thing that had happened was that I had watched Maria give birth to Happy, and for some reason that made a difference.

Dad drove me to Portland, and on the way he tried to tell me what it would be like at the hospital. "You have to keep reminding yourself," he said, "that it's still Molly. That's the hard thing, for me. Every time I go in her room, it takes me by surprise, seeing all that **machinery**. It seems to **separate** you from her. You have to look past it, and see that it's still Molly. Do you understand?"

I shook my head. "No," I said.

Dad sighed. "Well, I'm not sure I do either. But listen, Meg—when you think of Molly, how do you think of her?"

I was quiet for a minute, thinking. "I guess mostly I think of how she used to laugh. And then I think of how, even after she got sick, she used to run out in the field on sunny mornings, looking for new flowers. I used to watch her, sometimes, from the window."

"That's what I mean. That's the way I think of Molly, too. But when you get to the hospital, you'll see that everything is different for Molly now. It will make you feel strange, because you're outside of it; you're not part of it.

"She'll be very sleepy. That's because of the drugs they're

giving her, so that she'll feel comfortable. And she can't talk to you, because there's a tube in her **throat** to help her breathe.

"She'll look like a stranger to you, at first. And it'll be **scary**. But she can hear you, Meg. Talk to her. And you'll realize that underneath all that **stuff**, the tubes and needles and medicines, our Molly is still there. You have to remember that. It makes it easier.

"And, Meg?" He was driving very carefully, following the white line in the center of the curving road.

"What?"

"One more thing. Remember, too, that Molly's not in any pain, and she's not scared. It's only you and I and Mom, now, who are hurting and **frighten**ed.

"This is a hard thing to explain, Meg, but Molly is handling this thing very well by herself. She needs us, for our love, but she doesn't need us for anything else now." He **swallow**ed hard and said, "Dying is a very **solitary** thing. The only thing we can do is be there when she wants us there."

I had brought the little vase of pussy willows with me. I **shift**ed them on my **lap**, and reached over and **squeeze**d Dad's hand for a minute.

Mom met us at the hospital; the three of us had lunch together in the first-floor coffee shop. We talked mostly about Happy.

"I was the first one to hold him, Mom," I told her. "I think he smiled at me."

Mom looked as if she was remembering something. She started to speak, stopped and was silent for a minute, and then said what she had been thinking. "I remember when Molly was born. It's a very special time."

She told me that Molly was awake, that she knew I was coming, that she wanted me there. Then they took me upstairs.

She looked so small. For the first time in my life I felt older, bigger than Molly.

But not more beautiful. I would never feel more beautiful than Molly.

Her hair was completely gone. All those long blond curls were no longer part of Molly; the **translucent** skin of her face and head were like the fine **china** of an **antique** doll against the white pillow of the hospital bed. Above her, **label**ed glass bottles and plastic bags **dangle**d from a metal **rack**; through the tubes that led from them to the **vein**s in Molly's left arm, I watched the **solution**s **drip** slowly, like tears. The tube that entered her throat was held firmly in place with clean **adhesive** tape against her skin. I tried to separate all those things from Molly in my mind. Even though pain was **knot**ted inside me like a fist, I saw the way the **lash**es of her closed eyes were **outlined** on her cheek in perfect curving lines; I followed with my eyes the moving, **blur**red patterns of sunshine from the window on her bed, as the leaves of the trees outside moved and **swept** the sun across her hands and arms.

"Molly," I said. She opened her eyes, found me there, and smiled. She waited for me to talk to her.

"Molly, the baby is born."

She smiled again, very sleepily.

"It's a boy. He was born in the brass bed, the way they wanted. He came very quickly. Ben was all set to wait for hours, but Maria kept laughing and saying, 'No, Ben, it's coming right away!' And it did. Ben picked him up and put him on Maria's stomach, and he **curl**ed **up** and went to sleep."

She was watching me, listening. For a moment it was as if we were home again, in our beds, talking in the dark.

"Then Ben gave him to me, and I carried him to the **doorway** and showed him that the sun was coming up. I told him the birds were singing to him.

"Will came over later and brought them a big **bouquet** of wild flowers. I don't know the names—you would, though. All yellow and white.

"Ben and Maria and Will all said to tell you they love you."

152

She reached out and took my hand and squeezed it. Her hand was not as strong as Happy's.

"Ben and Maria asked me if I would make another copy of the picture of you holding the Queen Anne's lace. They want to hang it on the wall in the living room."

But she wasn't listening anymore. She had turned her head to one side and closed her eyes. Her hand **slip**ped gently out of mine and she was asleep again. I put the little vase of pussy willows on the table beside her bed, where she would see it when she woke up. Then I left her there alone.

On the drive home, I told my father, "Will Banks said a line from a **poem** to me once. He said, 'It is Margaret you **mourn** for,' and I told him I never mourn for myself. But I think he was right. So much of my sadness is because I miss Molly. I even miss fighting with her."

My father pulled me over close to him on the seat of the car and put his arm around me. "You've been great through all of this, Meg," he said. "I'm sorry I haven't told you that before. I've been busy mourning for myself too."

Then we sang the rest of the way home. We sang "Michael, Row Your Boat Ashore,*" mostly **off-key**, and we made up **verse**s for everybody. We sang "Dad's boat is

---

★ Michael, Row Your Boat Ashore '육지로 배를 저어요'라는 동요.

a Book boat," "Mom's boat is a Quilt boat," "Meg's boat is a Camera boat," "Ben and Maria's boat is a Happy boat," and "Will's boat is a House boat," which **struck** us both as much funnier than it really was. Finally, we sang "Molly's boat is a Flower boat," and when we finished that verse, we were turning down the **dirt road** to home.

Two weeks later she was gone. She just closed her eyes one afternoon and didn't ever open them again. Mom and Dad brought the pussy willows back for me to keep.

# *11*

Time goes on, and your life is still there, and you have to live it. After a while you remember the good things more often than the bad. Then, **gradually**, the empty silent parts of you fill up with sounds of talking and laughter again, and the **jagged** edges of sadness are softened by memories.

Nothing will be the same, ever, without Molly. But there's a whole world waiting, still, and there are good things in it.

It was September, and time to leave the little house that

had begun to seem like home.

I answered the knock at the front door and then went upstairs to the **study**. Dad was sitting at his desk, just staring **gloomily** at the piles of paperclipped pages that he had **arrange**d in some order on the floor.

"Dad, Clarice Callaway is at the door with some man. She says she hates to bother you at such a bad time, but."

"But she is going to do it anyway, right?" He **sigh**ed and got up. At the front door I heard Clarice introducing him to the man who was standing there holding a **briefcase** and looking **impatient** and **annoy**ed. Dad brought them inside, asked Mom to make some coffee, and the three of them sat down in the living room.

I went back to the darkroom where I was trying to pack. I was going to have a darkroom in town; Dad had already hired a couple of his students to build the **shelves** and do the **plumbing** and **wiring** in what had been a **maid**'s room, many years ago, on the third floor of the house there. It would, in fact, be a larger, better **equip**ped darkroom than the one I'd had all summer, so it wasn't that that was making me **depress**ed. And Will Banks had almost completed work on the darkroom that he was building for himself, in what had been a **pantry** of his little house. So my going away wasn't going to mean the end of Will's interest and **enthusiasm** or skill, and it couldn't have

156

been that that was making me feel sad as I packed up my negatives and **chemical**s and tools. I guess it was just that we wouldn't be doing it together anymore, Will and I.

It is hard to give up the being together with someone.

I **seal**ed the packing boxes with tape, wrote "Darkroom" on them, and carried them to a corner of the kitchen. There were other boxes there already; Mom had been packing for several days. There were boxes marked "Dishes," "Cooking **Utensil**s," and "**Linen**s." We'd been living like campers all week, eating from paper plates, finishing up the **odds and ends** in the **refrigerator**, making meals from the last few things in Mom's little garden.

There was a box marked "Quilt." Two nights before, my mother had **snap**ped off a **thread**, looked at the quilt in surprise, and said, "I think it's finished. How can it be finished?" She turned it all around, looking for some corner or **spot** that she'd forgotten, but every inch was covered with the **neat**, close-together rows of her tiny **stitch**es. She stood up and **laid** it out on the big kitchen table. There they were, all those orderly, **geometric** patterns of our past, Molly's and mine. All those bright **square**s of color: in the center, the **pale** pinks and yellows of our baby dresses; farther out, in carefully organized rows, the little **flowery** prints and the bright **plaid**s of the years when we were little girls; and at the edges, the more **subdue**d and **faded** denims and corduroys* of our growing up.

"It really is," she said slowly. "It's all done." Then she folded it and put it in the box.

Now I could hear her serving coffee in the living room. There was an **argument** going on. I could hear the quick, angry voices of the visitors, and suddenly I heard my mother's soft voice say, "That's not *fair*," the way I had so often said the same thing to Molly.

There was silence in the living room for a moment after Mom said that. Then I heard my father say, "There's no point in our continuing to discuss this. Let's go down the road to see Will. You should have gone to see him first, Mr. Huntington."

Dad came into the kitchen to use the phone. "Will?" he said. "Your **nephew** is here. Can we come down?"

Dad **grin**ned as he listened to the reply. I could imagine what Will was saying; I had never heard him say a good word about his sister's son.

"Will," said Dad on the phone. "*You* know that, and *I* know that. **Nevertheless**, we have to be **civilized**. Now calm down. We'll be there in a few minutes."

After he **hung up**, he said to me, "Meg, run over to Ben

---

★ denims and corduroys 데님과 코듀로이. 둘다 직물 이름으로, 데님(denim)은 주로 청바지를 만드는 데 쓰이는 푸른색의 질긴 면직물이고, 코듀로이(corduroy)는 보통 코르덴 혹은 골덴이라고 부르는 골이 지게 짠 직물이다.

and Maria's, would you? Tell them you'll stay with Happy if they'll meet us at Will's house to talk to his nephew from Boston."

When he went back into the living room, I heard Clarice Callaway say, "I haven't finished my coffee."

And I heard my father reply, "Clarice, I hate to **inconvenience** you, but." I could tell from his voice that it gave him a lot of **satisfaction**, saying it.

I loved taking care of Happy. That was another thing I hated about moving back to town, that I wouldn't have a chance to watch him grow bigger and learn things. Already he was holding his head up and looking around. The **newborn** baby part of him was already in the past, after only a month; now he was a little person, with big eyes, a loud voice, and a **definite personality**. Maria said he was like Ben, with a **screwball** sense of humor and no respect for **propriety**. Ben said he was like Maria: **illogical, assertive**, and a **showoff**. Maria **whack**ed Ben with a dish towel when he said that, and Ben grinned and said, "See what I mean?"

I just thought he was Happy, not like anyone else but himself.

When Ben and Maria came back from Will's, I asked them what was going on. Maria rolled her eyes and said, "*I don't know. Craziness, that's what's going on.*"

Ben was **roar**ing with laughter. "Meg, I have to show you something." He went to the **closet** and got the box with the album of wedding pictures.

"I've already seen them, Ben. I know you're married. I told my father so. Clarice can't still be worrying about *that*."

"No, no, *look*, **dummy**," said Ben. He **flip**ped through the heavy pages of colored photographs until he found the one he wanted. It was of a crowd of wedding guests, middle-aged people, drinking champagne. In the center of the crowd, looking terribly proper and at the same time a little **silly** from the champagne, was Will Banks' nephew.

"It's Martin Huntington!" Ben was **practically doubled up**, laughing. "I couldn't believe it. I walked into Will's house, and there was this **jerk** with a **lawyer suit** on, holding a briefcase, and he looked at me with my jeans and my **beard**, as if he didn't want to get too close for fear of being **infect**ed with some **disease**. And when I realized who he was, I **held out** my hand—you should have been there, Meg—and said, "Mr. Huntington, don't you remember me? I'm Ben Brady.""

"How do you know *him?*" I asked.

"He's been a junior partner* in my father's law firm* for

---

★ junior partner 법률사무소, 회계법인, 컨설팅 회사 등에서의 높은 지위를 '파트너'라고 하는데, 회사의 이익을 공유하는 '동업자'에서 유래한 말이다. junior partner는 낮은 직급의 파트너를 말한다.
＊ law firm 법률사무소.

years," laughed Ben. "Oh, you should have seen it, Meg. He stood there in Will's living room with his mouth open, and then he said in that **pompous** way he has, 'Well, Benjamin. I, ah, of course had no idea that, ah, it was you living in my family's house. Ah, of course, this does, ah, add a certain **element** of, ah, **awkward**ness to these **proceedings**.'

"'Proceedings!' Can you imagine, calling a discussion in Will Banks' living room 'proceedings'? That's so **typical** of Martin Huntington. I can't wait to tell my father!"

"But what's going to happen?"

Ben **shrugg**ed. "I don't know. But I'm going to call my father. I know what I'd like to have happen. I'd like to buy this house from Will, if my dad will lend me the money for a down payment.* I'd like Happy to grow up here. How about that, Hap? Hey, Maria, doesn't that kid ever stop eating?"

Maria was **nursing** Happy. She grinned at Ben. "He's gonna **take after** his old man," she said.

Back home, my parents were in the living room drinking the **reheat**ed coffee. The **rug** was rolled up, and the curtains were gone from the windows. Little by little the house was being emptied of everything that had been ours.

---

★ down payment 할부금의 계약금, 첫 불입금.

"Ben wants to buy the house," I told them. "And they'd live here always." I sighed, kicked off my shoes, and brushed away the pieces of dead leaves that were stuck to my socks and jeans. Everything in the field seemed to be dying.

"Well, that's **terrific!**" said my father. "Why are you looking so **glum?**"

"I'm not sure," I answered. "I guess because we're leaving. Next summer everything will be the same for *them*, but what about us?"

Mom and Dad were quiet for a minute. Finally Dad said, "Listen, Meg. This house will still be here next summer. We *could* **rent** it again. But Mom and I have talked about it, and we're just not sure."

"There are so many sad memories for us here, Meg," my mother said quietly.

"By next summer, though," I suggested, "maybe it would be easier. Maybe it would be fun to remember Molly in this house."

Mom smiled. "Maybe. We'll wait and see."

The three of us stood up; Mom headed for the kitchen, to finish the packing there. Dad started up the stairs to his study.

"You know," he said, stopping halfway up the **staircase**. "At one point in the book, I wrote that the use

162

of **coincidence** is an **immature literary device**. But when Ben walked into Will's living room today and said, 'Mr. Huntington, don't you remember me?,' well—"

He stood there thinking for a moment. Then he starred talking to himself.

"If I **rearrange**d the ninth chapter," he **mutter**ed, "to make it **correspond** to—" He walked slowly up the rest of the stairs, muttering. At the top of the stairs he stood, looked into the study at the piles of pages, then turned and called down to us **triumphant**ly, "Lydia! Meg! The book is *finished!* It only needs rearranging! I didn't realize it until now!"

So the **manuscript** was packed, too, and in great bold capital letters, Dad wrote on the box, "BOOK."

The next day, the **moving van** came. Will Banks, Ben, and Maria, holding Happy, stood in the **driveway** of the little house, and **wave**d good-bye.

It was the end of September when my father came home after his classes one day and told me, "Meg, **comb** your hair. I want you to go **someplace** with me."

Usually he doesn't notice or care if my hair is combed, so I knew it was someplace special. I even washed my face and changed from **sneaker**s into my school shoes. I **grab**bed a jacket—it was getting **chilly**: the kind of September air that smells of **pumpkin**s, apples, and dead leaves—and got into the car. Dad drove me to the university museum, the big stone building with bronze **statue**s in front of it.

"Dad," I whispered as we went up the wide steps, "I have seen the Renaissance★ collection a thousand times. If you're going to make me take that guided tour *again*, I'll—"

"Meg," he said. "Will you please **hush**?"

The lady at the front desk knew Dad. "Dr. Chalmers," she said, "I was so sorry to hear about your daughter."

"Thank you," said my father. "This is my other daughter, Meg. Meg, this is Miss Amato."

I shook her hand, and she looked at me curiously.

"Oh," she said, as if she were surprised. Didn't she know that Dad had another daughter? "*Oh*," she said again. "The photography **exhibition** is in the west **wing**, Dr. Chalmers."

I hadn't even heard about a photography exhibition. Not surprising, because I'd been so busy, fixing up the new darkroom, and getting ready for school. I had a sudden **sink**ing feeling as Dad and I walked toward the west wing.

"Dad," I said, "you didn't **submit** any of my photographs to an exhibition, did you?"

"No," he said, shaking his head. "I would never have

---

★ Renaissance 르네상스. 14~16세기 유럽의 문예 부흥기.

164

done that without asking your **permission**, Meg. Someday you'll do that yourself."

The huge white-walled room was filled with **framed** photographs on each wall. The sign at the entrance to the room was carefully lettered in Gothic **script**:* *Faces of New England*. As I walked around the room, I recognized the names of many of the photographers: famous names, names I had seen in magazines and in books of photographs that I had taken from the library. The photographs were all of people: the old, **gaunt** faces of farmers who live on the back roads; the **weathered**, **wrinkle**d faces of their wives; the **eager**-eyed, sunshine-**speckled** faces of children.

And suddenly there was my face. It was a large photograph, against a white **mount**, framed in a narrow black frame, and it was not just the coincidence of a stranger who happened to look like me; it was my face. It was taken at an angle; the wind was blowing my hair, and I was looking off in the distance somewhere, far beyond the **meticulous**ly **trim**med edges of the photograph or the **rigid confine**s of its frame. The outline of my neck and **chin** and half-turned cheek was sharp against the **blur**red and **subtle** shapes of **pine** trees in the background.

I knew, though I had not known it then, that Will had

---

★ Gothic script 고딕체. 획이 굵은 활자체.

taken it. He had taken it in the village **cemetery** the day we **buried** Molly there and **heap**ed her grave with goldenrod.

There was something of Molly in my face. It **startled** me, seeing it. The line that **defined** my face, the line that **separated** the darkness of the trees from the light that curved into my **forehead** and cheek was the same line that had once **identified** Molly by its shape. The way I held my shoulders was the way she had held hers. It was a **transient** thing, I knew, but when Will had held the camera and released the **shutter** for one five-hundredth of a second, he had captured it and made **permanent** whatever of Molly was in me. I was **grateful**, and glad.

I went close to read what was written below the photograph. The title was "Fringed Gentian"; on the other side was his signature: *William Banks.*

"Dad," I said, "I have to go back. I have to see Will. I promised him."

My father took me back on the weekend. I remembered, in the car, what a long trip it had seemed last winter, when we went for the first time to the house in the country. Now the distance seemed short. Perhaps it is part of a place becoming familiar that makes it seem closer; perhaps it is just a part of growing up

There was Will, with his head inside the open **hood** of his truck. He stood up straight when we drove in, **wiped** his hands, and **chuckle**d, "Spark plugs.*"

"Will, I came so you could show me the fringed gentian. I'm sorry I forgot."

"You didn't forget, Meg," he told me. "It wasn't time until now."

My father waited at Will's house while we walked across the fields. Almost all of the flowers were gone. Ben and Maria's house was closed up tight and empty, although the curtains Maria had made still hung at the windows. They had gone back so that Ben could complete the last course for his **master's degree** at Harvard.

"They'll be back," said Will, watching me look at the house, with its paint still new and its garden still **tidy** and **weed**ed, even though the vegetables were gone. "The house is theirs now. Maybe next summer you can help Happy learn to walk."

Maybe. Maybe there would be another summer filled with flowers and the laughter of a little boy whose life was still **brand-new**.

Will went right to the place on the side of the woods where the spruce tree was beside the birches. I had forgotten the spot that he had pointed out months before, but this was his land; he knew it like his life. He pushed

---

★ spark plug 점화 플러그. 가솔린엔진 따위에서 혼합가스에 점화하는 장치.

aside the **underbrush** and led me to the place where he knew the gentians would be growing. It was very quiet there. The ground was mostly **moss**, and the sunlight came down through the tall trees in **patch**es, lighting the deep green here and there in patterns like the patchwork of a quilt.

The little **clump** of fringed gentians stood alone, the purple **blossom**s at the tops of straight **stem**s that grew up toward the sunlight from the **damp** earth. Will and I stood and looked at them together.

"They're my favorite flower," he told me, "I suppose because they're the last of the season. And because they grow here all alone, not caring whether anyone sees them or not."

"They're beautiful, Will," I said; and they were.

"'It tried to be a rose,'" Will said, and I knew he was **quoting** again, "'and failed, and all the summer laughed: but just before the snows there came a purple creature that **ravish**ed all the hill; and summer hid her forehead, and **mockery** was still.'"

"Will," I said, as we turned to leave the woods, "you should have been a **poet**."

He laughed. "A truck **mechanic** would have been more **practical**."

I fell a little way behind him as we walked back across

the field, wanting to capture every image in my mind. Even the goldenrod was gone. The tall grasses had turned **brownish** and **brittle**, like the sepia tones$^\star$ of an old and faded photograph. In my mind, in quick **sequence**s as if a film were stopping and starting, I saw Molly again. I saw her standing in the grass when it was green, her arms full of flowers; with the wind in her hair, with her quick smile, reaching for the next flower, and the next. The **float**ing **pollen drift**ed in patterns through the sunlight around her, as she looked back over her shoulder, laughing.

Somewhere, for Molly, I thought suddenly, it would be summer still, summer always.

Across the field I saw the little house that had been our house. And ahead of me I saw Will. I watched as he walked toward home, pushing the grass aside with his heavy stick, and realized that he was **lean**ing on it as he walked, that he needed its support. Walking through the **rocky** field wasn't as easy for him as it was for me. I understood then what Ben had told me once, about knowing and accepting that bad things will happen, because I understood, watching him, that someday Will would be gone from me too.

I ran to **catch up**. "Will," I said, "do you know that the picture of me is hanging in the university museum?"

---

★ sepia tones 세피아 색조. 암갈색 혹은 흑갈색. 세피아(sepia)는 오징어 먹물을 원료로 한 잉크에서 그 색과 이름이 유래했다.

He nodded. "Do you mind?"

I shook my head. "You made me beautiful," I said **shy**ly.

"Meg," he laughed, putting one arm over my shoulders, "you were beautiful **all along**."

# *Afterword*
## LOIS LOWRY

If my sister, Helen, were alive today she would be seventy-two years old. It makes me **chuckle** to write those words. Gray hair? Bifocals? Maybe a little extra weight? No way. For me Helen will always be young and slim and blond.

And so, too, Molly will always, for Meg, be young.

When I wrote the book that would be called *A Summer to Die*, I was remembering my own sister, who had been lost to **cancer** years before. People **frequent**ly ask if that makes the book, then, **autobiography**.

No. Not really. Parts of it are real and true, but I wrote it as **fiction**. The setting is different; the family is different; even the type of illness is different. (And I am happy to point out that the illness that takes Molly's life in the book is very often **curable** today.)

But here's what was real: the feelings. The relationship between the sisters—best friends and worst enemies, **sidekick**s and buddies—complete with the **jealousies** and **bicker**ing, as well as **fierce**, protective love. The anger, **helpless**ness, and **anguish** that **overcome** an entire family caught in an unfair, **inescapable** situation.

"After a while," Meg says in the book, "you remember the good things more often than the bad." That has been true for me. I remember Helen **giggling**. I remember the two of us fighting over who was taking up too much room in the backseat. How we borrowed each other's clothes (and even once dated the same boy). Somehow, magically, **merciful**ly, I no longer remember her ill. That's because mostly what is real is the way life continues, and the way people become able to **absorb** loss, to value memories, and to say goodbye.

# A Summer to Die

## LOIS LOWRY

WORK BOOK

A Summer to Die

1판 1쇄   2011년 10월  4일
2판 2쇄   2023년  1월 25일

지은이   Lois Lowry
기획   이수영
책임편집   김보경 이수영
콘텐츠제작및감수   김보경 이제원 Megan Manley
저작권   이수영 Marie Frenett
마케팅   김보미 정경훈

펴낸이   이수영
펴낸곳   롱테일북스
출판등록   제2015-000191호
주소   04033 서울특별시 마포구 양화로 113, 3층(서교동, 순흥빌딩)
전자메일   help@ltinc.net

ISBN  979-11-91343-89-2   14740

# *Contents*

## '아동 도서계의 노벨상!' 미국 최고 권위의 아동 문학상

뉴베리 상(Newbery Award)은 미국 도서관 협회에서 해마다 미국 아동 문학 발전에 가장 크게 이바지한 작가에게 수여하는 아동 문학상입니다. 1922년에 시작된 이 상은 미국에서 가장 오랜 역사를 지닌 아동 문학상이자, '아동 도서계의 노벨상'이라 불릴 만큼 높은 권위를 자랑하는 상입니다.

뉴베리 상은 그 역사와 권위만큼이나 심사 기준이 까다롭기로 유명한데, 심사단은 책의 주제 의식은 물론 정보의 깊이와 스토리의 정교함, 캐릭터와 문체의 적정성 등을 꼼꼼히 평가하여 수상작을 결정합니다.

그해 최고의 작품으로 선정된 도서에게는 '뉴베리 메달(Newbery Medal)'이라고 부르는 금색 메달을 수여하며, 최종 후보에 올랐던 주목할 만한 작품들에게는 '뉴베리 아너(Newbery Honor)'라는 이름의 은색 마크를 수여합니다.

뉴베리 상을 받은 도서는 미국의 모든 도서관에 비치되어 더 많은 독자들을 만나게 되며, 대부분 수십에서 수백만 부가 판매되는 베스트셀러가 됩니다. 뉴베리 상을 수상한 작가는 그만큼 필력과 작품성을 인정받게 되어, 수상 작가의 다른 작품들 또한 수상작 못지않게 커다란 주목과 사랑을 받습니다

## 왜 뉴베리 수상작인가?
## 쉬운 어휘로 쓰인 '검증된' 영어원서!

뉴베리 수상작들은 '검증된 원서'로 국내 영어 학습자들에게 큰 사랑을 받고 있습니다. 뉴베리 수상작이 원서 읽기에 좋은 교재인 이유는 무엇일까요?

1. 아동 문학인 만큼 어휘가 어렵지 않습니다.
2. 어렵지 않은 어휘를 사용하면서도 '문학상'을 수상한 만큼 문장의 깊이가 상당합니다.
3. 적당한 난이도의 어휘와 깊이 있는 문장으로 구성되어 있기 때문에 초등 고학년부터 성인까지, 영어 초보자부터 실력자까지 모든 영어 학습자들이 읽기에 좋습니다.

실제로 뉴베리 수상작은 국제중·특목고에서는 입시 필독서로, 대학교에서는 영어 강독 교재로 다양하고 폭넓게 활용되고 있습니다. 이런 이유로 뉴베리 수상작은 한국어 번역서보다 오히려 원서가 훨씬 많이 판매되는 기현상을 보이고 있습니다.

## '베스트 오브 베스트'만을 엄선한 「뉴베리 컬렉션」

「뉴베리 컬렉션」은 뉴베리 메달 및 아너 수상작, 그리고 뉴베리 수상 작가의 유명 작품들을 엄선하여 한국 영어 학습자들을 위한 최적의 교재로 재탄생시킨 영어 원서 시리즈입니다.

1. 어휘 수준과 문장의 난이도, 분량 등 국내 영어 학습자들에게 적합한 정도를 종합적으로 검토하여 선정하였습니다.
2. 기존 원서 독자층 사이의 인기도까지 감안하여 최적의 작품들을 선별하였습니다.
3. 판형이 좁고 글씨가 작아 읽기 힘들었던 원서 디자인을 대폭 수정하여, 판형을 시원하게 키우고 읽기에 최적화된 영문 서체를 사용하여 가독성을 극대화하였습니다.
4. 함께 제공되는 워크북은 어려운 어휘를 완벽하게 정리하고 이해력을 점검하는 퀴즈를 덧붙여 독자들이 원서를 보다 쉽고 재미있게 읽을 수 있도록 구성하였습니다.
5. 기존에 높은 가격에 판매되어 구입이 부담스러웠던 오디오북을 부록으로 제공하여 리스닝과 소리 내어 읽기에까지 원서를 두루 활용할 수 있도록 했습니다.

**로이스 로리(Lois Lowry)**는 1937년 하와이 호놀룰루에서 태어난 미국의 청소년 문학 작가입니다. 언니의 죽음을 자전적으로 다룬 첫 소설 「그 여름의 끝(A Summer to Die)」으로 단숨에 독자들을 사로잡은 그녀는, 2차 세계대전을 배경으로 인간의 존엄성과 가치를 되새기게 하는 문제작 「별을 헤아리며(Number the Stars)」로 1990년 첫 번째 뉴베리 메달을 수상했습니다. 이어 1994년에는 인간의 어두운 면을 파헤치며 미래 사회에 대한 질문을 던진 수작 「기억 전달자(The Giver)」로 다시 뉴베리 메달을 수상했는데, 한 작가가 뉴베리 아너도 아닌 메달을 두 번이나 수상한 것은 극히 이례적인 일로 그녀의 뛰어난 작품성을 확인할 수 있는 단적인 예라고 할 수 있습니다.

「A Summer to Die」는 로이스 로리가 40세의 나이로 처음 쓴 소설입니다. 주인공 메그(Meg)와 그녀의 언니 몰리(Molly)는 자매이지만 전혀 다른 성격을 가지고 있습니다. 몰리는 예쁘고 명랑하여 많은 사람들의 인기를 한 몸에 받지만 동생 메그는 내성적이며 비판적이고 때로는 괴팍하기까지 합니다. 어느 날 대학교수인 아버지의 책 집필을 위해 가족 전체는 시골 마을의 작은 오두막으로 이사를 가게 되고, 덕분에 같은 방을 쓰게 된 메그와 몰리는 매일 티격태격 싸우곤 합니다. 한편 메그는 가족이 살고 있는 오두막의 주인 윌 뱅크스(Will Banks)와 친구가 되고 그에게 사진을 현상하는 법을 가르쳐줍니다. 사교적이지 못한 메그에게 윌 뱅크스는 아주 좋은 친구가 되어 줍니다. 그러던 와중 언니 몰리는 원인을 알 수 없는 코피에 시달리다 건강이 심각하게 나빠지고 급기야 병원에 입원하게 됩니다. 남겨진 메그는 몰리에 대한 죄책감과 몰리를 고치지 못하는 의사들에 대한 원망으로 하루하루를 보냅니다.

이 책은 「The Giver」, 「Number the Stars」 등으로 지금은 미국 최고의 아동 소설 작가로 올라선 로이스 로리의 첫 소설이라는 기념비적 작품입니다. 게다가 작가가 어린 시절 실제로 사망했던 자신의 언니를 떠올리며 쓴 자전적 이야기라 더욱 특별한 의미가 있기도 합니다. 첫 작품답지 않게 감수성 넘치는 문체는 단숨에 독자들을 사로 잡았고 그녀를 지금과 같이 유명작가의 반열에 오르게 했습니다.

# 이 책의 구성

## 원서 본문

내용이 담긴 원서 본문입니다.
원어민이 읽는 일반 원서와 같은 텍스트지만, 암기해야 할 중요 어휘들은 볼드체로 표시되어 있습니다. 이 어휘들은 지금 들고 계신 워크북에 챕터별로 정리되어 있습니다.

학습 심리학 연구 결과에 따르면, 한 단어씩 따로 외우는 단어 암기는 거의 효과가 없다고 합니다. 단어를 제대로 외우기 위해서는 문맥(context) 속에서 단어를 암기해야 하며, 한 단어당 문맥 속에서 15번 이상 마주칠 때 완벽하게 암기할 수 있다고 합니다.

이 책의 본문에서는 중요 어휘를 볼드체로 강조하여, 문맥 속의 단어들을 더 확실히 인지(word cognition in context)하도록 돕고 있습니다. 또한 대부분의 중요 단어들은 다른 챕터에서도 반복해서 등장하기 때문에 이 책을 읽는 것만으로도 자연스럽게 어휘력을 향상시킬 수 있습니다.

또한 본문 하단에는 내용 이해를 돕기 위한 '각주'가 첨가되어 있습니다. 각주는 군이 암기할 필요는 없지만, 알아 두면 도움이 될 만한 정보를 설명하고 있습니다. 각주를 참고하면 스토리를 더 깊이 있게 이해할 수 있어 원서를 읽는 재미가 배가됩니다.

## 워크북(Workbook)

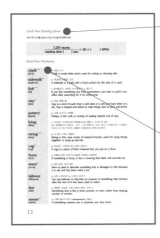

### Check Your Reading Speed

해당 챕터의 단어 수가 기록되어 있어, 리딩 속도를 측정할 수 있습니다. 특히 리딩 속도를 중시하는 독자들이 유용하게 사용할 수 있습니다.

### Build Your Vocabulary

본문에 볼드 표시되어 있는 단어들이 정리되어 있습니다. 리딩 전·후에 반복해서 보면 원서를 더욱 쉽게 읽을 수 있고, 어휘력도 빠르게 향상될 것입니다.

단어는 〈스펠링 – 빈도 – 발음기호 – 품사 – 한글 뜻 – 영문 뜻〉 순서로 표기되어 있으며 빈도 표시(★)가 많을수록 필수 어휘입니다. 반복해서 등장하는 단어는 빈도 대신 '복습'으로 표기되어 있습니다. 품사는 아래와 같이 표기했습니다.

**n.** 명사 ┃ **a.** 형용사 ┃ **ad.** 부사 ┃ **vi.** 자동사 ┃ **vt.** 타동사 ┃ **v.** 자·타동사 모두 쓰이는 동사

**conj.** 접속사 ┃ **prep.** 전치사 ┃ **int.** 감탄사 ┃ **phrasal v.** 구동사 ┃ **idiom** 숙어 및 관용구

### Comprehension Quiz

간단한 퀴즈를 통해 읽은 내용에 대한 이해력을 점검해 볼 수 있습니다.

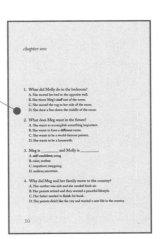

## 「뉴베리 컬렉션」 이렇게 읽어 보세요!

아래와 같이 프리뷰(Preview) → 리딩(Reading) → 리뷰(Review) 세 단계를 거치면서 읽으면, 더욱 효과적으로 영어 실력을 향상할 수 있습니다.

### 1. 프리뷰(Preview) : 오늘 읽을 내용을 먼저 점검하자!

• 워크북을 통해 오늘 읽을 챕터에 나와 있는 단어들을 쭉 훑어봅니다. 어떤 단어들이 나오는지, 내가 아는 단어와 모르는 단어는 어떤 것들이 있는지 가벼운 마음으로 살펴봅니다.

• 평소처럼 하나하나 쓰면서 암기하려고 하지는 마세요! 익숙하지 않은 단어들을 주의 깊게 보되, 어차피 리딩을 하면서 점차 익숙해질 단어라는 것을 기억하며 빠르게 훑어봅니다.

• 뒤 챕터로 갈수록 '복습'이라고 표시된 단어들이 늘어나는 것을 알 수 있습니다. '복습' 단어인데도 여전히 익숙하지 않다면 더욱 신경을 써서 봐야겠죠? 매일매일 꾸준히 읽는다면, 익숙한 단어들이 점점 많아진다는 것을 몸으로 느낄 수 있습니다.

### 2. 리딩(Reading) : 내용에 집중하며 빠르게 읽어 나가자!

• 프리뷰를 마친 후 바로 리딩을 시작합니다. 방금 살펴봤던 어휘들을 문장 속에서 다시 만나게 되는데, 이 과정에서 단어의 쓰임새와 어감을 자연스럽게 익히게 됩니다.

• 모르는 단어나 이해되지 않는 문장이 나오더라도 멈추지 말고 전체적인 맥락을 파악하면서 속도감 있게 읽어 나가세요. 이해되지 않는 문장들은 따로 표시를 하되, 일단 넘어가고 계속 읽는 것이 좋습니다. 뒷부분을 읽다 보면 자연히 이해가 되는 경우도 있고, 정 이해가 되지 않는 부분은 리딩을 마친 이후에 따로 리뷰하는 시간을 가지면 됩니다. 문제집을 풀듯이 모든 문장을 분석하면서 원서를 읽는 것이 아니라, 리딩을 할 때는 리딩에만, 리뷰를 할 때는 리뷰에만 집중하는 것이 필요합니다.

• 볼드 처리된 단어의 의미가 궁금하더라도 워크북을 바로 펼치지 마세요. 정 궁금하다면 한 번씩 참고하는 것도 나쁘진 않지만, 워크북과 원서를 번갈아 보면서 읽는 것은 리딩의 흐름을 끊고 단어 하나하나에 집착하는 좋지 않은 리딩 습관을 심어 줄 수 있습니다.

• 같은 맥락에서 번역서를 구해 원서와 동시에 번갈아 보는 것도 좋은 방법이 아닙니다. 한글 번역을 가지고 있다고 해도 일단 영어로 읽을 때는 영어에만 집중하고 어느 정도 분량을 읽은 후에 번역서와 비교하도록 하세요. 모든 문장을

일일이 번역해서 완벽하게 이해하려는 것은 오히려 좋지 않은 리딩 습관을 심어 주어 장기적으로는 바람직하지 않은 결과를 얻을 수 있습니다. 처음부터 완벽하게 이해하려고 하는 것보다는 빠른 속도로 2~3회 반복해서 읽는 방식이 실력 향상에 더 도움이 됩니다. 만일 반복해서 읽어도 내용이 전혀 이해되지 않아 곤란하다면 책 선정에 문제가 있다고 할 수 있습니다. 그럴 때는 좀 더 쉬운 책을 골라 실력을 다진 뒤 다시 도전하는 것이 좋습니다.

• 초보자라면 분당 150단어의 리딩 속도를 목표로 잡고 리딩을 합니다. 분당 150단어는 원어민이 말하는 속도로, 영어 학습자들이 리스닝과 스피킹으로 넘어가기 위해 가장 기초적으로 달성해야 하는 단계입니다. 분당 50~80단어 정도의 낮은 리딩 속도를 가지고 있는 경우는 대부분 영어 실력이 부족해서라기보다 '잘못된 리딩 습관'을 가지고 있어서 그렇습니다. 이해력이 조금 떨어진다고 하더라도 분당 150단어까지는 속도에 대한 긴장감을 놓치지 말고 속도감 있게 읽어 나가도록 하세요.

### 3. 리뷰(Review) : 이해력을 점검하고 꼼꼼하게 다시 살펴보자!

• 해당 챕터의 Comprehension Quiz를 통해 이해력을 점검해 봅니다.
• 오늘 만난 어휘들을 다시 한번 복습합니다. 이때는 읽으면서 중요하다고 생각했던 단어를 연습장에 써 보면서 꼼꼼하게 외우는 것도 좋습니다.
• 이해가 되지 않는다고 표시해 두었던 부분도 주의 깊게 분석해 봅니다. 다시 한번 문장을 꼼꼼히 읽고, 어떤 이유에서 이해가 되지 않았는지 생각해 봅니다. 따로 메모를 남기거나 노트를 작성하는 것도 좋은 방법입니다.
• 사실 꼼꼼히 리뷰하는 것은 매우 고된 과정입니다. 원서를 읽고 리뷰하는 시간을 가지는 것이 영어 실력 향상에 많은 도움이 되기는 하지만, 이 과정을 철저히 지키려다가 원서 읽기의 재미를 반감시키는 것은 바람직하지 않습니다. 그럴 때는 차라리 리뷰를 가볍게 하는 것이 좋을 수 있습니다. '내용에 빠져서 재미있게', 문제집에서는 상상도 못할 '많은 양'을 읽으면서, 매일매일 조금씩 꾸준히 실력을 키워 가는 것이 원서를 활용하는 기본적인 방법이며, 영어 공부의 왕도입니다. 문제집 풀듯이 원서 읽기를 시도하고 접근해서는 실패할 수밖에 없습니다.
• 이런 방식으로 원서를 끝까지 다 읽었다면, 다시 반복해서 읽거나 오디오북을 활용하는 등 다양한 방식으로 원서 읽기를 확장해 나갈 수 있습니다. 이에 대한 자세한 안내가 워크북 말미에 실려 있습니다.

*chapter one*

1. What did Molly do in the bedroom?
   A. She moved her bed to the opposite wall.
   B. She threw Meg's stuff out of the room.
   C. She moved the rug to her side of the room.
   D. She drew a line down the middle of the room.

2. What does Meg want in the future?
   A. She wants to accomplish something important.
   B. She wants to have a different name.
   C. She wants to be a world-famous painter.
   D. She wants to be a housewife.

3. Meg is _____ and Molly is _____.
   A. self-confident; smug
   B. calm; restless
   C. impatient; easygoing
   D. restless; uncertain

4. Why did Meg and her family move to the country?
   A. Her mother was sick and she needed fresh air.
   B. Her parents retired and they wanted a peaceful lifestyle.
   C. Her father needed to finish his book.
   D. Her parents didn't like the city and wanted a new life in the country.

5. How many years apart are Meg and Molly?
   A. 1
   B. 2
   C. 3
   D. 4

6. Molly liked to _____ and Meg liked to _____.
   A. be alone; have lots of friends
   B. do cheerleading; paint and take photos
   C. paint; go for long walks
   D. explore; stay at home

7. What was true about the house in the country?
   A. It was very big.
   B. It had many places for privacy and escape.
   C. It had four bedrooms.
   D. It was over 100 years old.

1분에 몇 단어를 읽는지 리딩 속도를 측정해보세요.

$$\frac{3{,}251 \text{ words}}{\text{reading time (} \quad \text{) sec}} \times 60 = ( \qquad ) \text{ WPM}$$

*Build Your Vocabulary*

**chalk**\*\*\*
[tʃɔ́ːk]

n. 분필, 초크
Chalk is small white sticks used for writing or drawing with.

**sidewalk**\*\*
[sáidwɔ́ːk]

n. (포장한) 보행로, 인도
A sidewalk is a path with a hard surface by the side of a road.

**fish**\*\*\*
[fiʃ]

v. 끌어올리다, 꺼내다; 낚시질하다; n. 물고기
If you fish something out from somewhere, you take or pull it out, often after searching for it for some time.

**clay**\*\*
[kléi]

n. 점토, 찰흙; 흙
Clay is a kind of earth that is soft when it is wet and hard when it is dry. Clay is shaped and baked to make things such as pots and bricks.

**pottery**\*
[pátəri]

n. 도예; 도자기 (그릇들)
Pottery is the craft or activity of making objects out of clay.

**lying**
[láiiŋ]

v. 니에(눕다, 누워있다)의 현재분사(ing) 형태; a. 드러누워 있는
lie는 현재분사가 되면서 −ie가 −y로 변한다는 것과, '눕다, 누워있다'와 '거짓말하다'라는 두 가지 의미의 스펠링이 동일하다는 점에 유의하자.

**string**\*\*\*
[striŋ]

n. 끈, 줄; v. 묶다, 매달다
String is thin rope made of twisted threads, used for tying things together or tying up parcels.

**rug**\*\*
[rʌg]

n. (방바닥·마루에 까는) 깔개, 양탄자
A rug is a piece of thick material that you put on a floor.

**fuzzy**
[fʌzi]

a. 보풀로 덮힌; (머리가) 곱슬한; 흐릿한, 어렴풋한
If something is fuzzy, it has a covering that feels soft and like fur.

**worn**\*\*
[wɔːrn]

a. 닳아 해진, 써서 낡은
Worn is used to describe something that is damaged or thin because it is old and has been used a lot.

**leftover**
[léftòuvər]

a. 남은, 나머지의; n. 나머지, 찌꺼기
You use leftover to describe an amount of something that remains after the rest of it has been used or eaten.

**flat**\*
[flǽt]

a. 평평한, 균일한, 고른; 바람이 빠진, 구멍 난
Something that is flat is level, smooth, or even, rather than sloping, curved, or uneven.

**amaze**\*\*
[əméiz]

vt. 깜짝 놀라게 하다 (amazement n. 놀람)
If something amazes you, it surprises you very much.

12

**ceiling***\*\*\*
[síːliŋ]

n. 천장; 최고 한도
A ceiling is the horizontal surface that forms the top part or roof inside a room.

**neat***\*\*
[níːt]

a. 깔끔한, 산뜻한; (구어) 굉장한, 멋진 (neatly ad. 깔끔하게)
A neat place, thing, or person is tidy and smart, and has everything in the correct place.

**mess***\*\*
[més]

n. 엉망진창인 상태; (개 · 고양이의) 똥; v. 망쳐놓다, 방해하다
If you say that something is a mess or in a mess, you think that it is in an untidy state.

**wavy**
[wéivi]

a. 굽이치는, 물결 모양의
A wavy line has a series of regular curves along it.

**slob**
[slɑb]

n. (지저분한) 게으름뱅이, 굼벵이
If you call someone a slob, you mean that they are very lazy and untidy.

**ignore***\*
[ignɔ́ːr]

vt. 무시하다, 모르는 체하다
If you ignore someone or something, you pay no attention to them.

**academic***
[æ̀kədémik]

a. 학구적인, 학문의; 학업의, 학교의 (unacademic a. 학구[학문]적이 아닌)
Academic is used to describe work, or a school, college, or university, that places emphasis on studying and reasoning rather than on practical or technical skills.

**generalize***
[dʒénərəlàiz]

v. 일반화하다; 개괄하다, 법칙화하다
If you generalize, you say something that seems to be true in most situations or for most people, but that may not be completely true in all cases.

**accomplish***\*\*
[əká(ɔ́)mpliʃ]

vt. 이루다, 성취하다, 완수하다
If you accomplish something, you succeed in doing it.

**content***\*\*
[kəntént]

a. (자기가 가진 것에) 만족하는; 기꺼이 …하려 하는; vt. 만족시키다; n. 만족
If you are content with something, you are willing to accept it, rather than wanting something more or something better.

**restless***\*
[réstlis]

a. 침착하지 못한, 불안한; 가만히 있지 못하는, 끊임없는
If you are restless, you are bored, impatient, or dissatisfied, and you want to do something else.

**impatient***\*
[impéiʃənt]

a. 성급한, 조급한, 참을성 없는
If you are impatient, you are easily irritated by things.

**uncertain***\*
[ʌnsɔ́ːrtn]

a. 확신이 없는, 잘 모르는; 불확실한, 불안정한
If you are uncertain about something, you do not know what you should do, what is going to happen, or what the truth is about something.

**fearful***\*
[fíərfəl]

a. 걱정[염려]하는; 무시무시한, 무서운
If you are fearful of something, you are afraid of it.

**determined***
[ditɔ́ːrmind]

a. 결연한, 굳게 결심한
If you are determined to do something, you have made a firm decision to do it and will not let anything stop you.

| | |
|---|---|
| **hasty**<br>[héisti] | a. 급한, 성급한<br>If you describe a person or their behavior as hasty, you mean that they are acting too quickly, without thinking carefully. |
| **impetuous**<br>[impétʃuəs] | a. 성급한, 충동적인<br>If you describe someone as impetuous, you mean that they are likely to act quickly and suddenly without thinking or being careful. |
| **miserable**<br>[mízərəbl] | a. 비참한, 우울한, 형편없는<br>If you are miserable, you are very unhappy. |
| **sort out** | phrasal v. 선별하다, 분류하다; 문제를 해결하다<br>If you sort out a problem or the details of something, you do what is necessary to solve the problem or organize the details. |
| **assured**<br>[əʃúərd] | a. 자신 있는; 보증된, 확실한<br>Someone who is assured is very confident and relaxed. |
| **easygoing**<br>[íːzigóuiŋ] | a. 태평스러운, 안이한<br>If you describe someone as easygoing, you mean that they are not easily annoyed, worried, or upset, and you think this is a good quality. |
| **self-confident**<br>[sélf-kánfədənt] | a. 자신감 있는<br>Someone who is self-confident behaves confidently because they feel sure of their abilities or value. |
| **downright**<br>[dáunràit] | a. 순전한, 완전한<br>You use downright to emphasize unpleasant or bad qualities or behavior. |
| **smug**<br>[smʌg] | a. 의기양양한, 우쭐해 하는<br>If you say that someone is smug, you are criticizing the fact they seem very pleased with how good, clever, or lucky they are. |
| **put together** | phrasal v. 구성하다, 편집하다; 모으다, 합계하다<br>If you put something together, you join its different parts to each other so that it can be used. |
| **represent**<br>[reprizént] | vt. 대표하다, 나타내다, 표현하다<br>To represent an idea or quality means to be a symbol or an expression of that idea or quality. |
| **ambition**<br>[æmbíʃən] | n. 야망, 포부<br>If you have an ambition to do or achieve something, you want very much to do it or achieve it. |
| **logic**<br>[lá(ɔ)dʒik] | n. 논리, 타당성; 논리학<br>The logic of a conclusion or an argument is its quality of being correct and reasonable. |
| **unmatched**<br>[ʌnmǽtʃt] | a. 짝이 없는, 부조화의; (아무도) 필적할 수 없는<br>If you describe something as unmatched, you are emphasizing that it is better or greater than all other things of the same kind. |
| **crumple**<br>[krʌ́mpl] | v. 구기다, 구겨지다, 쭈글쭈글하게 하다; n. 주름 (crumpled a. 구겨진, 뒤틀린)<br>If you crumple something such as paper or cloth, or if it crumples, it is squashed and becomes full of untidy creases and folds. |

14

**poem**\*\*\*
[póuəm]

n. (한 편의) 시; 운문, 시적인 문장
A poem is a piece of writing in which the words are chosen for their beauty and sound and are carefully arranged, often in short lines which rhyme.

**shed**\*\*
[ʃed]

① v. (눈물을) 흘리다, 내뿜게 하다, 발하다, 발산하다 ② n. 오두막, 창고
If you shed tears, you cry.

**solitary**\*\*
[sálitèri]

a. 혼자 하는, 홀로 있는
A solitary person or object is alone, with no others near them.

**brick**\*\*
[brík]

n. 벽돌
Bricks are rectangular blocks of baked clay used for building walls, which are usually red or brown.

**strike**\*\*\*
[straik]

v. (시계가) 치다, 알리다; (세게) 치다, 부딪치다; (…하다는) 인상[느낌]을 주다
When a clock strikes, its bells make a sound to indicate what the time is.

**chime**\*\*
[tʃaim]

n. 시간을 알리는 종; v. (종 · 시계가) 울리다
A chime is a ringing sound made by a bell, especially when it is part of a clock.

**define**\*\*
[difáin]

v. 윤곽을 분명히 나타내다; (단어 · 구의 뜻을) 정의하다
(well defined a. 명확한; 알기 쉬운)
If you define something, you show, describe, or state clearly what it is and what its limits are, or what it is like.

**silhouette**\*
[sìluét]

n. 윤곽, 실루엣; vt. …의 그림자를 비추다
A silhouette is the solid dark shape that you see when someone or something has a bright light or pale background behind them.

**ivy**\*
[áivi]

n. [식물] 담쟁이덩굴 (ivied a. 담쟁이로 장식된)
Ivy is an evergreen plant that grows up walls or along the ground.

**face**\*\*\*
[féis]

n. (시계 등의) 문자반; 얼굴
The face of a clock or watch is the surface with the numbers or hands on it, which shows the time.

**in the middle of nowhere**

idiom 멀리 인적이 끊긴
If you say that a place is in the middle of nowhere, you mean that it is a long way from other places.

**seldom**\*\*\*
[séldəm]

ad. 드물게, 거의 …않는
If something seldom happens, it happens only occasionally.

**measure**\*\*\*
[méʒər]

v. (치수 · 양 등을) 측정하다, 재다; n. 조치, 정책; 척도, 기준
If you measure a quantity that can be expressed in numbers, such as the length of something, you discover it using a particular instrument or device, for example a ruler.

**study**\*\*\*
[stʌ́di]

n. 서재, 집무실; v. 배우다, 공부하다
A study is a room in a house which is used for reading, writing, and studying.

**stop by**

idiom 들르다, 방문하다
If you stop by somewhere, you make a short visit to a person or place.

**drop in**

idiom (구어) 잠깐 들르다
If you drop in on someone, you visit them informally, usually without having arranged it.

**porch**\*\*\*
[pɔːrtʃ]

n. (건물 입구에 지붕이 얹혀 있고 흔히 벽이 둘러진) 현관, 포치
A porch is a sheltered area at the entrance to a building, which has a roof and sometimes has walls.

**embarrass**\*\*
[embǽrəs]

v. 당황스럽게[어색하게] 만들다; 곤란하게 하다 (embarrassed a. 쑥스러운, 어색한)
If something or someone embarrasses you, they make you feel shy or ashamed.

**disturb**\*\*
[distə́ːrb]

v. 방해하다, 어지럽히다
If you disturb someone, you interrupt what they are doing and upset them.

**invite**\*\*\*
[inváit]

vt. 초청하다, 초대하다
If you invite someone to something such as a party or a meal, you ask them to come to it.

**noodle**
[núːdl]

n. (밀가루로 만든) 국수; 면류
Noodles are long, thin, curly strips of pasta, which are used especially in Chinese and Italian cooking.

**lettuce**\*
[létis]

n. [식물] 상추 (a head of lettuce idiom 양상추 한 포기)
A lettuce is a plant with large green leaves that is the basic ingredient of many salads.

**peel**\*\*
[piːl]

v. 껍질을 벗기다; (껍질 · 피부가) 벗겨지다; n. (과일 · 채소의 두꺼운) 껍질
When you peel fruit or vegetables, you remove their skins.

**carrot**\*
[kǽrət]

n. 당근
Carrots are long, thin, orange-colored vegetables. They grow under the ground, and have green shoots above the ground.

**stew**\*
[stjuː]

n. 스튜(고기와 채소를 넣고 국물이 좀 있게 해서 천천히 끓인 요리)
A stew is a meal which you make by cooking meat and vegetables in liquid at a low temperature.

**linger**\*\*
[líŋgər]

vi. 오래 머무르다, 떠나지 못하다
When something lingers, it continues to exist for a long time, often much longer than expected.

**exhaust**\*\*
[igzɔ́ːst]

vt. (연구 · 과제 등을) 철저히 규명하다; 기진맥진하게 만들다
If you have exhausted a subject or topic, you have talked about it so much that there is nothing more to say about it.

**argument**\*\*
[áːrgjəmənt]

n. 언쟁, 논의, 말다툼
An argument is a conversation in which people disagree with each other angrily or noisily.

**anecdote**\*\*
[ǽnikdòut]

n. 일화
An anecdote is a short, amusing story about a real person or event.

**dialectic**
[dàiəléktik]

a. 변증법적 (방식)
People refer to the dialectic or dialectics of a situation when they are referring to the way in which two very different forces or factors work together, and the way in which their differences are resolved.

16

**synthesis***
[sínθəsis]

n. 종합, 통합; 합성
A synthesis of different ideas or styles is a mixture or combination of these ideas or styles.

**irony****
[áiərəni]

n. 비꼼, 반어법
Irony is a subtle form of humor which involves saying things that you do not mean.

**break up**

idiom 웃음을 터뜨리다; 부서지다, 끝이 나다
If something breaks someone up, it causes them to lose control and begin to laugh or cry.

**stern****
[stə́:rn]

a. 엄한, 단호한
Stern words or actions are very severe.

**full of bull**

idiom 과장된, 허풍선이의
If you say that something is full of bull, you mean that it is complete nonsense or absolutely untrue.

**figure*****
[fígjər]

v. (…일 거라고) 생각[판단]하다; 계산하다; n. 모습, 형태; 계산, 숫자
If you figure that something is the case, you think or guess that it is the case.

**fireplace****
[faiərplèis]

n. (벽)난로
In a room, the fireplace is the place where a fire can be lit and the area on the wall and floor surrounding this place.

**dirt road**
[də́:rt róud]

n. 비포장도로
Dirt road is a rough road in the country that is made from hard earth.

**idiot***
[ídiət]

n. 바보, 얼간이
If you call someone an idiot, you are showing that you think they are very stupid or have done something very stupid.

**consolidate***
[kənsálədèit]

vt. 통합하다, 결합하다; 강화하다, 굳건하게 하다
To consolidate a number of small groups or firms means to make them into one large organization.

**grin****
[grín]

v. 이를 드러내고 싱긋 웃다; n. 싱긋 웃음
When you grin, you smile broadly.

**laxative**
[lǽksətiv]

n. 설사약, 완하제(배변을 쉽게 하는 약이나 음식)
A laxative is food or medicine that you take to make you go to the toilet.

**concern*****
[kənsə́:rn]

n. 우려, 걱정; v. 영향을 미치다, 관련되다; …를 걱정스럽게[우려하게] 만들다
Concern is worry about a situation.

**umpteen**
[ʌmptí:n]

a. 아주 많은, 무수한
Umpteen can be used to refer to an extremely large number of things or people.

**watercolor***
[wɔ́:tə:rkʌ̀lə:r]

n. (pl.) 수채화 그림물감; 수채화(법)
Watercolors are paints that you mix with water, not oil, and use for painting pictures.

| | |
|---|---|
| **beat out** | phrasal v. 물리치다, 따라잡다<br>If you beat out someone in a competition, you defeat them. |
| **groan**\*\*<br>[gróun] | v. 신음하다, 끙끙거리다; n. 신음, 끙 하는 소리<br>If you groan, you make a long, low sound because you are in pain, or because you are upset or unhappy about something. |
| **all of a sudden** | idiom 갑자기, 뜻밖에, 돌연히<br>If something happens all of a sudden, it happens quickly and unexpectedly. |
| **stuff**\*\*\*<br>[stʌf] | n. 것(들), 물건, 물질; vt. 채워 넣다, 속을 채우다<br>You can use stuff to refer to things such as a substance, a collection of things, events, or ideas, or the contents of something in a general way without mentioning the thing itself by name. |
| **every now and then** | idiom 가끔, 때때로, 이따금<br>If you do something every now and then, you do it sometimes, but not very often. |
| **astonish**\*\*<br>[əstá(ɔ́)niʃ] | vt. 깜짝 놀라게 하다 (astonishment n. 놀라움, 경악)<br>If something or someone astonishes you, they surprise you very much. |
| **priority**\*<br>[praiɔ́(:)rəti] | n. 우선 사항; 우선, 우선권<br>If someting is a priority, it is more important than other things and should be dealt with first. |
| **frown**\*\*<br>[fráun] | n. 찌푸린 얼굴; vi. 눈살을 찌푸리다, 얼굴을 찡그리다<br>A frown is an expression of displeasure. |
| **fuss**\*\*<br>[fʌs] | v. 야단법석하다, 안절부절못하다; n. 호들갑, 야단 법석<br>If you fuss, you worry or behave in a nervous, anxious way about unimportant matters or rush around doing unnecessary things. |
| **skip**\*\*<br>[skip] | v. 건너뛰다, 생략하다; 뛰어다니다, 깡충깡충 뛰다<br>If you skip something that you usually do or something that most people do, you decide not to do it. |
| **fit**\*\*\*<br>[fit] | v. (물건·장소에) 끼워 맞추다, 끼우다; 적합하다; a. 적합한<br>If you fit something into a particular space or place, you put it there. |
| **outfit**\*\*<br>[áutfit] | n. 한 벌의 옷, 복장<br>An outfit is a set of clothes. |
| **substitute**\*\*<br>[sʌ́bstitju:t] | n. (다른 누구·무엇을) 대신하는 사람[것]; v. 대신하다, 대치되다<br>A substitute is something that you have or use instead of something else. |
| **pretend**\*\*<br>[priténd] | v. 가장하다, …인 체하다; a. 가짜의<br>If you pretend that something is the case, you act in a way that is intended to make people believe that it is the case, although in fact it is not. |
| **sympathetic**\*\*<br>[simpəθétik] | a. 동정심 있는, 인정 있는; 마음에 드는<br>If you are sympathetic to someone who is in a bad situation, you are kind to them and show that you understand their feelings. |

18

**phony**
[fóuni]

a. (구어) 가짜의, 허위의, 겉치레의; n. 가짜, 위조품; vt. 위조하다, 속이다
If you describe something as phony, you disapprove of it because it is false rather than genuine.

**pleat**
[plíːt]

vt. 주름을 잡다; n. 주름, 플리트 (pleated a. 주름을 잡은)
A pleated piece of clothing has pleats in it.

**arrange**\*\*\*
[əréindʒ]

v. 정리하다, 배열하다; 준비하다
If you arrange things somewhere, you place them in a particular position, usually in order to make them look attractive or tidy.

**sideways**\*
[sáidwèiz]

ad. (한쪽 부분이 앞을 향하도록) 옆으로 비스듬히
Sideways means from or towards the side of something or someone.

**figure out**

phrasal v. …을 생각해내다, 발견하다
If you figure out a solution to a problem or the reason for something, you succeed in solving it or understanding it.

**physical**\*\*
[fízikəl]

a. 신체의, 육체의; 물리적인, 물질의
Physical qualities, actions, or things are connected with a person's body, rather than with their mind.

**bother**\*\*
[báðər]

v. 일부러 …하다, 애를 쓰다; 귀찮게 하다, 괴롭히다, 폐 끼치다
If you do not bother to do something, you do not do it, consider it, or use it because you think it is unnecessary.

**might as well**

idiom …하는 편이 낫다
If you say that you might as well do something, or that you may as well do it, you mean that you will do it although you do not have a strong desire to do it and may even feel slightly unwilling to do it.

**enemy**\*\*\*
[énəmi]

n. 적, 경쟁 상대
If someone is your enemy, they hate you or want to harm you.

**closet**\*\*
[klázit]

n. 벽장, 찬장
A closet is a piece of furniture with doors at the front and shelves inside, which is used for storing things.

**stairway**\*
[stéərwèi]

n. (통로로서의) 계단, 층계
A stairway is a staircase or a flight of steps, inside or outside a building.

**attic**\*\*
[ǽtik]

n. 다락(방)
An attic is a room at the top of a house just below the roof.

**privacy**\*
[práivəsi]

n. 사생활, 프라이버시; 은둔
If you have privacy, you are in a place or situation which allows you to do things without other people seeing you or disturbing you.

**curl up**

phrasal v. (눕거나 앉아서) 몸을 웅크리다
If you curl up, your body forms a curved or round shape.

**tack**\*
[tæk]

vt. 압정으로 고정시키다; n. 압정
If you tack something to a surface, you pin it there with tacks or drawing pins.

**bug***
[bʌg]

v. (구어) 귀찮게 굴다; n. 곤충; 결함
If someone or something bugs you, they worry or annoy you.

**thumbtack**
[θʌ́mtæ̀k]

n. 압정, 제도핀; vt. 압정으로 고정시키다
A thumbtack is a short pin with a broad flat top which is used for fastening papers or pictures to a board, wall, or other surface

**respond****
[rispánd]

vi. 응답하다, 대답하다
When you respond to something that is done or said, you react to it by doing or saying something yourself.

**staircase***
[stéərkèis]

n. (건물 내부에 난간으로 죽 이어져 있는) 계단
A staircase is a set of stairs inside a building.

**slant****
[slænt]

v. 기울어지다, 비스듬해지다; n. 경사, 비스듬함
Something that slants is sloping, rather than horizontal or vertical.

**pine*****
[páin]

n. 소나무 (재목)
A pine tree or a pine is a tall tree which has very thin, sharp leaves and a fresh smell. Pine trees have leaves all year round.

**moving van**
[múːviŋ væn]

n. 이삿짐 트럭
A moving van is a vehicle used to transport furniture and other possessions when people move to a new home.

**snowy****
[snóui]

a. 눈이 많은; 순백의
A snowy place is covered in snow.

**driveway***
[dráivwèi]

n. (도로에서 집·차고까지의) 진입로
A driveway is a piece of hard ground that leads from the road to the front of a house or other building.

**fade****
[feid]

vi. 바래다, 시들다, 희미해지다 (faded a. 시든, 빛깔이 바랜)
When a colored object fades or when the light fades it, it gradually becomes paler.

**bookcase****
[búkkèis]

n. 책장, 책꽂이, 서가
A bookcase is a piece of furniture with shelves that you keep books on.

**rectangle***
[réktæ̀ŋgl]

n. 직사각형
A rectangle is a four-sided shape whose corners are all ninety degree angles.

**frame*****
[freim]

n. 틀, 액자; 구조, 골격; vt. 틀[액자]에 넣다, 테를 두르다
The frame of a picture or mirror is the wood, metal, or plastic that is fitted around it, especially when it is displayed or hung on a wall.

**icicle***
[áisikəl]

n. 고드름
An icicle is a long pointed piece of ice hanging down from a surface, which forms when water comes slowly off the surface, and freezes as it falls.

**roof*****
[rúːf]

n. 지붕; vt. 지붕을 해 덮다
The roof of a building is the covering on top of it that protects the people and things inside from the weather.

20

**melt**\*\*\*
[mélt]

v. 녹다, 녹이다, 용해하다; (감정 등이) 누그러지다; n. 용해
When a solid substance melts or when you melt it, it changes to a liquid, usually because it has been heated.

**abandon**\*\*
[əbǽndən]

vt. 버리다; 단념하다, 그만두다 (abandoned a. 버려진, 황폐한)
If you abandon a place, thing, or person, you leave the place, thing, or person permanently or for a long time.

**meadow**\*\*
[médou]

n. 목초지, 초원
A meadow is a field which has grass and flowers growing in it.

**couch**\*\*
[kautʃ]

n. (기댈 수 있는 등받이와 팔걸이가 있는) 소파, 긴 의자
A couch is a long, comfortable seat for two or three people.

**sprinkle**\*\*
[spríŋkl]

vt. (액체·분말 따위를) 뿌리다, 끼얹다, 붓다
If you sprinkle a thing with something such as a liquid or powder, you scatter the liquid or powder over it.

**slip**\*\*\*
[slip]

① v. 미끄러지다, 미끄러지게 하다; n. 미끄럼, 실수 ② n. (작은 종이) 조각
If you slip, you accidentally slide and lose your balance.

**flowered**
[fláuərd]

a. 꽃무늬로 장식한, 꽃으로 덮인
Flowered paper or cloth has a pattern of flowers on it.

**gesture**\*\*
[dʒéstʃər]

n. 몸짓; vi. 몸짓을[신호를] 하다
A gesture is a movement that you make with a part of your body, especially your hands, to express emotion or information.

**wave**\*\*\*
[wéiv]

n. (팔·손·몸을) 흔들기; 파도, 물결; (머리카락의) 웨이브;
v. 손을 흔들다, 신호하다; 파도치다
A wave is a move of your hand from side to side in the air, usually in order to say hello or goodbye to someone.

**block**\*\*\*
[blák]

vt. (길 등을) 막다, 방해하다; n. 덩어리; 블록, 도시의 한 구획
If you block someone's way, you prevent them from going somewhere or entering a place by standing in front of them.

**barn**\*\*
[bɑːrn]

n. (농가의) 헛간, 광
A barn is a building on a farm in which crops or animal food can be kept.

**attach**\*\*
[ətǽtʃ]

vt. 붙이다, 달다; 소속시키다 (attached a. 덧붙여진, 첨부된)
If you attach something to an object, you join it or fasten it to the object.

**typewriter**\*
[táipràitər]

n. 타자기
A typewriter is a machine with keys which are pressed in order to print letters, numbers, or other characters onto paper.

**cinnamon**\*
[sínəmən]

n. 계피
Cinnamon is a sweet spice used for flavoring food.

**pumpkin**\*
[pʌ́mpkin]

n. 호박
A pumpkin is a large, round, orange vegetable with a thick skin.

## chapter two

1. Who always likes Molly?
   A. Cheerleaders
   B. Boys
   C. Meg's friends
   D. Teachers

2. Meg thought that Molly was _____.
   A. mean
   B. beautiful
   C. very smart
   D. impatient

3. What was Will Banks doing outside?
   A. Fixing his truck
   B. Repairing his house
   C. Walking his dog
   D. Shoveling his driveway

4. Why was Meg's house in the country special to Will?
   A. His wife grew up in the house.
   B. He built the house.
   C. His grandfather built the house.
   D. His best friend used to live in the house.

5. What was NOT true about Will?

    A. He had a wife named Margaret.

    B. He sometimes rented out two of his houses.

    C. He moved to the city when he was a young man.

    D. He carved his name into the closet floor when he was young.

6. What did Meg do in Will's kitchen?

    A. She made him some hot tea.

    B. She took his picture.

    C. She told Will about her sister.

    D. She had lunch.

7. Why did Meg feel warm deep down inside?

    A. She was happy to meet a new friend.

    B. She had an idea for a beautiful painting.

    C. She drank a lot of tea.

    D. Will called her beautiful.

*Check Your Reading Speed*

1분에 몇 단어를 읽는지 리딩 속도를 측정해보세요.

$$\frac{3,455 \text{ words}}{\text{reading time ( ) sec}} \times 60 = (\quad) \text{ WPM}$$

*Build Your Vocabulary*

**stick it out**

idiom (구어) 참다, 끝까지 버티다
If you stick it out, you keep going and endure something difficult.

**alike**\*\*
[əláik]

a. 비슷한; ad. 마찬가지로, 같게
If two or more things are alike, they are similar in some way.

**enthusiastic**\*\*
[inθù:ziǽstik]

a. 열광적인, 열렬한
If you are enthusiastic about something, you show how much you like or enjoy it by the way that you behave and talk.

**birdseed**
[bə́:rdsi:d]

n. 새 모이
Birdseed is a mixture of various kinds of seeds for feeding birds.

**feeder**\*
[fí:dər]

n. (새·동물의) 먹이통
A feeder is a container that you fill with food for birds or animals.

**stop by**<sup>복습</sup>

idiom 들르다, 방문하다
If you stop by somewhere, you make a short visit to a person or place.

**announcement**\*\*
[ənáunsmənt]

n. 발표, 공표, 공고 (birth announcement n. 출생 통지)
An announcement is a statement made to the public or to the media which gives information about something that has happened or that will happen.

**brick**<sup>복습</sup>
[brík]

n. 벽돌
Bricks are rectangular blocks of baked clay used for building walls, which are usually red or brown.

**every now and then**<sup>복습</sup>

idiom 가끔, 때때로, 이따금
If you do something every now and then, you do it sometimes, but not very often.

**sleepwalker**
[slí:pwɔ̀:kər]

n. 몽유병자
Someone who is a sleepwalker walks around while sleeping.

**typewriter**<sup>복습</sup>
[táipràitər]

n. 타자기
A typewriter is a machine with keys which are pressed in order to print letters, numbers, or other characters onto paper.

**rip**\*
[ríp]

v. 찢다, 잡아찢다, 풀어내다; n. 찢어진 틈, 잡아 찢음
(rip up phrasal v. 갈기갈기 찢다)
When something rips or when you rip it, you tear it forcefully with your hands or with a tool such as a knife.

24

**crumple**<sup>복습</sup>
[krʌ́mpl]

v. 구기다, 구겨지다, 쭈글쭈글하게 하다; n. 주름
If you crumple something such as paper or cloth, or if it crumples, it is squashed and becomes full of untidy creases and folds.

**clatter**\*\*
[klǽtər]

vt. 달가닥달가닥 울리게 하다; n. 달가닥달가닥하는 소리; 떠들썩한 소리
If you say that people or things clatter somewhere, you mean that they move there noisily.

**mutter**\*\*
[mʌ́tər]

v. 중얼거리다, 불평하다; n. 중얼거림, 불평
If you mutter, you speak very quietly so that you cannot easily be heard, often because you are complaining about something.

**preoccupied**\*
[priːάkjupàid]

a. (어떤 생각 · 걱정에) 사로잡힌, 정신이 팔린
If you are preoccupied, you are thinking a lot about something or someone, and so you hardly notice other things.

**scrap**\*\*
[skræp]

n. (종이 · 옷감 등의) 조각; vt. 긁어내다; 문지르다; 부스러기로 만들다
A scrap of something is a very small piece or amount of it.

**material**\*\*\*
[mətíəriəl]

n. 직물, 천; (물건의) 재료; a. 물질의, 물질적인
Material is cloth.

**yucky**
[jʌ́ki]

a. 역겨운, 구역질나는
Something yucky is disgusting or very unpleasant.

**embroider**\*
[embrɔ́idər]

v. 수놓다, 수를 놓다, 장식하다 (hand-embroidered a. 손으로 수놓은)
If something such as clothing or cloth is embroidered with a design, the design is stitched into it.

**all of a sudden**<sup>복습</sup>

idiom 갑자기, 뜻밖에, 돌연히
If something happens all of a sudden, it happens quickly and unexpectedly.

**have[get] a grip on**

idiom …을 파악하다, 이해하다; 사로잡다, 장식하다
If you have a grip on yourself, you make an effort to control or improve your behavior or work.

**study**<sup>복습</sup>
[stʌ́di]

n. 서재, 집무실; v. 배우다, 공부하다
A study is a room in a house which is used for reading, writing, and studying.

**fond**\*\*\*
[fάnd]

a. 정다운, 다정한; 좋아하는
You use fond to describe people or their behavior when they show affection.

**lovable**\*
[lʌ́vəbl]

a. 사랑스러운, 귀여운
If you describe someone as lovable, you mean that they have attractive qualities, and are easy to like.

**forgetful**\*
[fərgétfəl]

a. 잘 잊어 먹는, 건망증이 있는
Someone who is forgetful often forgets things.

**frustration**\*
[frʌ́streiʃən]

n. 좌절, 실패, 낙담; 장애물
Frustration is the feeling of being frustrated.

**confusion**\*\*
[kənfjúːʒən]

n. 혼란, 혼동, 뒤죽박죽
Confusion is a situation in which everything is in disorder, especially because there are lots of things happening at the same time.

**rage**\*\*
[réidʒ]

v. 날뛰다; 격노하다; 노하게 하다 n. 격노, 분노; 열광
You can refer to the strong anger that someone feels in a particular situation as a particular rage, especially when this results in violent or aggressive behavior.

**caring**
[kéəriŋ]

a. 배려하는, 보살피는
If someone is caring, they are affectionate, helpful, and sympathetic.

**go beyond**

phrasal v. …을 넘어서다
If something goes beyond, it is greater or better than expected.

**complicated**\*\*
[kámplikèitid]

a. 복잡한; 풀기[이해하기] 어려운
If you say that something is complicated, you mean it has so many parts or aspects that it is difficult to understand or deal with.

**puzzle**\*\*
[pʌzl]

v. 어리둥절하게[이해할 수 없게] 만들다; n. 수수께끼, 어려운 문제
(puzzling a. 곤혹하게 하는, 헷갈리게 하는)
If something puzzles you, you do not understand it and feel confused.

**telescope**\*
[téləskòup]

n. 망원경
A telescope is a long instrument shaped like a tube, which has lenses inside it that make distant things seem larger and nearer when you look through it.

**watcher**
[wátʃər]

n. 연구가, 관찰자
A watcher is a person who watches.

**neighborhood**\*\*
[néibərhùd]

n. 근처, 인근, 이웃
A neighborhood is one of the parts of a town where people live.

**loan**\*\*
[lóun]

v. 빌려 주다; n. 대부(貸付), 대여
If you loan something to someone, you lend it to them.

**skin**\*\*\*
[skin]

v. (피부가) 까지다, 벗겨지다; n. 피부, (동물의) 가죽
If you skin your body, you scrape, or rub off your skin.

**dreg**
[dreg]

n. (보통 pl.) 잔재, 찌꺼기, 마지막 부분; 하찮은 것, 쓰레기
The dregs of a liquid are the last drops left at the bottom of a container, together with any solid bits that have sunk to the bottom.

**wrinkle**\*\*
[ríŋkl]

v. 구겨지다, 주름[구김살]이 생기다; n. 주름, 잔주름 (wrinkled a. 주름진)
When someone's skin wrinkles or when something wrinkles it, lines start to form in it because the skin is getting old or damaged.

**block**\*\*\*
[blák]

n. 블록, 도시의 한 구획; 덩어리; vt. (길 등을) 막다, 방해하다
A block in a town is an area of land with streets on all its sides.

26

**get used to**

idiom …에 익숙해지다
If you get used to something or someone, you become familiar with it or get to know them, so that you no longer feel that the thing or person is unusual or surprising.

**glance**\*\*\*
[glæns]

v. 흘긋 보다, 잠깐 보다; n. 흘긋 봄
If you glance at something or someone, you look at them very quickly and then look away again immediately.

**forehead**\*\*
[fɔ́:rhèd]

n. 이마
Your forehead is the area at the front of your head between your eyebrows and your hair.

**wave**복습
[wéiv]

n. (머리카락의) 웨이브; (팔 · 손 · 몸을) 흔들기; 파도, 물결;
v. 손을 흔들다, 신호하다; 파도치다
If someone's hair has waves, it curves slightly instead of being straight.

**eerie**
[íəri]

a. 섬뜩한, 기분 나쁜, 무시무시한
If you describe something as eerie, you mean that it seems strange and frightening, and makes you feel nervous.

**hold one's breath**

idiom (흥분 · 공포 등으로) 숨을 죽이다
If you say that someone is holding their breath, you mean that they are waiting anxiously or excitedly for something to happen.

**tongue**\*\*\*
[tʌ́ŋ]

n. 혀; 말, 말씨 (stick out one's tongue idiom 혀를 내밀다)
Your tongue is the soft movable part inside your mouth which you use for tasting, eating, and speaking.

**hang around**

idiom 배회하다, 서성거리다
If you hang around, you stay in the same place doing nothing, usually because you are waiting for something or someone.

**dirt road**복습
[dɔ́:rt róud]

n. 비포장도로
Dirt road is a rough road in the country that is made from hard earth.

**pantry**\*
[pǽntri]

n. 식료품 저장실
A pantry is a small room or large cupboard in a house, usually near the kitchen, where food is kept.

**stretch**\*\*\*
[stretʃ]

v. 뻗치다, 잡아 늘이다; 늘어나다; n. 뻗침
Something that stretches over an area or distance covers or exists in the whole of that area or distance.

**curly**\*
[kɔ́:rli]

a. 곱슬곱슬한
Curly hair is full of curls.

**stringy**
[stríŋi]

a. (머리카락이 길고 가늘며) 지저분한; (씹기 어렵게) 섬유질이 많은
Stringy hair is thin and unattractive.

**mean to**

idiom 계획하다, 의도하다
If you mean to do something, you intend or plan to do it.

**settle down**

phrasal v. (상황 · 흥분 따위가) 진정되다, 차분해지다
If a situation or a person that has been going through a lot of problems or changes settles down, they become calm.

**fate**\*\*\*
[feit]

n. 운명, 숙명; 죽음, 최후
Fate is a power that some people believe controls and decides everything that happens, in a way that cannot be prevented or changed.

**particular**\*\*\*
[pərtíkjələr]

a. 특정한, 특별한, 특유의
You use particular to emphasize that you are talking about one thing or one kind of thing rather than other similar ones.

**bundle up**

phrasal v. 옷을 껴입다; 꾸리다, 한 묶음으로 만들다
If you bundle up, you dress in a lot of warm clothes, usually because the weather is very cold. If you bundle someone up, you dress them in a lot of warm clothes.

**abandon**<sup>복습</sup>
[əbǽndən]

vt. 버리다; 단념하다, 그만두다 (abandoned a. 버려진, 황폐한)
If you abandon a place, thing, or person, you leave the place, thing, or person permanently or for a long time.

**driveway**<sup>복습</sup>
[dráivwèi]

n. (도로에서 집·차고까지의) 진입로
A driveway is a piece of hard ground that leads from the road to the front of a house or other building.

**plow**\*\*
[plau]

v. 갈다, 갈아 일구다; n. 쟁기
When someone plow an area of land, they turn over the soil using a plow.

**stamp**\*\*\*
[stæmp]

v. (발을) 구르다, 짓밟다; 날인하다; n. 우표, 인지; 도장
If you stamp or stamp your foot, you lift your foot and put it down very hard on the ground, for example because you are angry.

**blind**\*\*\*
[bláind]

a. 눈먼, 장님인; vt. 눈멀게 하다; n. 블라인드
Someone who is blind is unable to see because their eyes are damaged.

**silly**\*\*
[síli]

a. 익살맞은, 어리석은, 바보 같은; n. 바보, 멍청이
If you say that someone or something is silly, you mean that they are foolish, childish, or ridiculous.

**square**\*\*\*
[skwɛə:r]

a. 정사각형의; 공명정대한; n. 광장; 정사각형
A square is a shape with four sides that are all the same length and four corners that are all right angles.

**chimney**\*\*
[tʃímni]

n. 굴뚝
A chimney is a pipe through which smoke goes up into the air, usually through the roof of a building.

**sag**
[sæg]

v. (가운데가) 축 처지다, 늘어지다; 약화되다
When something sags, it hangs down loosely or sinks downwards in the middle.

**shabby**\*\*
[ʃǽbi]

a. 낡아빠진, 허름한; 초라한
Shabby things or places look old and in bad condition.

**weather**\*\*\*
[wéðər]

v. 풍화되다; 비바람을 맞게 하다; n. 날씨, 기상
(weathered a. 풍화된; 비바람에 씻긴)
If something such as wood or rock weathers or is weathered, it changes color or shape as a result of the wind, sun, rain, or cold.

28

**scary**
[skέəri]

a. 무서운, 두려운
Something that is scary is rather frightening.

**beat-up**
[bíːt-ʌ́p]

a. (구어) 오래 써서 낡은, 닳은
A beat-up car or other object is old and in bad condition.

**weatherbeaten**
[wéðərbiːtn]

a. 비바람에 시달린, 비바람을 맞아 온
Something that is weatherbeaten is rough and slightly damaged after being outside for a long time.

**cousin***
[kʌ́zn]

n. 사촌, 종형제
Your cousin is the child of your uncle or aunt.

**elderly***
[éldərli]

a. 나이가 지긋한, 중년이 지난
You use elderly as a polite way of saying that someone is old.

**frail****
[freil]

a. 약한, 부서지기 쉬운, 무른
Weak or unhealthy, or easily damaged, broken or harmed.

**thump**
[θʌ́mp]

v. 탁치다, 두드리다, 부딪치다; n. 쿵하는 소리, 치기, 두드리기
If you thump something, you hit it hard, usually with your fist.

**snowbank**
[snóubæ̀ŋk]

n. (산허리 · 계곡의) 눈더미
A snowbank is a mound or heap of snow.

**hood****
[hud]

n. 자동차 보닛, 덮개; 두건
The hood of a car is the metal cover over the engine at the front.

**woolen****
[wúlən]

a. 양털로 만든, 양털의 모직으로 만든
Woolen clothes or materials are made from wool or from a mixture of wool and artificial fibers.

**automatic****
[ɔ́ːtəmæ̀tik]

a. 자동의, 기계적인 (automatically ad. 자동적으로)
An automatic action is one that you do without thinking about it.

**mitten***
[mítn]

n. 벙어리장갑
Mittens are gloves which have one section that covers your thumb and another section that covers your four fingers together.

**smear***
[smíər]

n. (기름기 등이 묻은) 얼룩, 자국; v. (기름을) 바르다, 칠하다; (잉크 등이) 번지다
A smear is a dirty or oily mark.

**grease****
[gríːs]

n. 기름, 지방분; v. 기름을 바르다[치다]
Grease is a thick, oily substance which is put on the moving parts of cars and other machines in order to make them work smoothly.

**spice****
[spais]

n. 향신료, 양념, 양념류; vt. …에 양념을 치다
A spice is a part of a plant, or a powder made from that part, which you put in food to give it flavor.

**wipe****
[waip]

vt. 닦다, 닦아 내다; n. 닦음, 닦아 냄
If you wipe something, you rub its surface to remove dirt or liquid from it.

**greasy***
[gríːsi]

a. 기름투성이의, 기름에 전
Something that is greasy has grease on it or in it.

**rag**\*\*
[ræg]
n. 해진 천, 누더기
Rags are old torn clothes.

**apologize**\*\*
[əpálədʒàiz]
v. 사과하다, 사죄하다
When you apologize to someone, you say that you are sorry that you have hurt them or caused trouble for them.

**toe**\*\*
[tóu]
n. 발가락
Your toes are the five movable parts at the end of each foot.

**numb**\*
[nʌm]
a. (얼어서) 마비된; 감각을 잃은; vt. 감각을 잃게 하다; 망연자실케 하다
If a part of your body is numb, you cannot feel anything there.

**envision**
[invíʒən]
vt. (미래의 일을) 상상하다, 구상하다, 마음속에 그리다
If you envision something, you imagine that it is true, real, or likely to happen.

**hesitate**\*\*
[hézətèit]
v. 주저하다, 머뭇거리다, 망설이다
If you hesitate, you do not speak or act for a short time, usually because you are uncertain, embarrassed, or worried about what you are going to say or do.

**thorough**\*\*
[θɔ́ːrou]
a. 철저한, 완전한; 절대적인 (thoroughly ad. 완전히, 철저히)
Thorough is used to emphasize the great degree or extent of something.

**harmless**\*\*
[háːrmlis]
a. 해롭지 않은, 무해한
If you describe someone or something as harmless, you mean that they are not important and therefore unlikely to annoy other people or cause trouble.

**company**\*\*\*
[kʌ́mpəni]
n. 함께 있음, (집에 온) 손님; 동료, 일행; 회사 v. 따르다, 동행하다
Company is having another person or other people with you, usually when this is pleasant or stops you feeling lonely.

**fall apart**
phrasal v. 산산조각나다, 부서지다
If something falls apart, it is old or in bad condition and breaks into pieces.

**oriental**\*\*
[ɔ́ːriéntl]
a. 동양의, 동양인의
Oriental means coming from or associated with eastern Asia.

**rug**\*\*\*
[rʌg]
n. (방바닥 · 마루에 까는) 깔개, 융단
A rug is a piece of thick material that you put on a floor.

**shade**\*\*\*
[ʃeid]
n. 색조, 색깔; 그늘, 그림자; (얼굴의 어두운) 기색; vt. 그늘지게 하다, 어둡게 하다
A shade of a particular color is one of its different forms. For example, emerald green and olive green are shades of green.

**fireplace**\*\*\*
[faiərplèis]
n. (벽)난로
In a room, the fireplace is the place where a fire can be lit and the area on the wall and floor surrounding this place.

**mantel**
[mǽntl]
n. 벽난로 선반, 벽난로를 감싸고 있는 장식
A mantel is a wood or stone shelf which is the top part of a border round a fireplace.

30

**pitcher**[**] 
[pítʃər] 

① n. 물 주전자 ② n. 투수, 피처 
A pitcher is a jug. 

**polish**[**] 
[páliʃ] 

v. (윤이 나도록) 닦다, 광을 내다; n. 광택제; 광택, 윤 
(polished a. (잘 닦아서) 윤[광]이 나는) 
If you polish something, you put polish on it or rub it with a cloth 
to make it shine. 

**chest**[**] 
[tʃest] 

n. 상자, 궤; 가슴, 흉곽 
A chest is a large, heavy box used for storing things. 

**drawer**[**] 
[dró:ər] 

n. 서랍 
A drawer is part of a desk, chest, or other piece of furniture that 
is shaped like a box and is designed for putting things in. 

**stove**[**] 
[stóuv] 

n. 스토브, 난로; (요리용) 화로; v. 난로로 데우다 
A stove is a piece of equipment which provides heat, either for 
cooking or for heating a room. 

**kettle**[**] 
[kétl] 

n. 주전자, 솥 
A kettle is a container with a lid, handle and a spout, used for 
boiling water. 

**pine**[복습] 
[páin] 

n. 소나무 (재목) 
A pine tree or a pine is a tall tree which has very thin, sharp leaves 
and a fresh smell. Pine trees have leaves all year round. 

**laid** 
[leid] 

v. LAY(두다, 눕혀놓다; 알을 낳다)의 과거 · 과거분사 
lie—lay—lain(눕다, 누워있다)와 의미와 스펠링을 헷갈리지 않도록 주의하자. 

**weave**[**] 
[wi:v] 

v. (wove—woven) (옷감 · 카펫 · 바구니 등을) 짜다, 엮다 
If you weave cloth or a carpet, you make it by crossing threads 
over and under each other using a frame or machine. 

**scrub**[**] 
[skrʌb] 

v. 북북 문지르다, 세척하다, 비벼서 씻다 
If you scrub something, you rub it hard in order to clean it, using 
a stiff brush and water. 

**kindergarten**[*] 
[kíndərgà:rtn] 

n. 유치원 
A kindergarten is an informal kind of school for very young children, 
where they learn things by playing. 

**pottery**[복습] 
[pátəri] 

n. 도자기 (그릇들); 도예 
You can use pottery to refer to pots, dishes, and other objects 
which are made from clay and then baked in an oven until they 
are hard. 

**gleam**[**] 
[glí:m] 

vi. 번득이다, 빛을 반사하다; (얼굴 · 눈이 감정으로) 빛나다; 
n. 번득임; 어스레한 빛 
If an object or a surface gleams, it reflects light because it is shiny 
and clean. 

**combination**[**] 
[kàmbənéiʃən] 

n. 조합, 결합, 화합 
A combination of things is a mixture of them. 

**closet**[복습] 
[klázit] 

n. 벽장, 찬장 
A closet is a piece of furniture with doors at the front and shelves 
inside, which is used for storing things.

**carve**\*\*
[kɑːrv]

vt. 새기다, 조각하다
If you carve writing or a design on an object, you cut it into the surface of the object.

**refinish**
[riːfíniʃ]

vt. (목재 · 가구 등의) 표면을 다시 끝손질하다
If you refinish something such as furniture and wood, you change or restore the surface of them.

**spank**\*
[spæŋk]

v. 찰싹 때리다; n. 찰싹 때리기
If someone spanks a child, they punish them by hitting them on the bottom several times with their hand.

**rude**\*\*
[ruːd]

a. 무례한, 버릇없는
When people are rude, they act in an impolite way towards other people or say impolite things about them.

**bride**\*\*
[bráid]

n. 새색시, 신부
A bride is a woman who is getting married or who has just got married.

**gone**\*\*\*
[gɔ́ːn]

a. (완곡) 죽은; 지나간, 과거의; v. GO의 과거분사
When someone is gone, they have left the place where you are and are no longer there.

**tempt**\*\*
[tempt]

vt. 유혹하다, 부추기다
Something that tempts you attracts you and makes you want it, even though it may be wrong or harmful.

**pipe**\*\*\*
[paip]

n. 담배 파이프; (액체 · 기체가 흐르는) 관, 파이프
A pipe is an object which is used for smoking tobacco.

**hired man**

n. 고용인, 머슴
A hired man is a laborer on a farm or ranch.

**cottage**\*\*
[kɑ́(ɔ́)tidʒ]

n. (시골에 있는) 작은 집
A cottage is a small house, usually in the country.

**rent**\*\*
[rént]

v. 세놓다, 임대하다; 세내다, 임차하다
If you rent something to someone, you let them have it and use it in exchange for a sum of money which they pay you regularly.

**wilderness**\*\*
[wíldərnis]

n. 황무지, 황야; 야생
A wilderness is a large area of land that has never been developed or farmed.

**solitude**\*\*
[sɑ́(ɔ́)litjuːd]

n. 고독, 외로움
Solitude is the state of being alone, especially when this is peaceful and pleasant.

**stimulate**\*\*
[stímjulèit]

v. 자극하다, 격려[고무]하다
To stimulate something means to encourage it to begin or develop further.

**carpentry**
[kɑ́ːrpəntri]

n. 목수 일; 목공
Carpentry is the activity of making and repairing wooden things.

**straighten**\*\*
[stréitn]

v. (자세를) 바로 하다; 똑바르게 되다[하다]
If you are standing in a relaxed or slightly bent position and then you straighten, you make your back or body straight and upright.

32

**plaid*** [plæd]
n. 격자무늬 옷감
Plaid is material with a check design on it.

**honor**\*\*\* [ánər]
vt. 영광을 베풀다; 존경하다, 공경하다; n. 명예, 영예 (honored a. 명예로운)
If someone is honored, they are given public praise or an award for something they have done.

**harsh**\*\* [haːrʃ]
a. 거친; (소리 따위가) 귀에 거슬리는; 가혹한
Something that is harsh is so hard, bright, or rough that it seems unpleasant or harmful.

**gesture**<sup>복습</sup> [dʒéstʃər]
vi. 몸짓을[신호를] 하다; n. 몸짓
If you gesture, you use movements of your hands or head in order to tell someone something or draw their attention to something.

**awkward**\*\* [ɔ́ːkwərd]
a. 어색한, 불편한, 곤란한
Someone who feels awkward behaves in a shy or embarrassed way.

**inept** [inépt]
a. 솜씨 없는, 서투른
If you say that someone is inept, you are criticizing them because they do something with a complete lack of skill.

**make up for**
idiom 뒤진 것을 만회하다, 벌충하다
To make up for something means to do something good for somebody because you have treated them badly or because they have done something good for you.

**composition**\*\* [kàmpəzíʃən]
n. (그림 · 사진의) 구도, 구성
When you talk about the composition of something, you are referring to the way in which its various parts are put together and arranged.

**unload*** [ʌnlóud]
v. (카메라에서) 필름을 빼내다; (차 · 배 등의) 짐을 내리다
To unload a camera or other piece of equipment means to put film, tape, or data out of it after use.

**expose**\*\* [ikspóuz]
vt. 노출시키다; 드러내다, 폭로하다 (exposed a. (필름 등이) 노출된)
To expose something that is usually hidden means to uncover it so that it can be seen.

**sting**\*\* [stiŋ]
v. 따끔거리다; 찌르다, 쏘다; n. 찌름, 쏨 (stinging a. 찌르는 듯이 아픈, 얼얼한)
If a part of your body stings, or if a substance stings it, you feel a sharp pain there.

*chapter three*

1. How might Will's nephew cause trouble?
   A. He wants control over Will's property.
   B. He wants to live in Will's house.
   C. He wants Will to move to Boston.
   D. He wants to use the land near Will's house to grow crops.

2. What was Mom doing with the fabric in the living room?
   A. She was making Molly a dress.
   B. She was making clothing for Molly and Meg.
   C. She was making curtains for the living room.
   D. She was making a quilt.

3. What would Meg and Dad make together?
   A. A study area
   B. A board game
   C. A darkroom
   D. A camera

4. Why did Meg think it was fun when Molly was sick?
   A. Molly would go for walks with her.
   B. She could read Molly stories that she wrote.
   C. Molly would play board games with her.
   D. Molly would do her hair and makeup.

5. Why was Molly a nuisance when she was sick?

    A. She was grouchy.

    B. She spent a lot of time with her friends.

    C. She took board games too seriously.

    D. She took too long to get ready for school.

6. Molly _____ often while she was sick.

    A. saw her friends

    B. had nosebleeds

    C. had stomachaches

    D. cried

7. Where did Molly want to go in the summer?

    A. On a family vacation

    B. Boston

    C. A summer camp

    D. Their city house

*Check Your Reading Speed*

1분에 몇 단어를 읽는지 리딩 속도를 측정해보세요.

$$\frac{3{,}082 \text{ words}}{\text{reading time ( ) sec}} \times 60 = (\quad) \text{ WPM}$$

*Build Your Vocabulary*

**melt**<sup>복습</sup>
[mélt]

v. 녹다, 녹이다, 용해하다; (감정 등이) 누그러지다; n. 용해
When a solid substance melts or when you melt it, it changes to a liquid, usually because it has been heated.

**bury**\*\*\*
[béri]

vt. 파묻다, 매장하다; 묻다
To bury something means to put it into a hole in the ground and cover it up with earth.

**mess**<sup>복습</sup>
[més]

n. (개 · 고양이의) 똥; 엉망진창인 상태; v. 망쳐놓다, 방해하다
A mess is something liquid or sticky that has been accidentally dropped on something.

**mitten**<sup>복습</sup>
[mítn]

n. 벙어리장갑
Mittens are gloves which have one section that covers your thumb and another section that covers your four fingers together.

**toss**\*\*
[tɔ́:s]

v. 던지다, 내던지다, 버리다; n. 던져 올림; 위로 던짐
If you toss something somewhere, you throw it there lightly, often in a rather careless way.

**frozen**\*\*
[fróuzən]

v. FREEZE(얼다, 얼어붙다)의 과거 분사; a. 얼어붙은, 결빙한
If the ground is frozen it has become very hard because the weather is very cold.

**recite**\*\*
[risáit]

vt. 암송하다, 낭독하다
When someone recites a poem or other piece of writing, they say it aloud after they have learned it.

**poem**<sup>복습</sup>
[póuəm]

n. (한 편의) 시; 운문, 시적인 문장
A poem is a piece of writing in which the words are chosen for their beauty and sound and are carefully arranged, often in short lines which rhyme.

**cruel**\*\*
[krú:əl]

a. (crueler–cruelest) 잔혹한, 무자비한
Someone who is cruel deliberately causes pain or distress to people or animals.

**scrub**<sup>복습</sup>
[skrʌb]

v. 북북 문지르다, 세척하다, 비벼서 씻다
If you scrub something, you rub it hard in order to clean it, using a stiff brush and water.

**downright**<sup>복습</sup>
[dáunràit]

a. 순전한, 완전한
You use downright to emphasize unpleasant or bad qualities or behavior.

36

**bitter*** 
[bítər]

a. 혹독한, 매서운; 쓴, 쓰라린
Bitter weather, or a bitter wind, is extremely cold.

**operate****
[á(ɔ́)pəreit]

v. 작동하다, 움직이다, 운영하다; 수술하다
When you operate a machine or device, or when it operates, you make it work.

**get[have] a grip on . . .** 복습

idiom ⋯을 파악하다, 이해하다; 사로잡다, 장악하다
If you get a grip on yourself, you make an effort to control or improve your behavior or work.

**grip**
[grip]

v. 잡다, 움켜잡다; (마음을) 사로잡다, (관심[주의]을) 끌다;
n. 잡음, 붙듦, 움켜쥠; 손잡이
If you grip something, you take hold of it with your hand and continue to hold it firmly.

**blend****
[blend]

v. 섞(이)다, 혼합하다
If you blend substances together or if they blend, you mix them together so that they become one substance.

**stark***
[stɑ:rk]

a. 삭막한, 황량한; 냉혹한
Something that is stark is very plain in appearance.

**carve** 복습
[kɑ:rv]

vt. 새기다, 조각하다
If you carve writing or a design on an object, you cut it into the surface of the object.

**fascinate***
[fǽsineit]

v. 매혹하다, 황홀케 하다 (fascinating a. 매력적인, 대단히 흥미로운)
If something fascinates you, it interests and delights you so much that your thoughts tend to concentrate on it.

**lean****
[lí:n]

① v. 기대다, 의지하다; 상체를 굽히다, 기울이다 ② a. 야윈, 마른
If you lean on or against someone or something, you rest against them so that they partly support your weight.

**scruffy**
[skrʌ́fi]

a. (구어) 단정치 못한, 지저분한
Someone or something that is scruffy is dirty and untidy.

**company** 복습
[kʌ́mpəni]

n. 함께 있음, (집에 온) 손님; 동료, 일행; 회사 v. 따르다, 동행하다
Company is having another person or other people with you, usually when this is pleasant or stops you feeling lonely.

**master*** 
[mǽ(ɑ́:)stər]

n. 달인, 명수; 주인; v. ⋯을 완전히 익히다, ⋯에 숙달하다
If you say that someone is a master of a particular activity, you mean that they are extremely skilled at it.

**cabinetmaker**
[kǽbənitmèikər]

n. 고급 가구 제작자
A cabinetmaker is a person who makes high-quality wooden furniture.

**fortune*** 
[fɔ́:rtʃən]

n. 부, 재산; 운, 행운
Someone who has a fortune has a very large amount of money.

**teeny**
[tí:ni]

a. (= tiny) (구어) 작은, 조그마한
If you describe something as teeny, you are emphasizing that it is very small.

**nephew****
[néfju:]

n. 조카
Someone's nephew is the son of their sister or brother.

**bother** [복습]
[báðər]

v. 귀찮게 하다, 괴롭히다, 폐 끼치다; 일부러 …하다, 애를 쓰다
If something bothers you, or if you bother about it, it worries, annoys, or upsets you.

**property** [***]
[prá(ɔ́)pərti]

n. 부동산, 소유지; 재산, 자산; 성질, 특성
A property is a building and the land belonging to it.

**antique** [*]
[æntíːk]

n. (귀중한) 골동품; a. (귀중한) 골동품인
An antique is an old object such as a piece of china or furniture which is valuable because of its beauty or rarity.

**apparently** [**]
[əpǽrəntli]

ad. 보기에, 외관상으로; 분명히, 명백히
You use apparently to refer to something that seems to be true, although you are not sure whether it is or not.

**declare** [***]
[diklέər]

v. 선고하다, 선언하다; 단언하다
If you declare something, you state officially and formally that it exists or is the case.

**incompetent** [*]
[inkámpətənt]

a. (업무 · 과제 등에 대해) 무능한, 기술이 부족한
If you describe someone as incompetent, you are criticizing them because they are unable to do their job or a task properly.

**cottage** [복습]
[ká(ɔ́)tidʒ]

n. (시골에 있는) 작은 집
A cottage is a small house, usually in the country.

**inn** [**]
[ín]

n. (작은) 호텔, 여관
An inn is a small hotel or pub, usually an old one.

**brick** [복습]
[brík]

n. 벽돌
Bricks are rectangular blocks of baked clay used for building walls, which are usually red or brown.

**chimney** [복습]
[tʃímni]

n. 굴뚝
A chimney is a pipe through which smoke goes up into the air, usually through the roof of a building.

**roof** [복습]
[rúːf]

n. 지붕; vt. 지붕을 해 덮다
The roof of a building is the covering on top of it that protects the people and things inside from the weather.

**shutter** [**]
[ʃʌ́tər]

n. 덧문, 셔터; (카메라의) 셔터
Shutters are wooden or metal covers fitted on the outside of a window.

**envision** [복습]
[invíʒən]

vt. (미래의 일을) 상상하다, 구상하다, 마음속에 그리다
If you envision something, you imagine that it is true, real, or likely to happen.

**parking lot**
[páːrkiŋ lat]

n. 주차장
A parking lot is an area of ground where people can leave their cars.

**shrug** [*]
[ʃrʌ́g]

v. (양 손바닥을 내보이면서 어깨를) 으쓱하다; n. (어깨를) 으쓱하기
If you shrug, you raise your shoulders to show that you are not interested in something or that you do not know or care about something.

38

**loony**
[lú:ni]

n. 괴짜; a. 미친, 이상한
If you refer to someone as a loony, you mean that they behave in a way that seems mad, strange, or eccentric.

**ridiculous**\*\*
[ridíkjuləs]

a. 터무니없는; 웃기는, 우스꽝스러운
If you say that something or someone is ridiculous, you mean that they are very foolish.

**literature**\*\*
[lítəritʃər]

n. 문학, 문예; 문헌
Novels, plays, and poetry are referred to as literature, especially when they are considered to be good or important.

**break up**<sup>복습</sup>

idiom 웃음을 터뜨리다; 부서지다, 끝이 나다
If something breaks someone up, it causes them to lose control and begin to laugh or cry.

**lying**<sup>복습</sup>
[láiiŋ]

v. 니E(눕다, 누워있다)의 현재분사(ing) 형태; a. 드러누워 있는
lie는 현재분사가 되면서 -ie가 -y로 변한다는 것과, '눕다, 누워있다'와 '거짓말하다'라는 두 가지 의미의 스펠링이 동일하다는 점에 유의하자.

**stack**\*
[stæk]

n. 더미; 많음, 다량; v. 쌓다, 쌓아올리다
A stack of things is a pile of them.

**crumple**<sup>복습</sup>
[krámpl]

v. 구기다, 구겨지다, 쭈글쭈글하게 하다; n. 주름 (crumpled a. 구겨진, 뒤틀린)
If you crumple something such as paper or cloth, or if it crumples, it is squashed and becomes full of untidy creases and folds.

**sail**\*\*\*
[séil]

v. 미끄러지듯 나아가다; 항해하다; n. 배의 돛; 항해, 보트타기
If a person or thing sails somewhere, they move there smoothly and fairly quickly.

**pipe**<sup>복습</sup>
[paip]

n. 담배 파이프; (액체 · 기체가 흐르는) 관, 파이프
A pipe is an object which is used for smoking tobacco.

**silly**<sup>복습</sup>
[síli]

a. 익살맞은, 어리석은, 바보 같은; n. 바보, 멍청이
If you say that someone or something is silly, you mean that they are foolish, childish, or ridiculous.

**develop**\*\*\*
[divéləp]

v. [사진] 현상하다; 발달하다, 개발하다
To develop photographs means to make negatives or prints from a photographic film.

**expert**\*\*
[ékspə:rt]

a. 숙련된, 노련한; n. 전문가, 숙련가
Someone who is expert at doing something is very skilled at it.

**consultant**\*
[kənsáltənt]

n. 컨설턴트, 상담자
A consultant is a person who advises people on a particular subject.

**storeroom**
[stɔ́:rrù:m]

n. 저장실, 광
A storeroom is a room in which you keep things until they are needed.

**passageway**\*
[pǽsidʒwèi]

n. 복도, 통로
A passageway is a long narrow space with walls or fences on both sides, which connects one place or room with another.

**barn**<sup>복습</sup>
[bɑ:rn]

n. (농가의) 헛간, 광
A barn is a building on a farm in which crops or animal food can be kept.

**heater***
[híːtər]

n. 난방 장치, 난로, 가열기
A heater is a piece of equipment or a machine which is used to raise the temperature of something, especially of the air inside a room or a car.

**shelf****
[ʃelf]

n. (pl. shelves) 선반
A shelf is a flat piece which is attached to a wall or to the sides of a cupboard for keeping things on.

**expose**복습
[ikspóuz]

vt. 노출시키다; 드러내, 폭로하다
To expose something that is usually hidden means to uncover it so that it can be seen.

**equipment****
[ikwípmənt]

n. 장비, 설비
Equipment consists of the things which are used for a particular purpose, for example a hobby or job.

**might as well**복습
[ ]

idiom …하는 편이 낫다
If you say that you might as well do something, or that you may as well do it, you mean that you will do it although you do not have a strong desire to do it and may even feel slightly unwilling to do it.

**sigh*****
[sái]

v. 한숨 쉬다; n. 한숨, 탄식
When you sigh, you let out a deep breath, as a way of expressing feelings such as disappointment, tiredness, or pleasure.

**what the heck**

idiom 아무렴 어때
You say 'what the heck' to indicate that you do not care about a bad aspect of an action or situation.

**tray****
[tréi]

n. 쟁반, 음식 접시; 서류함
A tray is a flat piece of wood, plastic, or metal, which usually has raised edges and which is used for carrying things, especially food and drinks.

**chemical****
[kémikəl]

n. 화학 물질; a. 화학의, 화학적인
Chemicals are substances that are used in a chemical process or made by a chemical process.

**thermometer****
[θərmá(ɔ́)mitər]

n. 온도계
A thermometer is an instrument for measuring temperature.

**filter***
[fíltər]

n. [사진·광학] 필터, 여광기; 여과 장치; v. 여과하다, 거르다
A filter is a device through which sound or light is passed and which blocks or reduces particular sound or light frequencies.

**stuff**복습
[stʌf]

n. 것(들), 물건, 물질; vt. 채워 넣다, 속을 채우다
You can use stuff to refer to things such as a substance, a collection of things, events, or ideas, or the contents of something in a general way without mentioning the thing itself by name.

**triumphant****
[traiʌ́mfənt]

a. 의기양양한; 승리를 얻은, 성공한 (triumphantly ad. 의기양양하게)
Someone who is triumphant has gained a victory or succeeded in something and feels very happy about it.

**terrific**
[tərífik]

a. 아주 좋은, 멋진, 훌륭한
If you describe something or someone as terrific, you are very pleased with them or very impressed by them.

**typical***
[típikəl]

a. 전형적인, 대표적인
If a particular action or feature is typical of someone or something, it shows their usual qualities or characteristics.

**obvious****
[ábviəs]

a. 명백한, 분명한
If something is obvious, it is easy to see or understand.

**one's face fall**

idiom 실망하다
If your face fall, you suddenly look disappointed or upset.

**all along**

idiom 처음부터, 내내, 계속
If something have been there all along, it is there from the very beginning.

**insurmountable**
[insərmáuntəbl]

a. 대처[극복]할 수 없는, 이겨내기 어려운
A problem that is insurmountable is so great that it cannot be dealt with successfully.

**agonize**
[ǽgənàiz]

v. 고민하다, 고뇌하다
If you agonize over something, you feel very anxious about it and spend a long time thinking about it.

**resolve****
[rizálv]

v. (문제 등을) 해결하다; 결심하다; 분해하다, 용해하다
To resolve a problem, argument, or difficulty means to find a solution to it.

**out of nowhere**

idiom 갑자기, 난데없이
If you say that something or someone appears out of nowhere, you mean that they appear suddenly and unexpectedly.

**solution****
[səlúːʃən]

n. 해답, 해결; 용해, 용액
A solution to a problem or difficult situation is a way of dealing with it so that the difficulty is removed.

**tap****
[tǽp]

① v. 가볍게 두드리다; n. 가볍게 두드리기; ② n. 주둥이, (수도 등의) 꼭지
If you tap something, you hit it with a quick light blow or a series of quick light blows.

**subconscious**
[sʌbkánʃəs]

n. 잠재의식; a. 잠재의식의, 어렴풋이 의식하는
Your subconscious is the part of your mind that can influence you or affect your behavior even though you are not aware of it.

**plural****
[plúərəl]

n. [문법] 복수; 복수형(의 말); a. 복수의
The plural of a noun is the form of it that is used to refer to more than one person or thing.

**stitch****
[stitʃ]

v. 바느질하다; 꿰매다; n. 한 바늘, 한 땀
If you stitch cloth, you use a needle and thread to join two pieces together or to make a decoration.

**cringe**
[krindʒ]

vi. 움츠리다, 움찔하다
If you cringe at something, you feel embarrassed or disgusted, and making a slight movement.

**let's face it**

idiom 현실을 직시해라
You use the expression 'let's face it' when you are stating a fact or making a comment about something which you think the person you are talking to may find unpleasant or be unwilling to admit.

**be better off**

idiom 더 낫다
If you say that someone would be better off doing something, you are advising them to do it or expressing the opinion that it would benefit them to do it.

**striped**
[stráipt]

a. 줄무늬가 있는, 줄이 쳐져 있는
Something that is striped has stripes on it.

**throw up**

phrasal v. 토하다
When someone throws up, they vomit.

**roomful**
[rú(:)mful]

n. 방 하나 가득
A roomful of people or things is a room that is full of them.

**plaid**<sup>복습</sup>
[plæd]

n. 격자무늬 옷감
Plaid is material with a check design on it.

**due**\*\*\*
[dju:]

n. 내야 할 돈, 부과금; 당연히 지불되어야 할 것;
a. …하기로 되어 있는, …할 예정인
Dues are sums of money that you give regularly to an organization that you belong to, for example a social club or trade union, in order to pay for being a member.

**scold**\*\*
[skóuld]

v. 꾸짖다, 잔소리하다
If you scold someone, you speak angrily to them because they have done something wrong.

**embroidery**\*
[embróidəri]

n. 자수, 수놓기
Embroidery consists of designs stitched into cloth.

**nostalgic**
[nɑstǽldʒik]

a. 옛날을 그리워하는; 향수에 젖은
Nostalgic things cause you to think affectionately about the past.

**affectionate**\*\*
[əfékʃənit]

a. 애정 어린, 다정한, 인정 많은 (affectionately ad. 애정을 담고)
If you are affectionate, you show your love or fondness for another person in the way that you behave towards them.

**burst out**

phrasal v. 버럭 소리를 지르다; 갑자기 …하기 시작하다
If someone bursts out something, they say it suddenly and loudly.

**couch**<sup>복습</sup>
[kautʃ]

n. (기댈 수 있는 등받이와 팔걸이가 있는) 소파, 긴 의자
A couch is a long, comfortable seat for two or three people.

**neat**<sup>복습</sup>
[ní:t]

a. (구어) 굉장한, 멋진; 산뜻한, 깔끔한
If you say that something is neat, you mean that it is very good.

**flu**\*
[flú:]

n. 독감
Flu is an illness which is similar to a bad cold but more serious. It often makes you feel very weak and makes your muscles hurt.

**fixture**[*]
[fíkstʃər]

n. 고정[붙박이] 세간
Fixtures are pieces of furniture or equipment, for example baths and sinks, which are fixed inside a house or other building and which stay there if you move.

**dice**[*]
[dáis]

n. 주사위
A dice is a small cube which has between one and six spots or numbers on its sides, and which is used in games to provide random numbers.

**giggle**[*]
[gígl]

v. 낄낄 웃다; n. 낄낄 웃음
If someone giggles, they laugh in a childlike way, because they are amused, nervous, or embarrassed.

**thump**[복습]
[θʌmp]

n. 쿵하는 소리, 치기, 두드리기; v. 탁치다, 부딪치다
A thump is a loud, dull sound by hitting something.

**wipe out**

phrasal v. (…을) 완전히 파괴하다, 없애 버리다
To wipe out someone is to defeat them easily in a sports competition.

**mutter**[복습]
[mʌ́tər]

v. 중얼거리다, 불평하다; n. 중얼거림, 불평
If you mutter, you speak very quietly so that you cannot easily be heard, often because you are complaining about something.

**cheat**[**]
[tʃíːt]

v. 규칙을 어기다; 속이다; n. 사기
When someone cheats, they do not obey a set of rules which they should be obeying, for example in a game or exam.

**nuisance**[**]
[njúːsns]

n. 성가신 것, 방해물, 골칫거리
If you say that someone or something is a nuisance, you mean that they annoy you or cause you a lot of problems.

**grouchy**
[gráutʃi]

a. 불평이 많은, 잘 투덜거리는
If someone is grouchy, they are very bad-tempered and complain a lot.

**scroungy**
[skráundʒi]

a. 지저분한, 더러운
Something that is scroungy is dirty or shabby.

**pale**[**]
[péil]

a. 창백한, 핼쑥한; (색깔이) 엷은; v. 창백해지다
If someone looks pale, their face looks a lighter color than usual, usually because they are ill, frightened, or shocked.

**mess around**

phrasal v. 빈둥거리다
If you mess around, you spend time doing things without any particular purpose or without achieving anything.

**nerve**[**]
[nəːrv]

n. 용기; 뻔뻔스러움, 무례; 신경, 신경과민
If you refer to someone's nerves, you mean their ability to cope with problems such as stress, worry, and danger.

**charge**[***]
[tʃɑːrdʒ]

v. 돌진하다, 돌격하다; 청구하다; 충전하다; n. (상품·서비스에 대한) 요금
If you charge towards someone or something, you move quickly and aggressively towards them.

**examine**[***]
[igzǽmin]

v. 조사하다, 검토하다; 검사하다, 진찰하다
If you examine something, you look at it carefully.

**nosebleed**
[nóuzblìːd]

n. 코피
If someone has a nosebleed, blood comes out from inside their nose.

**adolescent**
[æ̀dəlésnt]

n. 청소년
Adolescent is used to describe young people who are no longer children but who have not yet become adults.

**nasal***
[néizəl]

a. 코의, 코에 관한; n. 콧소리, 비음
Nasal is used to describe things relating to the nose and the functions it performs.

**messy**
[mési]

a. 지저분한, 엉망인
Something that is messy is dirty or untidy.

**nasty**\*\*
[næsti]

a. 끔찍한, 형편없는; 못된, 고약한
Something that is nasty is very unpleasant to see, experience, or feel.

**spatter***
[spǽtər]

v. 튀(기)다, 흩어지다; n. (액체 등이) 튀는 것, 후두두 떨어지는 소리
If a liquid spatters a surface or you spatter a liquid over a surface, drops of the liquid fall on an area of the surface.

**dumb**\*\*
[dʌm]

a. 멍청한, 바보 같은; 벙어리의, 말을 못 하는
If you say that something is dumb, you think that it is silly and annoying.

**disgusting**\*\*
[disgʌ́stiŋ]

a. 구역질나는, 메스꺼운, 넌더리나는
If you say that something is disgusting, you are criticizing it because it is extremely unpleasant.

**argument**<sup>복습</sup>
[áːrgjəmənt]

n. 언쟁, 논의, 말다툼
An argument is a conversation in which people disagree with each other angrily or noisily.

**tidy**\*\*
[táidi]

a. 깔끔한, 단정한, 말쑥한; v. 치우다, 정돈하다
Something that is tidy is neat and is arranged in an organized way.

**preoccupied**<sup>복습</sup>
[priːɑ́kjupàid]

a. (어떤 생각 · 걱정에) 사로잡힌, 정신이 팔린
If you are preoccupied, you are thinking a lot about something or someone, and so you hardly notice other things.

**tuck***
[tʌk]

v. 밀어 넣다, 쑤셔 넣다; n. 접어 넣은 단
If you tuck something somewhere, you put it there so that it is safe, comfortable, or neat.

**stare**\*\*\*
[stɛər]

v. 응시하다, 뚫어지게 보다
If you stare at someone or something, you look at them for a long time.

**grin**<sup>복습</sup>
[grín]

n. 싱긋 웃음; v. 이를 드러내고 싱긋 웃다
A grin is a broad smile.

**groan**<sup>복습</sup>
[gróun]

v. 신음하다, 끙끙거리다; n. 신음, 끙 하는 소리
If you groan, you make a long, low sound because you are in pain, or because you are upset or unhappy about something.

**good-natured**[gúd-néitʃərd]
**a.** 온화한, 부드러운 (good-naturedly **ad.** 친절하게)
A good-natured person or animal is naturally friendly and does not get angry easily.

**amaze**<sup>복습</sup>
[əméiz]
**vt.** 깜짝 놀라게 하다 (amazed **a.** (대단히) 놀란)
If something amazes you, it surprises you very much.

**lettuce**<sup>복습</sup>
[létis]
**n.** [식물] 상추
A lettuce is a plant with large green leaves that is the basic ingredient of many salads.

**nuts**
[nʌts]
**a.** 미친, 제정신이 아닌
If you say that someone is nuts, you mean that they go crazy or are very foolish.

**grab**<sup>*</sup>
[græb]
**v.** 부여잡다, 움켜쥐다; **n.** 부여잡기
If you grab something, you take it or pick it up suddenly and roughly.

**clutch**<sup>**</sup>
[klʌtʃ]
**v.** (꽉) 움켜잡다; **n.** (자동차의) 클러치판; 움켜쥠
If you clutch at something or clutch something, you hold it tightly, usually because you are afraid or anxious.

**haughty**<sup>**</sup>
[hɔ́:ti]
**a.** 오만한, 거만한 (haughtily **ad.** 오만하게)
You use haughty to describe someone's behavior or appearance when you disapprove of the fact that they seem to be very proud and to think that they are better than other people.

**wad**
[wάd]
**n.** 뭉치, 다발; 많음, 다량
A wad of something such as paper or cloth is a tight bundle or ball of it.

**bleed**<sup>***</sup>
[bli:d]
**v.** 피를 흘리다, 피가 나다
When you bleed, you lose blood from your body as a result of injury or illness.

*chapter four*

1. What wasn't true at the beginning of the chapter?
   A. Tierney had asked Molly to go steady.
   B. Molly's nosebleeds had stopped.
   C. Meg had developed Will's photos.
   D. Meg's father had finished his book.

2. Where had Meg been spending most of her time?
   A. School
   B. Her bedroom
   C. Her darkroom
   D. Will's house

3. Will used to _____.
   A. be in the army
   B. bake blueberry pies
   C. work as a chef in Germany
   D. be a university professor in Boston

4. How did Molly compliment Meg?
   A. She said that Meg's photographs were good.
   B. She said that Meg was the smartest person she knew.
   C. She said that Meg's drawings were the best she'd ever seen.
   D. She said that Meg looked pretty in a photograph.

5. What did Molly often think about?
   A. Becoming a writer
   B. Getting married
   C. Being a successful businesswoman
   D. Getting sick

6. What did Meg see outside in the night?
   A. Will's truck
   B. A light from the empty house
   C. An ambulance
   D. A flashlight from Will's cottage

7. What happened to Molly in the night?
   A. She coughed up blood.
   B. She cut herself badly.
   C. She fell over some papers.
   D. She had a bad nosebleed.

*Check Your Reading Speed*

1분에 몇 단어를 읽는지 리딩 속도를 측정해보세요.

$$\frac{3{,}452 \text{ words}}{\text{reading time ( \quad ) sec}} \times 60 = ( \qquad ) \text{ WPM}$$

*Build Your Vocabulary*

| | |
|---|---|
| **all of a sudden**<sup>복습</sup> | **idiom** 돌연히, 갑자기, 뜻밖에<br>If something happens all of a sudden, it happens quickly and unexpectedly. |
| **blossom**\*\*<br>[blásəm] | **vi.** (나무 등이) 꽃 피다, 개화하다; 발전하다; **n.** (특히 과수의) 꽃, 개화<br>When a tree blossoms, it produces the flowers that appear before the fruit. |
| **go steady** | **idiom** (…와) 교제하다, 정식으로 사귀다<br>If you go steady, you have someone as a regular boyfriend or girlfriend. |
| **giggly**<br>[gígli] | **a.** 낄낄 웃는<br>Someone who is giggly keeps laughing in a childlike way, because they are amused, nervous, or drunk. |
| **bounce**\*<br>[bauns] | **v.** 깡충깡충 뛰다; 튀(게 하)다; **n.** 튐, 바운드<br>If someone bounces somewhere, they move there in an energetic way, because they are feeling happy. |
| **relapse**<br>[riléps] | **n.** (병의) 재발, 악화; **vi.** (이전 상태로) 다시 빠지다, 되돌아가다<br>If someone who is getting better after an illness has a relapse, they become ill again |
| **bleed**<sup>복습</sup><br>[bli:d] | **v.** 피를 흘리다, 피가 나다<br>When you bleed, you lose blood from your body as a result of injury or illness. |
| **prove**\*\*\*<br>[prú:v] | **v.** 입증하다, 증명하다<br>If something proves to be true or to have a particular quality, it becomes clear after a period of time that it is true or has that quality. |
| **nosebleed**<sup>복습</sup><br>[nóuzbli:d] | **n.** 코피<br>If someone has a nosebleed, blood comes out from inside their nose. |
| **stock**\*\*<br>[sták] | **n.** (기업의) 주식; 재고(품), 비축물; 가축, (농장) 동물<br>Stocks are shares in the ownership of a company, or investments on which a fixed amount of interest will be paid. |
| **develop**<sup>복습</sup><br>[divéləp] | **v.** [사진] 현상하다; 발달하다, 개발하다<br>To develop photographs means to make negatives or prints from a photographic film. |

48

**tuck**<sup>복습</sup>
[tʌk]

v. 밀어 넣다, 쑤셔 넣다; n. 접어 넣은 단
If you tuck something somewhere, you put it there so that it is safe, comfortable, or neat.

**drawer**<sup>복습</sup>
[drɔ́:ər]

n. 서랍
A drawer is part of a desk, chest, or other piece of furniture that is shaped like a box and is designed for putting things in.

**scare**<sup>**</sup>
[skɛə:r]

v. 겁주다, 놀라게 하다 (scared a. 무서워하는, 겁먹은)
If something scares you, it frightens or worries you.

**stiff**<sup>**</sup>
[stif]

ad. 완전히, 매우; 딱딱하게; a. 굳은, 뻣뻣한; 완강한, 완고한
If you are bored stiff, worried stiff, or scared stiff, you are extremely bored, worried, or scared.

**strip**
[strip]

① n. 길고 가느다란 조각 ② v. 옷을 벗다; (껍질을) 벗기다
A strip of something such as paper, cloth, or food is a long, narrow piece of it.

**genius**<sup>**</sup>
[dʒí:njəs]

n. 천재; 특별한 재능
A genius is a highly talented, creative, or intelligent person.

**cross one's fingers**

idiom (중지를 인지에 포개고) 행운을 빌다, 기도하다
If you cross your fingers, you put one finger on top of another and hope for good luck.

**tray**<sup>복습</sup>
[tréi]

n. 쟁반, 음식 접시; 서류함
A tray is a flat piece of wood, plastic, or metal, which usually has raised edges and which is used for carrying things, especially food and drinks.

**dim**<sup>**</sup>
[dím]

a. 어둑한, 흐릿한, 희미한; v. 어둑하게 하다, 흐려지다
Dim light is not bright.

**shade**<sup>복습</sup>
[ʃeid]

n. 색조, 색깔; 그늘, 그림자; (얼굴의 어두운) 기색; vt. 그늘지게 하다, 어둡게 하다
A shade of a particular color is one of its different forms. For example, emerald green and olive green are shades of green.

**drip**<sup>**</sup>
[drip]

v. 물방울이 떨어지다; 흠뻑 젖다
When something drips, drops of liquid fall from it.

**laid**<sup>복습</sup>
[leid]

v. LAY(두다, 눕혀놓다; 알을 낳다)의 과거 · 과거분사
lie—lay—lain(눕다, 누워있다)와 의미와 스펠링을 헷갈리지 않도록 주의하자.

**peel**<sup>복습</sup>
[pi:l]

v. 껍질을 벗기다; (껍질 · 피부가) 벗겨지다; n. (과일 · 채소의 두꺼운) 껍질
When you peel fruit or vegetables, you remove their skins.

**lean**<sup>복습</sup>
[lí:n]

① v. 기대다, 의지하다; 상체를 굽히다, 기울이다 ② a. 야윈, 마른
If you lean on or against someone or something, you rest against them so that they partly support your weight.

**determine**<sup>***</sup>
[ditə́:rmin]

v. 결정하다, 결심하다
If a particular factor determines the nature of a thing or event, it causes it to be of a particular kind.

**attic**<sup>복습</sup>
[ǽtik]

n. 다락(방)
An attic is a room at the top of a house just below the roof.

**station**\*\*\*
[stéiʃən]

vt. (군인을) 배치하다, 주둔시키다; n. 역, 정거장; 방송국; (육군 · 해군의) 주둔지
If soldiers or officials are stationed in a place, they are sent there to do a job or to work for a period of time.

**flunk**
[flʌŋk]

v. 낙제하다, (성적 불량으로 학교를) 그만두다, (시험에) 떨어지다
If you flunk an exam or a course, you fail to reach the required standard.

**officer**\*\*\*
[ɔ́:fisər]

n. 장교, 관리; 공무원
In the armed forces, an officer is a person in a position of authority.

**salute**\*\*
[səlú:t]

v. 경례하다, 인사하다; n. 경례, 인사
If you salute someone, you greet them or show your respect with a formal sign.

**stern**<sup>복습</sup>
[stə́:rn]

a. 엄한, 단호한
Someone who is stern is very serious and strict.

**rigid**\*
[rídʒid]

a. 엄격한, 융통성 없는; 뻣뻣한, 단단한
Laws, rules, or systems that are rigid cannot be changed or varied, and are therefore considered to be rather severe.

**puff**\*\*
[pʌf]

v. (담배 · 파이프 등을) 뻐끔뻐끔 피우다; (연기를) 내뿜다; n. 훅 불기, 입김
If someone puffs at a cigarette, cigar, or pipe, they smoke it.

**celebrate**\*\*
[séləbrèit]

vi. 축하하다; (의식 · 축전 등을) 거행하다
If you celebrate, you do something enjoyable because of a special occasion.

**be sick of . . .**

idiom ···에 넌더리가 나다
If you say that you are sick of something or sick and tired of it, you are emphasizing that you are very annoyed by it and want it to stop.

**enlarge**\*\*
[inlá:rdʒ]

v. 확대하다, 크게 하다; 커지다
To enlarge a photograph means to develop a bigger print of it.

**chalk**<sup>복습</sup>
[tʃɔ́:k]

n. 분필, 초크
Chalk is small white sticks used for writing or drawing with.

**messy**<sup>복습</sup>
[mési]

a. 지저분한, 엉망인
Something that is messy is dirty or untidy.

**tear**\*\*
[tiə:r]

① v. 찢다, 찢어지다; n. 찢음 ② n. 눈물
If you tear paper, cloth, or another material, or if it tears, you pull it into two pieces or you pull it so that a hole appears in it.

**glance**<sup>복습</sup>
[glæns]

v. 흘긋 보다, 잠깐 보다; n. 흘긋 봄
If you glance at something or someone, you look at them very quickly and then look away again immediately.

**scold**<sup>복습</sup>
[skóuld]

v. 꾸짖다, 잔소리하다
If you scold someone, you speak angrily to them because they have done something wrong.

**ridiculous**<sup>복습</sup>
[ridíkjuləs]

a. 터무니없는; 웃기는, 우스꽝스러운
If you say that something or someone is ridiculous, you mean that they are very foolish.

**step on . . .**    phrasal v. ···을 밟다
If you step on something, you put your foot on it or move your foot in that direction.

**in ... terms**    phrasal v. ···의 점에서 (보면), ···에 관하여
If you talk about something in terms of something or in particular terms, you are specifying which aspect of it you are discussing or from what point of view you are considering it.

**intense**\*\*
[inténs]    a. 심한, 강렬한, 격렬한 (intensely ad. 심하게)
Intense is used to describe something that is very great or extreme in strength or degree.

**assembly**\*\*
[əsémbli]    n. (학교에서의) 조회, 조례; 집회, 회의
In a school, assembly is a gathering of all the teachers and pupils at the beginning of every school day.

**curl up**<sup>복습</sup>    phrasal v. (눕거나 앉아서) 몸을 웅크리다
If you curl up, your body forms a curved or round shape.

**giggle**<sup>복습</sup>
[gígl]    v. 낄낄 웃다; n. 낄낄 웃음
If someone giggles, they laugh in a childlike way, because they are amused, nervous, or embarrassed.

**bride**<sup>복습</sup>
[bráid]    n. 새색시, 신부
A bride is a woman who is getting married or who has just got married.

**improve**\*\*\*
[imprú:v]    v. 개선하다, 진보하다, 나아지다
If something improves or if you improve it, it gets better.

**scary**<sup>복습</sup>
[skéəri]    a. 무서운, 두려운
Something that is scary is rather frightening.

**proportion**\*\*\*
[prəpó:rʃən]    n. 비율, 비; 크기; 균형
The proportion of one amount to another is the relationship between the two amounts in terms of how much there is of each thing.

**bouquet**\*
[bu:kéi]    n. 부케, 꽃다발
A bouquet is a bunch of flowers which is attractively arranged.

**keep in mind**    idiom (···을) 기억해 두다
If you tell someone to keep something in mind, you are reminding or warning them about something important which they should remember.

**thigh**\*\*
[θai]    n. 넓적다리
Your thighs are the top parts of your legs, between your knees and your hips.

**elbow**\*\*
[élbou]    n. 팔꿈치; vt. 팔꿈치로 쿡 찌르다
Your elbow is the part of your arm where the upper and lower halves of the arm are joined.

**waist**\*\*
[weist]    n. 허리
Your waist is the middle part of your body where it narrows slightly above your hips.

**bosom**[**]
[búzəm]

n. (여자의) 가슴
A woman's breasts are sometimes referred to as her bosom or her bosoms.

**glamorous**
[glǽmərəs]

a. 매혹적인, 매력에 찬
If you describe someone or something as glamorous, you mean that they are more attractive, exciting, or interesting than ordinary people or things.

**huffy**
[hʌ́fi]

a. 발끈 성을 내며, 홱 토라져서
Someone who is huffy is obviously annoyed or offended about something.

**cross one's eyes**

phrasal v. 눈을 사시로 만들다
If you cross your eyes, you make your eyes look towards each other.

**make a face**

idiom 얼굴을 찌푸리다, 침울한 표정을 짓다
If you make a face, you twist your face to indicate a certain mental or emotional state.

**thoughtful**[**]
[θɔ́:tfəl]

a. 생각에 잠긴, 생각이 깊은 (thoughtfully ad. 생각에 잠겨)
If you are thoughtful, you are quiet and serious because you are thinking about something.

**ignore**[복습]
[ignɔ́:r]

vt. 무시하다, 모르는 체하다
If you ignore someone or something, you pay no attention to them.

**dumb**[복습]
[dʌm]

a. 멍청한, 바보 같은; 벙어리의, 말을 못 하는
If you call a person dumb, you mean that they are stupid or foolish.

**pretend**[복습]
[priténd]

v. 가장하다, …인 체하다; a. 가짜의
If you pretend that something is the case, you act in a way that is intended to make people believe that it is the case, although in fact it is not.

**eyelash**
[ailæ̀ʃ]

n. 속눈썹
Your eyelashes are the hairs which grow on the edges of your eyelids.

**ruin**[***]
[rú:in]

v. 망치다, 엉망으로 만들다; n. 붕괴, 몰락
To ruin something means to severely harm, damage, or spoil it.

**sincere**[**]
[sinsíə:r]

a. 참된, 진지한, 진심의; 성실한 (sincerely ad. 마음으로부터, 진정으로)
If you say that someone is sincere, you approve of them because they really mean the things they say.

**intentional**[*]
[inténʃənəl]

a. 의도적인, 고의로 한 (intentionally ad. 의도적으로, 일부러)
Something that is intentional is deliberate.

**snide**
[snaid]

a. (은근히) 헐뜯는
A snide comment or remark is one which criticizes someone in an unkind and often indirect way.

**stringy**[복습]
[stríŋi]

a. (머리카락이 길고 가늘며) 지저분한; (씹기 어렵게) 섬유질이 많은
Stringy hair is thin and unattractive.

**blow up**

phrasal v. 화를 내다, 분통을 터뜨리다
If you blow up at someone, you lose your temper and shout at them.

**strike a pose**

idiom (그림 · 사진의) 포즈를 취하다
If you strike a pose, you sit, stand or lie in a position in order to attract attention.

**phony** 복습
[fóuni]

a. (구어) 엉터리의, 가짜의; n. 가짜, 위조품, 사기꾼; vt. 위조하다, 속이다
If you describe something as phony, you disapprove of it because it is false rather than genuine.

**sarcastic**\*\*
[sɑːrkǽstik]

a. 빈정대는, 비꼬는, 풍자적인 (sarcastically ad. 빈정대며, 비꼬아서)
Someone who is sarcastic says or does the opposite of what they really mean in order to mock or insult someone.

**embarrass** 복습
[embǽrəs]

v. 당황스럽게[어색하게] 만들다; 곤란하게 하다 (embarrassed a. 쑥스러운, 어색한)
If something or someone embarrasses you, they make you feel shy or ashamed.

**typical** 복습
[típikəl]

a. 전형적인, 대표적인
If a particular action or feature is typical of someone or something, it shows their usual qualities or characteristics.

**gesture** 복습
[dʒéstʃər]

n. 몸짓; vi. 몸짓을[신호를] 하다
A gesture is a movement that you make with a part of your body, especially your hands, to express emotion or information.

**pigpen**
[pígpèn]

n. 돼지우리
A pigpen is an enclosed place where pigs are kept on a farm.

**storm**\*\*\*
[stɔːrm]

vi. 돌진하다; 격노하다; n. 폭풍우
If you storm into or out of a place, you enter or leave it quickly and noisily, because you are angry.

**slam**\*
[slǽm]

v. (문 따위를) 탕 닫다, 세게 치다; 털썩 내려놓다; n. 쾅 (하는 소리)
If you slam a door or window or if it slams, it shuts noisily and with great force.

**apologize** 복습
[əpálədʒàiz]

v. 사과하다, 사죄하다
When you apologize to someone, you say that you are sorry that you have hurt them or caused trouble for them.

**call it quits**

idiom 비긴 것으로 하다; 그만두기로 하다
If you say that you are going to call it quits, you mean that you have decided to stop doing something or being involved in something.

**exercise**\*\*\*
[éksərsaiz]

n. 연습문제; 활동, 일; 운동, 체조; v. 운동하다
An exercise is a short activity or piece of work that you do, for example in school, which is designed to help you learn a particular skill.

**slide**\*\*
[sláid]

v. (slid–slidden) 미끄러지다, 미끄러지게 하다
If you slide somewhere, you move there smoothly and quietly.

**flutter**\*\*
[flʌ́tər]

v. (깃발 등이) 펄럭이다, (새 등이) 날갯짓하다; n. 펄럭임
If something thin or light flutters, or if you flutter it, it moves up and down or from side to side with a lot of quick, light movements.

**barn** 복습
[bɑːrn]

n. (농가의) 헛간, 광
A barn is a building on a farm in which crops or animal food can be kept.

**reflect**[**]
[riflékt]

v. 반사하다, 반영하다
When something is reflected in a mirror or in water, you can see its image in the mirror or in the water.

**rectangle**[복습]
[réktæŋgl]

n. 직사각형
A rectangle is a four-sided shape whose corners are all ninety degree angles.

**frighten**[**]
[fráitn]

v. 놀라게 하다, 섬뜩하게 하다; 기겁하다 (frightened a. 겁먹은, 무서워하는)
If something or someone frightens you, they cause you to suddenly feel afraid, anxious, or nervous.

**puzzle**[복습]
[pʌzl]

v. 어리둥절하게[이해할 수 없게] 만들다; n. 수수께끼, 어려운 문제
(puzzled a. 어리둥절하는, 얼떨떨한)
If something puzzles you, you do not understand it and feel confused.

**odd**[**]
[ɑd]

a. 이상한, 기묘한
If you describe someone or something as odd, you think that they are strange or unusual.

**ordinary**[***]
[ɔ́:rdənèri]

a. 보통의, 평범한 (ordinarily ad. 보통, 대개)
Ordinary people or things are normal and not special or different in any way.

**principle**[***]
[prínsipl]

n. 원칙, 원리; 주의, 근본 방침 (general principle n. 통칙, 원칙)
A principle is a general belief that you have about the way you should behave, which influences your behavior.

**horrible**[**]
[hɔ́:rəbl]

a. 끔찍한, 소름 끼치게 싫은; 무서운
You can call something horrible when it causes you to feel great shock, fear, and disgust.

**bury**[복습]
[béri]

vt. 묻다; 파묻다, 매장하다
If you bury your head or face in something, you press your head or face against it, often because you are unhappy.

**pillow**[**]
[pílou]

n. 베개
A pillow is a rectangular cushion which you rest your head on when you are in bed.

**stream**[***]
[strí:m]

n. (액체 · 기체의) 줄기, 흐름, 시내, 개울; v. 흐르다, 흘러나오다
A stream of smoke, air, or liquid is a narrow moving mass of it.

**spatter**[복습]
[spǽtər]

v. 튀(기)다, 흩어지다; n. (액체 등이) 튀는 것, 후두두 떨어지는 소리
If a liquid spatters a surface or you spatter a liquid over a surface, drops of the liquid fall on an area of the surface.

**linen**[**]
[línin]

n. 리넨 제품(침대 시트, 식탁보, 베갯잇 등); 리넨, 아마 섬유
Linen is tablecloths, sheets, pillowcases, and similar things made of cloth that are used in the home.

**reassure**[*]
[ri:əʃúə:r]

vt. 안심시키다
If you reassure someone, you say or do things to make them stop worrying about something.

**choke**[**]
[tʃouk]

v. 숨이 막히다; 질식시키다; n. 질식
When you choke or when something chokes you, you cannot breathe properly or get enough air into your lungs.

54

**whimper**[*]
[hwímpər]

vi. 훌쩍훌쩍 울다; (개 등이) 낑낑거리다; n. 흐느낌, 낑낑거림
If someone whimpers, they make quiet unhappy or frightened sounds, as if they are about to start crying.

**doorway**[**]
[dɔ́:rwèi]

n. 문간, 현관, 출입구
A doorway is a space in a wall where a door opens and closes.

**drench**[**]
[drentʃ]

vt. 흠뻑 젖게 하다
To drench something or someone means to make them completely wet.

**faint**[***]
[feint]

a. 희미한, 어렴풋한; vi. 기절하다
A faint sound, color, mark, feeling, or quality has very little strength or intensity.

**bare**[***]
[bέər]

a. 발가벗은, 살을 드러낸; 있는 그대로의
If a part of your body is bare, it is not covered by any clothing.

**miserable**[복습]
[mízərəbl]

a. 비참한, 우울한, 형편없는 (miserably ad. 비참하게, 불쌍하게)
If you describe a place or situation as miserable, you mean that it makes you feel unhappy or depressed.

**streak**[**]
[stri:k]

n. 줄 모양의 것; 기미, 경향; v. 줄을 긋다; 질주하다
A streak is a long stripe or mark on a surface which contrasts with the surface because it is a different color.

**startle**[**]
[stá:rtl]

v. 깜짝 놀라게 하다; 움찔하다; n. 깜짝 놀람
If something sudden and unexpected startles you, it surprises and frightens you slightly.

**unreal**[*]
[ʌnrí:əl]

a. 현실 같지 않은, 너무도 이상한
If you say that a situation is unreal, you mean that it is so strange that you find it difficult to believe it is happening.

**nightmare**[*]
[náitmɛər]

n. 악몽
A nightmare is a very frightening dream.

**gradual**[**]
[grǽdʒuəl]

a. 점진적인, 단계적인 (gradually ad. 점진적으로)
A gradual change or process occurs in small stages over a long period of time, rather than suddenly.

**guardian**[**]
[gá:rdiən]

n. 수호자; 후견인
The guardian of something is someone who defends and protects it.

**flowered**[복습]
[fláuərd]

a. 꽃으로 덮인, 꽃무늬로 장식한
Flowered paper or cloth has a pattern of flowers on it.

**sticky**[*]
[stíki]

a. 끈적거리는, 끈적끈적한, 달라붙는
A sticky substance is soft, or thick and liquid, and can stick to other things.

**stain**[**]
[stéin]

n. 얼룩, 오점; v. 더러워지다, 얼룩지게 하다
A stain is a mark on something that is difficult to remove.

**spread**[***]
[spréd]

v. 펴다, 펼치다; 뿌리다; n. 퍼짐, 폭, 넓이
If something such as a liquid, gas, or smoke spreads or is spread, it moves outwards in all directions so that it covers a larger area.

**terrify**\*\*
[térəfài]

vt. 무섭게[겁나게] 하다, 놀래다 (terrified a. 무서워하는, 겁먹은)
If something terrifies you, it makes you feel extremely frightened.

**reflection**\*\*
[riflékʃən]

n. 반사, 반영; (거울 · 물 등에 비친) 영상
A reflection is an image that you can see in a mirror or in glass or water.

## chapter five

1. What did Meg make for Molly and Will?
   A. Paintings
   B. Dinner
   C. Painted mugs
   D. Easter eggs

2. At dinner, why was Meg angry at her parents?
   A. Her parents didn't like the photos she took of Will.
   B. Her parents wouldn't let her give Molly a present.
   C. Her parents talked about Molly as if she weren't a person.
   D. Her parents didn't visit Molly at the hospital very often.

3. Why did Meg feel like crying after Will told her about the picture?
   A. Will said that he didn't like her pictures.
   B. Will's favorite picture was different than Meg's favorite.
   C. Will had the same feelings as Meg about her photo.
   D. Will only said nice things about her photos because he didn't want to be rude.

4. What would Will do for Meg?
   A. He would give her his camera for free.
   B. He would let Meg use his camera.
   C. He would let Meg take more pictures of him.
   D. He would buy Meg a new camera.

5. How would Meg help Will?

   A. She would show him how to use a camera.

   B. She would help him fix his truck.

   C. She would teach him how to use the darkroom.

   D. She would help him fix the big house.

6. Will forgot to ask Ben and Maria _____.

   A. if they were married

   B. if they would fix his house

   C. about their jobs

   D. about how much money they would pay in rent

7. What did Meg say she'd do for Molly at the end of the chapter?

   A. Teach her how to take photos

   B. Send in her summer camp application

   C. Teach her how to draw

   D. Take a picture of her

## Check Your Reading Speed

1분에 몇 단어를 읽는지 리딩 속도를 측정해보세요.

$$\frac{3{,}307 \text{ words}}{\text{reading time ( ) sec}} \times 60 = (\quad) \text{ WPM}$$

## Build Your Vocabulary

**hard-boiled**
[há:rd-bóild]

a. (달걀이) 완숙된; (사람이) 감정을 잘 드러내지 않는
A hard-boiled egg has been boiled in its shell until the whole of the inside is solid.

**dye**\*\*
[dai]

v. 물들이다, 염색하다
If you dye something such as hair or cloth, you change its color by soaking it in a special liquid.

**vinegar**\*\*
[vínigər]

n. 식초
Vinegar is a sharp-tasting liquid, usually made from sour wine or malt, which is used to make things such as salad dressing.

**rotten**\*\*
[rátn]

a. 썩은, 부패한; 형편없는, 끔찍한
If food, wood, or another substance is rotten, it has decayed and can no longer be used.

**fragile**\*
[frǽdʒəl]

a. 부서지기[손상되기] 쉬운
Something that is fragile is easily broken or damaged.

**depress**\*\*
[diprés]

vt. 우울하게 하다, 낙담시키다 (depressingly ad. 울적하게)
If someone or something depresses you, they make you feel sad and disappointed.

**pale**\*\*ᵇᵏ
[péil]

a. (색깔이) 엷은; 창백한, 핼쑥한; v. 창백해지다
If something is pale, it is very light in color or almost white.

**miniature**\*\*
[míniətʃər]

a. 아주 작은, 소형의; n. 축소 모형, 미니어처
Miniature is used to describe something which is very small, especially a smaller version of something which is normally much bigger.

**eggshell**
[égʃèl]

n. 달걀 껍질
An eggshell is the hard covering on the outside of an egg.

**delicate**\*\*
[délikit]

a. 섬세한, 고운; 예민한, 민감한
If something is delicate, it is easy to harm, damage, or break, and needs to be handled or treated carefully.

**intricate**\*
[íntrikit]

a. 뒤얽힌, 복잡한
You use intricate to describe something that has many small parts or details.

**varnish**\*
[vá:rniʃ]

vt. 니스를 칠하다, 광택을 내다; n. 니스, 광택제
If you varnish something, you paint it with an oily liquid which is painted onto wood or other material to give it a hard, clear, shiny surface.

60

**permanent**<sup>**</sup>
[pə́:rmənənt]

a. 변하지 않는, 영구적인, 영속하는
Something that is permanent lasts forever.

**cotton**<sup>***</sup>
[kátn]

n. 솜, 목화
Cotton is a type of cloth made from soft fibers from a particular plant.

**transfusion**
[trænsfjúːʒən]

n. [의학] 수혈
A transfusion is a process in which blood is injected into the body of a person who is badly injured or ill.

**bleed**<sup>복습</sup>
[bliːd]

v. 피를 흘리다, 피가 나다
When you bleed, you lose blood from your body as a result of injury or illness.

**specialist**<sup>*</sup>
[spéʃəlist]

n. 전문의; 전문가, 전공자
A specialist is a doctor who has special training in and knowledge of a particular area of medicine.

**advance**<sup>***</sup>
[ædvǽ(á:)ns]

v. 진보하다, 전진하다, 나아가다; 승진시키다 (advanced a. 진보한, 발달된)
To advance means to make progress, especially in your knowledge of something.

**figure out**<sup>복습</sup>

phrasal v. ···을 생각해내다, 발견하다
If you figure out a solution to a problem or the reason for something, you succeed in solving it or understanding it.

**tropical**<sup>*</sup>
[trɔ́pikəl]

a. 열대의, 열대지방의
Tropical means belonging to or typical of the tropics.

**disease**<sup>***</sup>
[dizíːz]

n. 병, 질환
A disease is an illness which affects people, animals, or plants, for example one which is caused by bacteria or infection.

**fool around**

idiom 빈둥거리며 세월을 보내다, 펀둥펀둥 지내다
If you fool around, you behave in a silly, dangerous, or irresponsible way.

**inject**<sup>**</sup>
[indʒékt]

vt. 주사하다, 주입하다, 삽입하다
To inject someone with a substance such as a medicine means to put it into their body using a device with a needle called a syringe.

**spine**<sup>*</sup>
[spáin]

n. 척추, 등뼈
Your spine is the row of bones down your back.

**creep**<sup>**</sup>
[kriːp]

n. (구어) 섬뜩해지는 느낌, 전율; vi. 살금살금 움직이다, 기다
If someone or something gives you the creeps, they make you feel very nervous or frightened.

**experiment**<sup>***</sup>
[ekspérimənt]

vi. 실험하다; n. 실험
If you experiment with something or experiment on it, you do a scientific test on it in order to discover what happens to it in particular conditions.

**clot**
[klɔt]

v. (혈액이나 크림이) 엉기다, 응고되다; n. 혈전
When blood clots, it becomes thick and forms a lump.

**clinical*** [klínikəl]

a. 임상의
Clinical means involving or relating to the direct medical treatment or testing of patients.

**specimen**** [spésəmən]

n. (의학 검사용) 시료; 표본; 견본, 샘플
A specimen is a single plant or animal which is an example of a particular species or type and is examined by scientists.

**reaction*** [riǽkʃən]

n. 반응. 반작용
If you have a reaction to a substance such as a drug, or to something you have touched, you are affected unpleasantly or made ill by it.

**side effect** [sáid ifékt]

n. (약물 등의) 부작용
The side effects of a drug are the effects, usually bad ones, that the drug has on you in addition to its function of curing illness or pain

**contraindication** [kàntrəindikéiʃən]

n. (특정 약물 · 치료의) 사용 금지 사유
Contraindications are specific medical reasons for not using a particular treatment for a medical condition in the usual way.

**pronounce**** [prənáuns]

v. 발음하다; 선언하다
To pronounce a word means to say it using particular sounds.

**application**** [ǽplikéiʃən]

n. 신청(서), 지원(서); 적용
An application for something such as a job or membership of an organization is a formal written request for it.

**fancy**** [fǽnsi]

a. (필요 이상으로) 복잡한; 장식이 많은, 색깔이 화려한;
v. 원하다, …하고 싶다; 생각[상상]하다
If you describe something as fancy, you mean that it is special, unusual, or elaborate, for example because it has a lot of decoration.

**pill**** [píl]

n. 알약. 환약
Pills are small solid round masses of medicine or vitamins that you swallow without chewing.

**spice**복습 [spais]

n. 향신료, 양념. 양념류; vt. …에 양념을 치다
A spice is a part of a plant, or a powder made from that part, which you put in food to give it flavor.

**encyclopedia** [ensàikloupí:diə]

n. 백과사전, 전문사전
An encyclopedia is a book or set of books in which facts about many different subjects or about one particular subject are arranged for reference, usually in alphabetical order.

**blossom**복습 [blásəm]

n. (특히 과수의) 꽃, 개화; vi. (나무 등이) 꽃 피다. 개화하다; 발전하다
Blossom is the flowers that appear on a tree before the fruit.

**intertwine** [intərtwáin]

v. 뒤얽다, 엮(이)다
If two or more things are intertwined or intertwine, they are closely connected with each other in many ways.

**complicated** <sup>복습</sup>
[kámplikèitid]

a. 복잡한; 풀기[이해하기] 어려운
If you say that something is complicated, you mean it has so many parts or aspects that it is difficult to understand or deal with.

**envelope** \*\*\*
[énvəlòup]

n. 봉투
An envelope is the rectangular paper cover in which you send a letter to someone through the post.

**concentrate** \*\*
[kánsəntrèit]

v. 집중하다, 집중시키다, 전념하다
If you concentrate on something, you give all your attention to it.

**catch up**

phrasal v. 따라잡다, 따라붙다; 뒤지지 않다
To catch up with someone means to reach the same standard, stage, or level that they have reached.

**freeze** \*\*
[frí:z]

v. (froze–frozen) 얼다, 얼어붙다; (기온이) 영하이다; n. 결빙
When it freezes outside, the temperature falls below freezing point.

**driveway** <sup>복습</sup>
[dráivwèi]

n. (도로에서 집ᆞ차고까지의) 진입로
A driveway is a piece of hard ground that leads from the road to the front of a house or other building.

**occasional** \*\*
[əkéiʒənəl]

a. 가끔의 (occasionally ad. 가끔)
Occasional means happening sometimes, but not regularly or often.

**muddy** \*\*
[mʌdi]

vt. 진흙으로 더럽히다, 혼탁하게 하다; a. 진흙투성이의; 흙탕물의, 탁한
If you muddy something, you cause it to be muddy.

**saw** \*\*
[sɔ:]

n. 톱; v. 톱으로 켜다, 톱질하다
A saw is a tool for cutting wood, which has a blade with sharp teeth along one edge.

**figure** <sup>복습</sup>
[fígjər]

n. 모습, 형태; 계산, 숫자; v. (…일 거라고) 생각[판단]하다; 계산하다
You refer to someone that you can see as a figure when you cannot see them clearly or when you are describing them.

**move in**

idiom 이사를 들다
When you move in somewhere, you begin to live there as your home.

**nephew** <sup>복습</sup>
[néfju:]

n. 조카
Someone's nephew is the son of their sister or brother.

**permission** \*\*
[pə:rmíʃən]

n. 허가, 허락, 승인
If someone who has authority over you gives you permission to do something, they say that they will allow you to do it.

**inn** <sup>복습</sup>
[ín]

n. (작은) 호텔, 여관
An inn is a small hotel or pub, usually an old one.

**distract** \*
[distrǽkt]

v. (마음ᆞ주의를) 흐트러뜨리다, 딴 데로 돌리다 (distracted a. (정신이) 산만해진)
If you are distracted, you are not concentrating on something because you are worried or are thinking about something else.

**spaceship** \*\*
[spéisʃip]

n. 우주선
A spaceship is a spacecraft that carries people through space.

**hood**<sup>복습</sup>
[hud]

n. 자동차 보닛, 덮개; 두건
The hood of a car is the metal cover over the engine at the front.

**approach**\*\*\*
[əpróutʃ]

v. 접근하다, 다가오다 n. 접근, 가까움
When you approach something, you get closer to it.

**straighten**<sup>복습</sup>
[stréitn]

v. (자세를) 바로 하다; 똑바르게 되다[하다]
If you are standing in a relaxed or slightly bent position and then you straighten, you make your back or body straight and upright.

**drop in**<sup>복습</sup>

idiom (구어) 잠깐 들르다
If you drop in on someone, you visit them informally, usually without having arranged it.

**kettle**<sup>복습</sup>
[kétl]

n. 주전자, 솥
A kettle is a container with a lid, handle and a spout, used for boiling water.

**fate**<sup>복습</sup>
[feit]

n. 운명, 숙명; 죽음, 최후
Fate is a power that some people believe controls and decides everything that happens, in a way that cannot be prevented or changed.

**hint**\*\*
[hínt]

v. 넌지시 말하다; 암시하다; n. 힌트, 암시
If you hint at something, you suggest it in an indirect way.

**perpetual**\*\*
[pərpétʃuəl]

a. 끊임없는, 영구의, 영원한
A perpetual feeling, state, or quality is one that never ends or changes.

**fistful**
[fístfùl]

n. 한 움큼, 한 줌
A fistful of things is the number of them that you can hold in your fist.

**overdue**
[òuvərdjúː]

a. (지불 · 반납 등의) 기한이 지난
An overdue library book has not been returned to the library, even though the date on which it should have been returned has passed.

**slip**<sup>복습</sup>
[slip]

① n. (작은 종이) 조각 ② v. 미끄러지다, 미끄러지게 하다; n. 미끄럼, 실수
A slip of paper is a small piece of paper.

**historical**\*\*
[histɔ́ːrikəl]

a. 역사학의; 역사적, 역사상의
Historical information, research, and discussion is related to the study of history.

**preservation**\*
[prèzərvéiʃən]

n. 유지, 보전; 보존, 보호
Preservation is the act of keeping something in its original state or in good condition.

**exercise**<sup>복습</sup>
[éksərsaiz]

n. 연습문제; 활동, 일; 운동, 체조; v. 운동하다
If you describe an activity as an exercise in a particular quality or result, you mean that it has that quality or result, especially when it was not intended to have it.

**irony**<sup>복습</sup>
[áiərəni]

n. 반어법; 빈정댐, 풍자
Irony is a subtle form of humor which involves saying things that you do not mean.

64

**preserve**\*\*\*
[prizə́:rv]

v. 보존하다, 유지하다
If you preserve something, you take action to save it or protect it from damage or decay.

**monument**\*\*
[mɑ́(ɔ́)njumənt]

n. 기념물, 기념비
A monument is something such as a castle or bridge which was built a very long time ago and is regarded as an important part of a country's history.

**have a crush on . . .**

idiom …에게 홀딱 반하다
If you have a crush on someone, you are in love with them but do not have a relationship with them.

**sigh**<sup>복습</sup>
[sái]

v. 한숨 쉬다; n. 한숨, 탄식
When you sigh, you let out a deep breath, as a way of expressing feelings such as disappointment, tiredness, or pleasure.

**wipe**<sup>복습</sup>
[waip]

vt. 닦다, 닦아 내다; n. 닦음, 닦아 냄
If you wipe something, you rub its surface to remove dirt or liquid from it.

**rag**<sup>복습</sup>
[ræg]

n. 해진 천, 누더기
Rags are old torn clothes.

**radiator**\*
[réidièitə:r]

n. (차량ㆍ항공기의) 냉각 장치, 라디에이터
The radiator in a car is the part of the engine which is filled with water in order to cool the engine.

**flat**<sup>복습</sup>
[flǽt]

a. (타이어 등이) 바람이 빠진, 구멍 난; 평평한, 균일한, 고른
A flat tire, ball, or balloon does not have enough air in it.

**disaster**\*\*
[dizǽ(á:)stər]

n. 참사, 재난, 재해
If you refer to something as a disaster, you are emphasizing that you think it is extremely bad or unacceptable.

**enemy**<sup>복습</sup>
[énəmi]

n. 적, 경쟁 상대
If someone is your enemy, they hate you or want to harm you.

**confront**\*\*
[kənfrʌ́nt]

vt. 직면하다, 마주치다, 맞서다
If you confront a difficult situation or issue, you accept the fact that it exists and try to deal with it.

**blush**\*\*
[blʌ́ʃ]

v. 얼굴을 붉히다, (얼굴이) 빨개지다; n. 얼굴을 붉힘, 홍조
When you blush, your face becomes redder than usual because you are ashamed or embarrassed.

**thoughtful**<sup>복습</sup>
[θɔ́:tfəl]

a. 생각에 잠긴, 생각이 깊은 (thoughtfully ad. 생각에 잠겨)
If you are thoughtful, you are quiet and serious because you are thinking about something.

**composition**<sup>복습</sup>
[kàmpəzíʃən]

n. (그림ㆍ사진의) 구도, 구성
When you talk about the composition of something, you are referring to the way in which its various parts are put together and arranged.

**combination**<sup>복습</sup>
[kàmbənéiʃən]

n. 조합, 결합, 화합
A combination of things is a mixture of them.

**shutter**<sup>복습</sup>
[ʃʌ́tə:r]

n. (카메라의) 셔터; 덧문, 셔터
The shutter in a camera is the part which opens to allow light through the lens when a photograph is taken.

**aperture**<sup>*</sup>
[ǽpərtʃùər]

n. (카메라의) 조리개; 구멍
In photography, the aperture of a camera is the size of the hole through which light passes to reach the film.

**blur**<sup>*</sup>
[blə:r]

n. 흐릿한 형체; v. 흐릿해지다, 흐릿하게 만들다
A blur is a shape or area which you cannot see clearly because it has no distinct outline or because it is moving very fast.

**ephemeral**
[ifémərəl]

a. 수명이 짧은, 단명하는
If you describe something as ephemeral, you mean that it lasts only for a very short time.

**sacrifice**<sup>***</sup>
[sǽkrifais]

v. 희생하다, 희생시키다; n. 희생
If you sacrifice something that is valuable or important, you give it up, usually to obtain something else for yourself or for other people.

**clarity**<sup>*</sup>
[klǽrəti]

n. 선명함, 명쾌함, 깨끗하고 맑음
Clarity is the quality of being clear in outline or sound.

**well up**

phrasal v. 솟아나다, 넘쳐 나오다
If liquids, for example tears, well up, they come to the surface and form a pool.

**bear**<sup>***</sup>
[bɛər]

① v. 참다, 견디다; (의무 · 책임을) 지다 ② n. 곰
If you bear an unpleasant experience, you accept it because you are unable to do anything about it.

**gulp**<sup>*</sup>
[gʌlp]

v. 꿀꺽꿀꺽 마시다; (긴장, 흥분으로) 꿀꺽 삼키다; n. 꿀꺽꿀꺽 마심
If you gulp something, you eat or drink it very quickly by swallowing large quantities of it at once.

**diminish**<sup>**</sup>
[dimíniʃ]

v. 줄어들다, 약해지다
When something diminishes, or when something diminishes it, it becomes reduced in size, importance, or intensity.

**enthusiasm**<sup>**</sup>
[inθú:ziæzm]

n. 열정, 열의, 열광
Enthusiasm is great eagerness to be involved in a particular activity which you like and enjoy or which you think is important.

**gruff**
[grʌf]

a. (목소리가) 걸걸한, 거친 (gruffly ad. 걸걸하게, 거칠게)
A gruff voice sounds low and rough.

**attic**<sup>복습</sup>
[ǽtik]

n. 다락(방)
An attic is a room at the top of a house just below the roof.

**filter**<sup>복습</sup>
[fíltər]

n. [사진 · 광학] 필터, 여광기; 여과 장치; v. 여과하다, 거르다
A filter is a device through which sound or light is passed and which blocks or reduces particular sound or light frequencies.

**undertake**<sup>**</sup>
[ʌ̀ndərtéik]

v. (undertook−undertaken) (책임을 맡아서) 착수하다, 진행하다; 약속하다, 동의하다
When you undertake a task or job, you start doing it and accept responsibility for it.

**eyesight**\*
[áisàit]

n. 시력
Your eyesight is your ability to see.

**wail**\*\*
[weil]

v. 울부짖다, 통곡하다, 흐느끼다; n. 울부짖음, 통곡
If someone wails, they make long, loud, high-pitched cries which express sorrow or pain.

**commodity**\*
[kəmá(ɔ́)diti]

n. (유용한) 것; 상품, 물품
A commodity is a valuable quality.

**instance**\*\*\*
[ínstəns]

n. 사례, 경우
An instance is a particular example or occurrence of something.

**underrate**\*
[ʌ̀ndərréit]

vt. 과소평가하다, 깔보다
If you underrate someone or something, you do not recognize how clever, important, or significant they are.

**grave**\*\*
[greiv]

① a. 엄숙한, 중대한, 근엄한, 의젓한, 위엄 있는 (gravely ad. 중대하게) ② n. 무덤
A grave event or situation is very serious, important, and worrying.

**examine**<sup>복습</sup>
[igzǽmin]

v. 조사하다, 검토하다; 검사하다, 진찰하다
If you examine something, you look at it carefully.

**recognition**\*\*
[rèkəgníʃən]

n. 알아봄, 인식; 인정, 승인
Recognition is the act of recognizing someone or identifying something when you see it.

**solemn**\*\*
[sá(ɔ́)ləm]

a. 엄숙한, 근엄한 (solemnly ad. 진지하게)
Someone or something that is solemn is very serious rather than cheerful or humorous.

**shallow**\*\*
[ʃǽlou]

a. 얕은, 얄팍한; n. 얕은 곳, 여울
A shallow container, hole, or area of water measures only a short distance from the top to the bottom.

**pine**<sup>복습</sup>
[páin]

n. 소나무 (재목)
A pine tree or a pine is a tall tree which has very thin, sharp leaves and a fresh smell. Pine trees have leaves all year round.

**muted**
[mjú:tid]

a. (색깔 · 빛 등이) 밝지 않은, 눈부시지 않은; (소리가) 조용한, 낮은
Muted colors are soft and gentle, not bright and strong.

**oriental**<sup>복습</sup>
[ɔ́:riéntl]

a. 동양의, 동쪽의
Oriental means coming from or associated with eastern Asia, especially China and Japan.

**rug**<sup>복습</sup>
[rʌg]

n. (방바닥 · 마루에 까는) 깔개, 융단
A rug is a piece of thick material that you put on a floor.

**shade**<sup>복습</sup>
[ʃeid]

n. 색조, 색깔; 그늘, 그림자; (얼굴의 어두운) 기색; vt. 그늘지게 하다, 어둡게 하다
A shade of a particular color is one of its different forms. For example, emerald green and olive green are shades of green.

**reflect**<sup>복습</sup>
[riflékt]

v. 반영하다, 반사하다
If something reflects an attitude or situation, it shows that the attitude or situation exists or it shows what it is like.

**well-tended**
[wél-téndid]

a. 잘 손질된
well (ad. 잘, 훌륭하게) + tend (v. 돌보다, 손질하다) + ed (과거분사형 어미)

**oval**[*]
[óuvəl]

a. 타원형의, 달걀 모양의; n. 타원체
Oval things have a shape that is like a circle but is wider in one direction than the other.

**outline**[**]
[áutlàin]

vt. 윤곽을 보여주다; n. 윤곽
You say that an object is outlined when you can see its general shape because there is light behind it.

**polish**[복습]
[pɑ́liʃ]

v. (윤이 나도록) 닦다, 광을 내다; n. 광택제; 광택, 윤
(polished a. (잘 닦아서) 윤[광]이 나는)
If you polish something, you put polish on it or rub it with a cloth to make it shine.

**brighten**[**]
[bráitn]

v. 빛나게 하다, 밝게 하다; 명랑하게 하다, 활기를 주다
When a light brightens a place or when a place brightens, it becomes brighter or lighter.

**rectangle**[복습]
[réktæ̀ŋgl]

n. 직사각형
A rectangle is a four-sided shape whose corners are all ninety degree angles.

**scoot**
[sku:t]

v. 내닫다, 뛰어나가다
If you scoot somewhere, you go there very quickly.

**rent**[복습]
[rént]

v. 세 놓다, 임대하다; 세내다, 임차하다
If you rent something to someone, you let them have it and use it in exchange for a sum of money which they pay you regularly.

**thesis**[*]
[θí:sis]

n. 학위 논문, 졸업 논문; 논제, 제목
A thesis is a long piece of writing based on your own ideas and research that you do as part of a university degree.

**typewriter**[복습]
[táipràitər]

n. 타자기
A typewriter is a machine with keys which are pressed in order to print letters, numbers, or other characters onto paper.

**wiring**
[wáiəriŋ]

n. 배선 (장치)
The wiring in a building or machine is the system of wires that supply electricity to the different parts of it.

**plumbing**
[plʌ́miŋ]

n. (건물의) 배관, 수도 시설
Plumbing is the work of connecting and repairing things such as water and drainage pipes, baths, and toilets.

**thaw**[*]
[θɔ:]

v. 녹다, 날씨가 풀리다
When ice, snow, or something else that is frozen thaws, it melts.

**sheepish**
[ʃí:piʃ]

a. 매우 수줍어하는; 양 같은
If you look sheepish, you look slightly embarrassed because you feel foolish or you have done something silly.

**confess**[**]
[kənfés]

v. 고백[자백]하다, 인정하다
If someone confesses to doing something wrong, they admit that they did it.

68

**burst out**<sup>복습</sup>

phrasal v. 갑자기 …하기 시작하다; 버럭 소리를 지르다
If someone bursts out laughing, crying, or making another noise, they suddenly start making that noise.

**occur**\*\*\*
[əkə́ːr]

vi. 생각이 떠오르다; 일어나다, 생기다
If a thought or idea occurs to you, you suddenly think of it or realize it.

**fond**<sup>복습</sup>
[fánd]

a. 좋아하는; 정다운, 다정한
If you are fond of someone, you feel affection for them.

**adore**\*\*
[ədɔ́ːr]

vt. 아주 좋아하다, 숭배하다
If you adore someone, you feel great love and admiration for them.

**environmental**\*
[invàiərənméntl]

a. 환경의 (environmentally ad. 환경적으로)
Environmental means relating to or caused by the surroundings in which someone lives or something exists.

**absurd**\*\*
[æbsə́ːrd]

a. 우스꽝스러운, 터무니없는
If you say that something is absurd, you are criticizing it because you think that it is ridiculous or that it does not make sense.

**thrill**\*\*
[θríl]

v. 열광시키다, 황홀하게 만들다; n. 흥분, 설렘
(thrilled a. 아주 흥분한, 신이 난)
If something thrills you, or if you thrill at it, it gives you a feeling of great pleasure and excitement.

**drag**\*\*\*
[drǽg]

n. 지겨운[짜증나는] 것; 견인, 끌기; v. 끌(리)다, 끌고 가다
If you say that something is a drag, you mean that it is unpleasant or very dull.

**what the heck**<sup>복습</sup>

idiom 아무렴 어때
You say 'what the heck' to indicate that you do not care about a bad aspect of an action or situation.

**hang up**

phrasal v. 전화를 끊다, 수화기를 놓다
If you hang up or you hang up the phone, you end a phone call.

## chapter six

1. What wasn't true at the beginning of the chapter?
   A. Will was learning to use the darkroom.
   B. Molly was at home.
   C. Dad was very stern with Molly.
   D. Ben and Maria moved into the big house.

2. What was a side effect of Molly's medicine?
   A. The skin on her nose was dry.
   B. Her skin was pale.
   C. She lost weight.
   D. Her hair started to fall out.

3. What present made Molly really happy?
   A. Pussy willows
   B. A chocolate bar
   C. A book
   D. A stack of magazines

4. Meg thought that Will _____.
   A. was a slow learner
   B. had a good memory
   C. wasn't good at developing photographs
   D. took the best pictures she'd ever seen

5. Why did Molly like talking to Maria?

   A. Maria liked to talk about babies.

   B. Maria showed Molly different kinds of flowers.

   C. Maria talked about Molly's illness.

   D. Maria showed Molly the improvements to the house.

6. In what way did Meg want to be like Molly?

   A. She wanted to get attention from boys.

   B. She wanted to do as well as Molly in school.

   C. She wanted to say the right things to people.

   D. She wanted to be as athletic as Molly.

7. What did Meg promise Will?

   A. To see his photograph collection at the end of the summer

   B. To come back and see the fringed gentian

   C. To give him copies of her photographs

   D. To make a book of the different flowers from the field

*Check Your Reading Speed*

1분에 몇 단어를 읽는지 리딩 속도를 측정해보세요.

$$\frac{3,796 \text{ words}}{\text{reading time (} \quad \text{) sec}} \times 60 = (\quad) \text{ WPM}$$

*Build Your Vocabulary*

**terrific**<sup>복습</sup>
[tərífik]

a. 아주 좋은, 멋진, 훌륭한
If you describe something or someone as terrific, you are very pleased with them or very impressed by them.

**thorough**<sup>복습</sup>
[θə́:rou]

a. 철저한, 완전한; 절대적인 (thoroughly ad. 완전히, 철저히)
Thorough is used to emphasize the great degree or extent of something.

**unbearable**<sup>*</sup>
[ʌnbéərəbəl]

a. 견딜 수 없는, 참을 수 없는
If you describe something as unbearable, you mean that it is so unpleasant, painful, or upsetting that you feel unable to accept it or deal with it.

**blame**<sup>***</sup>
[bleim]

vt. …의 탓으로 돌리다; 비난하다, 나무라다
If you blame a person or thing for something bad, you believe or say that they are responsible for it or that they caused it

**awful**<sup>**</sup>
[ɔ́:fəl]

a. 엄청 대단한, 아주 심한; 끔찍한, 지독한 (awfully ad. 정말, 몹시)
You can use awful with adjectives that describe a quality in order to emphasize that particular quality.

**lying**<sup>복습</sup>
[láiiŋ]

v. LIE(눕다, 누워있다)의 현재분사(ing) 형태; a. 드러누워 있는
lie는 현재분사가 되면서 -ie가 -y로 변한다는 것과, '눕다, 누워있다'와 '거짓말하다'라는 두 가지 의미의 스펠링이 동일하다는 점에 유의하자.

**apparently**<sup>복습</sup>
[əpǽrəntli]

ad. 보기에, 외관상으로; 분명히, 명백히
You use apparently to refer to something that seems to be true, although you are not sure whether it is or not.

**get used to . . .**<sup>복습</sup>

idiom …에 익숙해지다
If you get used to something or someone, you become familiar with it or get to know them, so that you no longer feel that the thing or person is unusual or surprising.

**specialist**<sup>복습</sup>
[spéʃəlist]

n. 전문의; 전문가, 전공자
A specialist is a doctor who has special training in and knowledge of a particular area of medicine.

**supposedly**
[səpóuzidli]

ad. 추정상, 아마도, 추측건대
You use supposedly to show that you do not believe that something you have been told is true.

72

**discharge**[dist∫á:rdʒ]

v. (어떤 장소나 직무에서) 떠나는 것을 허락하다, 석방하다; 배출하다, 방출하다
When someone is discharged from hospital, prison, or one of the armed services, they are officially allowed to leave, or told that they must leave.

**be at one's beck and call**

idiom 늘 …이 시키는 대로 하다
If one person is at another's beck and call, they have to be constantly available and ready to do whatever is asked, and this often seems unfair or undesirable.

**put up with . . .**

phrasal v. …을 참고 견디다, 참다
If you put up with something, you tolerate or accept it, even though you find it unpleasant or unsatisfactory.

**amaze**<sup>복습</sup>[əméiz]

vt. 깜짝 놀라게 하다 (amazing a. 놀랄 만한, 굉장한)
If something amazes you, it surprises you very much.

**tuna fish**[tjú:nə fi∫]

n. 참치, 다랑어
Tuna fish or tuna are large fish that live in warm seas and are caught for food.

**couch**<sup>복습</sup>[kaut∫]

n. (기댈 수 있는 등받이와 팔걸이가 있는) 소파, 긴 의자
A couch is a long, comfortable seat for two or three people.

**lettuce**<sup>복습</sup>

n. [식물] 상추
A lettuce is a plant with large green leaves that is the basic ingredient of many salads.

**scurry**<sup>*</sup>[skə́:ri]

vi. 종종걸음으로 달리다, 급히 가다
When people or small animals scurry somewhere, they move there quickly and hurriedly, especially because they are frightened.

**madam**<sup>**</sup>[mǽdəm]

n. 아씨, 부인, 마님
People sometimes say Madam as a very formal and polite way of addressing a woman whose name they do not know or a woman of superior rank.

**bite**<sup>**</sup>[bait]

n. 한 입, 물기; 물린 상처; v. 물다, 물어뜯다
A bite of something, especially food, is the action of biting it.

**drift**<sup>**</sup>[drift]

v. (서서히) 이동하다; (물·공기에) 떠가다, 부유하다; n. 취지, 경향, 추세; 표류
To drift somewhere means to move there slowly or gradually.

**bug**<sup>복습</sup>[bʌg]

v. (구어) 귀찮게 굴다; n. 곤충; 결함
If someone or something bugs you, they worry or annoy you.

**storm**<sup>복습</sup>[stɔ:rm]

vi. 돌진하다; 격노하다; n. 폭풍우
If you storm into or out of a place, you enter or leave it quickly and noisily, because you are angry.

**slam**<sup>복습</sup>[slǽm]

v. (문 따위를) 탕 닫다, 세게 치다; 털썩 내려놓다; n. 쾅 (하는 소리)
If you slam a door or window or if it slams, it shuts noisily and with great force.

**tantrum**[tǽntrəm]

n. 성질을 부림, 짜증을 냄
If a child has a tantrum, they lose their temper in a noisy and uncontrolled way.

**nap**[**] 
[næp]

n. 낮잠, 선잠 (take a nap idiom 잠깐 낮잠을 자다)
If you take a nap, you have a short sleep, usually during the day.

**grouchy**[복습]
[gráutʃi]

a. 불평이 많은, 잘 투덜거리는
If someone is grouchy, they are very bad-tempered and complain a lot.

**irritable**[*]
[írətəbəl]

a. 짜증을 (잘) 내는, 화가 난
If you are irritable, you are easily annoyed.

**stern**[복습]
[stə́:rn]

a. 엄한, 단호한
Stern words or actions are very severe.

**rude**[복습]
[ru:d]

a. 무례한, 버릇없는 (rudeness n. 무례함, 오만함)
When people are rude, they act in an impolite way towards other people or say impolite things about them.

**shape up**

idiom 태도를 개선하다
If you tell someone to shape up, you are telling them to start behaving in a sensible and responsible way.

**chuckle**[**]
[tʃʌ́kl]

vi. 킬킬 웃다; n. 킬킬 웃음
When you chuckle, you laugh quietly.

**tease**[**]
[ti:z]

v. 놀리다, 괴롭히다; 졸라대다; n. 골리기
To tease someone means to laugh at them or make jokes about them in order to embarrass, annoy, or upset them.

**lay down the law**

idiom 강압적으로 말하다
If you say that someone lays down the law, you are critical of them because they give other people orders and they think that they are always right.

**confuse**[**]
[kənfjú:z]

v. 어리둥절하게 하다, 혼동하다 (confused a. 당황한, 어리둥절한)
To confuse someone means to make it difficult for them to know exactly what is happening or what to do.

**tense**[*]
[tens]

a. 긴장한, 긴박한; 팽팽한; v. 긴장시키다
If you are tense, you are anxious and nervous and cannot relax.

**study**[복습]
[stʌ́di]

n. 서재, 집무실; v. 배우다, 공부하다
A study is a room in a house which is used for reading, writing, and studying.

**obnoxious**
[əbnákʃəs]

a. 아주 불쾌한, 몹시 기분 나쁜
If you describe someone as obnoxious, you think that they are very unpleasant.

**dreadful**[**]
[drédfəl]

a. 끔찍한, 지독한, 무시무시한
If you say that something is dreadful, you mean that it is very bad or unpleasant, or very poor in quality.

**transfusion**[복습]
[trænsfjú:ʒən]

n. [의학] 수혈
A transfusion is a process in which blood is injected into the body of a person who is badly injured or ill.

74

**cell**\*\*\*
[sél]

n. 세포; 작은 방, 독방 (blood cell n. 혈구)
A cell is the smallest part of an animal or plant that is able to function independently. Every animal or plant is made up of millions of cells.

**fall out**

phrasal v. (머리 · 이빨이) 빠지다, 떨어져 나가다
If something such as a person's hair or a tooth falls out, it comes out.

**pill**<sup>복습</sup>
[píl]

n. 알약, 환약
Pills are small solid round masses of medicine or vitamins that you swallow without chewing.

**side effect**<sup>복습</sup>
[sáid ifékt]

n. (약물 등의) 부작용
The side effects of a drug are the effects, usually bad ones, that the drug has on you in addition to its function of curing illness or pain

**sarcastic**<sup>복습</sup>
[sɑːrkǽstik]

a. 빈정대는, 비꼬는, 풍자적인 (sarcastically ad. 빈정대며, 비꼬아서)
Someone who is sarcastic says or does the opposite of what they really mean in order to mock or insult someone.

**comb**\*\*
[kóum]

n. 머리빗, 빗; v. 빗다, 빗질하다
A comb is a flat piece of plastic or metal with narrow pointed teeth along one side, which you use to tidy your hair.

**strand**
[strænd]

n. (실 · 전선 · 머리카락 등의) 가닥
A strand of something such as hair, wire, or thread is a single thin piece of it.

**wig**\*\*
[wíg]

n. 가발
A wig is a covering of false hair which you wear on your head.

**gross**\*\*
[gróus]

a. 역겨운, 지겨운, 추잡한; 전체의, 총체의; 중대한
If you describe something as gross, you think it is very unpleasant.

**stomp**
[stámp]

v. 발을 구르며 걷다; 발을 동동 구르다; n. 발구르기
If you stomp somewhere, you walk there with very heavy steps, often because you are angry.

**depress**<sup>복습</sup>
[diprés]

vt. 우울하게 하다, 낙담시키다
If someone or something depresses you, they make you feel sad and disappointed.

**handful**\*\*
[hǽndfùl]

n. (한) 줌, 움큼
A handful of something is the amount of it that you can hold in your hand.

**thrill**<sup>복습</sup>
[θríl]

v. 열광시키다, 황홀하게 만들다; n. 흥분, 설렘 (thrilled a. 아주 흥분한, 신이 난)
If something thrills you, or if you thrill at it, it gives you a feeling of great pleasure and excitement.

**rub**\*\*
[ráb]

v. 비비다, 문지르다; 스치다; n. 문지르기
If you rub against a surface or rub a part of your body against a surface, you move it backwards and forwards while pressing it against the surface.

**kitten**\*\*
[kítn]

n. 새끼 고양이
A kitten is a very young cat.

**blossom**<sup>복습</sup>
[blásəm]

vi. (나무 등이) 꽃 피다, 개화하다; 발전하다; n. (특히 과수의) 꽃, 개화
When a tree blossoms, it produces the flowers that appear before the fruit.

**arrange**<sup>복습</sup>
[əréindʒ]

v. 정리하다, 배열하다; 준비하다 (arrange flowers idiom 꽃꽂이 하다)
If you arrange things somewhere, you place them in a particular position, usually in order to make them look attractive or tidy.

**incredible**\*\*
[inkrédəbl]

a. 믿을 수 없는, 믿기 힘든
If you describe something or someone as incredible, you like them very much or are impressed by them, because they are extremely or unusually good.

**procedure**\*\*
[prosí:dʒər]

n. (어떤 일을 하는) 절차, 방법, 차례
A procedure is a way of doing something, especially the usual or correct way.

**develop**<sup>복습</sup>
[divéləp]

v. [사진] 현상하다; 발달하다, 개발하다
To develop photographs means to make negatives or prints from a photographic film.

**temperature**\*\*\*
[témpəritʃər]

n. 온도, 기온
The temperature of something is a measure of how hot or cold it is.

**proportion**<sup>복습</sup>
[prəpɔ́:rʃən]

n. 비율, 비; 크기; 균형
The proportion of one amount to another is the relationship between the two amounts in terms of how much there is of each thing.

**chemical**<sup>복습</sup>
[kémikəl]

n. 화학 제품; a. 화학의, 화학적인
Chemicals are substances that are used in a chemical process or made by a chemical process.

**fool around**<sup>복습</sup>

idiom 빈둥거리며 세월을 보내다, 펀둥펀둥 지내다
If you fool around, you behave in a silly, dangerous, or irresponsible way.

**technical**\*\*
[téknikəl]

a. 기술적인, 전문의 (technically ad. 기술적으로)
You use technical to describe the practical skills and methods used to do an activity such as an art, a craft, or a sport.

**immense**\*\*
[iméns]

a. 막대한, 무한한, 광대한 (immensely ad. 엄청나게, 막대하게)
If you describe something as immense, you mean that it is extremely large or great.

**agitate**\*\*
[ǽdʒitèit]

v. (액체를) 휘젓다; (마음을) 뒤흔들다
If you agitate something, you shake it so that it moves about.

**compensate**\*
[ká(ɔ́)mpenseit]

v. 보충하다, 보상하다; 보상금을 주다
If you compensate for a lack of something or for something you have done wrong, you do something to make the situation better.

**prolong**\*\*
[prəlɔ́:(ɔ́)ŋ]

vt. 연장시키다, 연장하다
To prolong something means to make it last longer.

**occur** 복습
[əkə́:r]

vi. 일어나다, 생기다; 생각이 떠오르다
When something occurs, it happens.

**interrupt**\*\*
[ìntərʌ́pt]

v. 가로막다, 저지하다, 중단하다
If you interrupt someone who is speaking, you say or do something that causes them to stop.

**impatient** 복습
[impéiʃənt]

a. 성급한, 조급한, 참을성 없는
If you are impatient, you are easily irritated by things.

**independent**\*\*
[ìndipéndənt]

a. 독립적인, 자립심이 강한, 자립적인
If someone is independent, they do not need help or money from anyone else.

**heck**
[hék]

n. 지옥(HELL의 완곡어); int. 젠장, 제기랄
People use a heck of to emphasize how big something is or how much of it there is.

**experiment** 복습
[ekspérimənt]

vi. 실험하다; n. 실험
If you experiment with something or experiment on it, you do a scientific test on it in order to discover what happens to it in particular conditions.

**agitation**\*\*
[ædʒətéiʃən]

n. (액체를) 휘저어 섞음; 불안, 동요
Agitation is the act of moving something vigorously.

**contrast**\*\*
[kɑ́(ɔ)ntrækt]

n. 콘트라스트(사진·그림에서 특수 효과를 위해 색이나 명암 차를 이용하는 것); 대조, 대비
Contrast is the degree of difference between the darker and lighter parts of a photograph, television picture, or painting.

**reduce**\*\*\*
[ridjú:s]

v. 줄이다, 축소하다
If you reduce something, you make it smaller in size or amount, or less in degree.

**moron**
[mɔ́:rɑ]

n. 바보 천치, 멍청이
If you refer to someone as a moron, you think that they are very stupid.

**ruin** 복습
[rú:in]

v. 망치다, 엉망으로 만들다; n. 붕괴, 몰락
To ruin something means to severely harm, damage, or spoil it.

**bellow**\*
[bélou]

v. (우렁찬 소리로) 고함치다
If someone bellows, they shout angrily in a loud, deep voice.

**genius** 복습
[dʒí:njəs]

n. 천재; 특별한 재능
A genius is a highly talented, creative, or intelligent person.

**disregard**\*
[dìsrigɑ́:rd]

vt. 무시하다, 묵살하다; n. 무시, 묵살
If you disregard something, you ignore it or do not take account of it.

**boundary**\*\*
[báundəri]

n. 경계(선), 한계(선)
The boundaries of something such as a subject or activity are the limits that people think that it has.

**propriety**\*
[prəpráiəti]

n. (행동의 도덕적·사회적) 적절성; 예의범절, 예절
Propriety is the quality of being socially or morally acceptable.

**permit*** 
[pərmít]

v. 허용하다, 허락하다, 허가하다
If someone permits something, they allow it to happen.

**productive** 
[prədʌ́ktiv]

a. 결실 있는, 생산적인; 생산하는, 산출하는
If you say that a relationship between people is productive, you mean that a lot of good or useful things happen as a result of it.

**snip** 
[snip]

v. (가위로) 자르다, 싹둑 베다; n. 싹둑 자름, 가위질
If you snip something, or if you snip at or through something, you cut it quickly using sharp scissors.

**thread*** 
[θred]

n. 실, 가닥; vt. 실을 꿰다
Thread or a thread is a long very thin piece of a material such as cotton, nylon, or silk, especially one that is used in sewing.

**striped**복습 
[stráipt]

a. 줄무늬가 있는, 줄이 처져 있는
Something that is striped has stripes on it.

**square**복습 
[skwɛə:r]

n. 정사각형; 광장; a. 정사각형의; 공명정대한;
A square is a shape with four sides that are all the same length and four corners that are all right angles.

**typewriter**복습 
[táipràitər]

n. 타자기
A typewriter is a machine with keys which are pressed in order to print letters, numbers, or other characters onto paper.

**chew** 
[tʃú:]

v. 씹다
If a person or animal chews an object, they bite it with their teeth.

**stem** 
[stem]

n. 줄기, 대
The stem of a pipe is the long thin part through which smoke is sucked.

**pipe**복습 
[paip]

n. 담배 파이프; (액체·기체가 흐르는) 관, 파이프
A pipe is an object which is used for smoking tobacco.

**machinery*** 
[məʃíːnəri]

n. 기계(류)
You can use machinery to refer to machines in general, or machines that are used in a factory or on a farm.

**discipline*** 
[dísiplin]

n. 훈련, 규율; vt. 훈련하다
Discipline is the practice of making people obey rules or standards of behavior, and punishing them when they do not.

**occasional**복습 
[əkéiʒənəl]

a. 가끔의 (occasionally ad. 가끔)
Occasional means happening sometimes, but not regularly or often.

**radiator**복습 
[réidièitə:r]

n. (차량·항공기의) 냉각 장치, 라디에이터
The radiator in a car is the part of the engine which is filled with water in order to cool the engine.

**measure**복습 
[méʒər]

v. (치수·양 등을) 측정하다, 재다; n. 조치, 정책; 척도, 기준
(measure off phrasal v. 재어서 자르다, 구획하다)
If you measure a quantity that can be expressed in numbers, such as the length of something, you discover it using a particular instrument or device, for example a ruler.

**groan** <sup>복습</sup>
[gróun]

v. 신음하다, 끙끙거리다; n. 신음, 끙 하는 소리
If you groan, you make a long, low sound because you are in pain, or because you are upset or unhappy about something.

**dull**\*\*
[dʌl]

a. 따분한, 재미없는; 흐릿한, 칙칙한
If you describe someone or something as dull, you mean they are not interesting or exciting.

**term**\*\*\*
[təːrm]

n. 학기, 기간; 용어, 말
A term is one of the periods of time that a school, college, or university divides the year into.

**miserable** <sup>복습</sup>
[mízərəbl]

a. 비참한, 우울한, 형편없는
If you are miserable, you are very unhappy.

**self-conscious**\*
[sélf-kánʃəs]

a. 남의 시선을 의식하는, 자의식이 강한; 사람 앞을 꺼리는, 수줍어하는
If you describe someone or something as self-conscious, you mean that they are strongly aware of who or what they are.

**what the heck** <sup>복습</sup>

idiom 아무렴 어때
You say 'what the heck' to indicate that you do not care about a bad aspect of an action or situation.

**resign**\*\*
[rizáin]

v. 단념하다, 포기하다; 사직[사임]하다; 물러나다
If you resign yourself to an unpleasant situation or fact, you accept it because you realize that you cannot change it.

**burst**\*\*\*
[bə́ːrst]

n. 돌발, 파열; v. 갑자기 …하다; 파열하다, 터지다
A burst of something is a sudden short period of it.

**spring**\*\*\*
[spríŋ]

v. 튀다, 뛰어오르다; n. 뜀, 뛰어오름; 봄; 샘
If something springs in a particular direction, it moves suddenly and quickly.

**all along** <sup>복습</sup>

idiom 처음부터, 내내, 계속
If something have been there all along, it is there from the very beginning.

**rocky**\*\*
[rɑ́ki]

a. 바위로 된, 바위[돌]투성이의
A rocky place is covered with rocks or consists of large areas of rock and has nothing growing on it.

**shady**\*
[ʃéidi]

a. 그늘이 드리워진, 그늘을 드리우는
You can describe a place as shady when you like the fact that it is sheltered from bright sunlight, for example by trees or buildings.

**glance** <sup>복습</sup>
[glæns]

v. 흘긋 보다, 잠깐 보다; n. 흘긋 봄
If you glance at something or someone, you look at them very quickly and then look away again immediately.

**grin** <sup>복습</sup>
[grín]

v. 이를 드러내고 싱긋 웃다; n. 싱긋 웃음
When you grin, you smile broadly.

**put on**

phrasal v. 가장하다, 꾸미다; 입다, 신다
If you put someone on, you mock or tease them.

**hoot**[*]
[hu:t]

v. 폭소를 터뜨리다; 콧방귀를 뀌다. 비웃다; (올빼미가) 부엉부엉 울다
If you hoot, you make a loud high-pitched noise when you are laughing or showing disapproval.

**phony**[복습]
[fóuni]

a. (구어) 가짜의, 허위의, 겉치레의; n. 가짜, 위조품; vt. 위조하다, 속이다
If you say that someone is phony, you disapprove of them because they are pretending to be someone that they are not in order to deceive people.

**haughty**[복습]
[hɔ́:ti]

a. 오만한, 거만한
You use haughty to describe someone's behavior or appearance when you disapprove of the fact that they seem to be very proud and to think that they are better than other people.

**twinkle**[*]
[twíŋkl]

v. 반짝반짝 빛나다, 깜빡이다; n. 반짝거림, 번득임
If you say that someone's eyes twinkle, you mean that their face expresses good humour or amusement.

**underbrush**[*]
[ʌ́ndərbrʌ̀ʃ]

n. (큰 나무 밑에 자라는) 덤불
Underbrush consists of bushes and plants growing close together under trees in a forest.

**clump**[*]
[klʌmp]

n. (촘촘히 붙어 자라는 나무 등의) 무리, 수풀
A clump of things such as trees or plants is a small group of them growing together.

**ignore**[복습]
[ignɔ́:r]

vt. 무시하다, 모르는 체하다
If you ignore someone or something, you pay no attention to them.

**resemble**[**]
[rizémbl]

vt. 닮다, 비슷[유사]하다
If one thing or person resembles another, they are similar to each other.

**remarkable**[**]
[rimá:rkəbl]

a. 놀랄 만한, 놀라운, 주목할 만한
Someone or something that is remarkable is unusual or special in a way that makes people notice them and be surprised or impressed.

**bloom**[**]
[blu:m]

v. 꽃이 피다, 개화하다; 번영시키다; n. 꽃, 개화
When a plant or tree blooms, it produces flowers. When a flower blooms, it opens.

**meantime**[**]
[mí:ntàim]

ad. 그동안에, 사이에
In the meantime or meantime means in the period of time between two events.

**investigate**[**]
[invéstigeit]

v. 조사하다, 살피다
If someone, especially an official, investigates an event, situation, or claim, they try to find out what happened or what is the truth.

**shrug**[복습]
[ʃrʌg]

v. (양 손바닥을 내보이면서 어깨를) 으쓱하다; n. (어깨를) 으쓱하기
If you shrug, you raise your shoulders to show that you are not interested in something or that you do not know or care about something.

**patch**[**]
[pætʃ]

n. (채소나 과일을 기르는) 작은 땅; (주변과는 다른 조그만) 부분
A patch of land is a small area of land where a particular plant or crop grows.

**dig**\*\*\*
[díg]

v. (dug-dug) (구멍 등을) 파다; n. (손가락이나 팔꿈치로) 쿡 찌르기
If you dig one thing into another or if one thing digs into another, the first thing is pushed hard into the second, or presses hard into it.

**chop**\*\*
[tʃɑp]

vt. 썰다, 다지다, 패다
If you chop something, you cut it into pieces with strong downward movements of a knife or an axe.

**lump**\*\*
[lʌmp]

n. 덩어리, 한 조각; v. 한 덩어리로 만들다
A lump of something is a solid piece of it.

**hoe**\*
[hou]

n. 괭이
A hoe is a gardening tool with a long handle and a small square blade, which you use to remove small weeds and break up the surface of the soil.

**sweat**\*\*
[swét]

n. 땀; v. 땀 흘리다
Sweat is the salty colorless liquid which comes through your skin when you are hot, ill, or afraid.

**bare**<sup>복습</sup>
[béər]

a. 발가벗은, 살을 드러낸; 있는 그대로의
If a part of your body is bare, it is not covered by any clothing.

**fade**<sup>복습</sup>
[feid]

vi. 바래다, 시들다, 희미해지다 (faded a. 시든, 빛깔이 바랜)
When a colored object fades or when the light fades it, it gradually becomes paler.

**handkerchief**\*\*
[hǽŋkərtʃif]

n. 손수건
A handkerchief is a small square piece of fabric which you use for blowing your nose.

**beard**\*\*
[bíərd]

n. (턱)수염
A man's beard is the hair that grows on his chin and cheeks.

**savior**\*
[séiviər]

n. 구원자, 구세주
A savior is a person who saves someone or something from danger, ruin, or defeat.

**rescue**\*\*
[réskju:]

vt. 구조하다, 구출하다; n. 구출, 구원
If you rescue someone, you get them out of a dangerous or unpleasant situation.

**slave**\*\*\*
[sléiv]

n. 노예; v. 노예처럼[고되게] 일하다
A slave is someone who is the property of another person and has to work for that person.

**labor**\*\*\*
[léibər]

n. 노동, 근로, 노력; 분만, 진통; v. 일하다, 노동하다
Labor is very hard work, usually physical work.

**pea**\*\*
[pi:]

n. 완두(콩)
Peas are round green seeds which grow in long thin cases and are eaten as a vegetable.

**burst out**<sup>복습</sup>

phrasal v. 갑자기 …하기 시작하다; 버럭 소리를 지르다
If someone bursts out laughing, crying, or making another noise, they suddenly start making that noise.

chapter six

81

**understatement**
[ʌ̀ndərstéitmənt]

n. 절제(된 표현)
If you say that a statement is an understatement, you mean that it does not fully express the extent to which something is true.

**shy**\*\*
[ʃai]

a. 부끄러워하는, 수줍어하는
A shy person is nervous and uncomfortable in the company of other people.

**pregnant**\*
[prégnənt]

a. 임신한
If a woman or female animal is pregnant, she has a baby or babies developing in her body.

**sleeve**\*\*
[sliːv]

n. (옷의) 소맷자락
The sleeves of a coat, shirt, or other item of clothing are the parts that cover your arms.

**rip**<sup>복습</sup>
[rip]

v. 찢다, 잡아 찢다, 뜯어내다; n. 찢어진 틈, 잡아 찢음
When something rips or when you rip it, you tear it forcefully with your hands or with a tool such as a knife.

**tan**\*\*
[tæn]

a. 황갈색의; n. 햇볕에 그을음; vt. (피부를) 햇볕에 태우다
Something that is tan is a light brown color.

**barely**\*\*
[béərli]

ad. 간신히, 가까스로; 거의 …않다
You use barely to say that something is only just true or only just the case.

**sideways**<sup>복습</sup>
[sáidwèiz]

ad. (한쪽 부분이 앞을 향하도록) 옆으로 비스듬히
Sideways means from or towards the side of something or someone.

**pregnancy**
[prégnənsi]

n. 임신
Pregnancy is the condition of being pregnant or the period of time during which a female is pregnant.

**mend**\*\*
[mend]

v. 수선하다, 고치다, 개선하다; n. 수선, 개량
If you mend something that is broken or not working, you repair it, so that it works properly or can be used.

**predict**\*\*
[pridíkt]

v. 예언하다, 예상하다
If you predict an event, you say that it will happen.

**detach**\*
[ditætʃ]

v. 떼다, 분리하다
If one thing detaches from another, it becomes separated from it.

**braid**\*
[breid]

n. (머리를) 땋은 것
A braid is a length of hair which has been divided into three or more lengths and then woven together.

**botanist**\*
[bátənist]

n. 식물학자
A botanist is a scientist who studies plants.

**flinch**
[flintʃ]

v. 움찔하다, 주춤하다, 위축되다
If you flinch, you make a small sudden movement, especially when something surprises you or hurts you.

**due**<sup>복습</sup>
[dju:]

a. …하기로 되어 있는, …할 예정인; n. 부과금; 당연히 지불되어야 할 것
If something is due at a particular time, it is expected to happen, be done, or arrive at that time.

**hack**<sup>*</sup>
[hǽk]

v. 자르다, 베다, 난도질하다
If you hack your way through an area such as a jungle or hack a path through it, you move forward, cutting back the trees or plants that are in your way.

**clod**<sup>*</sup>
[klɑd]

n. (흙 · 점토) 덩어리
A clod of earth is a large lump of earth.

**obvious**<sup>복습</sup>
[ábviəs]

a. 명백한, 분명한 (obviously ad. 분명히, 명백하게)
If something is obvious, it is easy to see or understand.

**politics**<sup>**</sup>
[pálətiks]

n. 정치, 정치학
Politics are the actions or activities concerned with achieving and using power in a country or society.

**stereo**<sup>*</sup>
[stériòu]

n. 스테레오(음악 재생 장치)
A stereo is a cassette or CD player with two speakers.

**diaper**
[dáiəpər]

n. (아기의) 기저귀
A diaper is a piece of soft towel or paper, which you fasten round a baby's bottom in order to soak up its urine and faeces.

**affectionate**<sup>복습</sup>
[əfékʃənit]

a. 애정 어린, 다정한, 인정 많은 (affectionately ad. 애정을 담고)
If you are affectionate, you show your love or fondness for another person in the way that you behave towards them.

**weed**<sup>**</sup>
[wí:d]

n. 잡초; v. 잡초를 뽑다
A weed is a wild plant that grows in gardens or fields of crops and prevents the plants that you want from growing properly.

**cradle**<sup>**</sup>
[kréidl]

n. 요람, 아기 침대
A cradle is a baby's bed with high sides.

**refinish**<sup>복습</sup>
[rì:fíniʃ]

vt. (목재 · 가구 등의) 표면을 다시 끝손질하다
If you refinish something such as furniture and wood, you change or restore the surface of them.

**get to one's feet**

idiom 일어서다
If you get to your feet, you stand up.

**awkward**<sup>복습</sup>
[ɔ́:kwərd]

a. 어색한, 불편한, 곤란한 (awkwardly ad. 어색하게, 거북하게)
Someone who feels awkward behaves in a shy or embarrassed way.

**smooth**<sup>***</sup>
[smú:ð]

v. 매끄럽게 하다; a. 매끄러운; 유창한
If you smooth something, you move your hands over its surface to make it smooth and flat.

**period**<sup>***</sup>
[píəriəd]

n. (여성의) 생리; 기간, 시기
When a woman has a period, she bleeds from her womb. This usually happens once a month, unless she is pregnant.

**embarrass**<sup>복습</sup>
[embǽrəs]

v. 당황스럽게[어색하게] 만들다; 곤란하게 하다
(embarrassed a. 쑥스러운, 어색한)
If something or someone embarrasses you, they make you feel shy or ashamed.

**haul**\*\*
[hɔ́:l]

vt. 운반하다; 세게 잡아당기다; n. 세게 잡아당김; 운송
If you haul something which is heavy or difficult to move, you move it using a lot of effort.

**roof**<sup>복습</sup>
[rú:f]

n. 지붕; vt. 지붕을 해 덮다
The roof of a building is the covering on top of it that protects the people and things inside from the weather.

**wander**\*\*\*
[wándər]

v. 거닐다, 돌아다니다; 방황하다; n. 유랑, 방랑
If you wander in a place, you walk around there in a casual way, often without intending to go in any particular direction.

**scrape**\*\*
[skreip]

v. (무엇을 떼어 내기 위해) 긁다, 긁어내다; n. 긁기, 긁힌 상처
If you scrape something from a surface, you remove it, especially by pulling a sharp object over the surface.

**organic**\*
[ɔ:rgǽnik]

a. 유기농의, 화학 비료를 쓰지 않는
Organic methods of farming and gardening use only natural animal and plant products to help the plants or animals grow and be healthy, rather than using chemicals.

**stuff**<sup>복습</sup>
[stʌf]

n. 것(들), 물건, 물질; vt. 채워 넣다, 속을 채우다
You can use stuff to refer to things such as a substance, a collection of things, events, or ideas, or the contents of something in a general way without mentioning the thing itself by name.

**mulch**
[mʌltʃ]

vt. 거름을 주다, 뿌리 덮개를 덮어 주다; n. 뿌리 덮개
To mulch plants means to put a layer of something such as old leaves or small pieces of wood which you put on the soil round plants in order to protect them and help them to grow.

**herb**\*
[hɔ́:rb]

n. 허브, 약초, 향초
A herb is a plant whose leaves are used in cooking to add flavor to food, or as a medicine.

**off-key**
[ɔ́:f-kí:]

a. 음정이 맞지 않는
When music is off-key, it is not in tune.

**nonplus**
[nɑnplʌ́s]

v. 어찌할 바를 모르게 하다 (nonplused a. 몹시 놀라 어쩔 줄 모르는)
If you are nonplussed, you feel confused and unsure how to react.

**furnish**\*\*\*
[fɔ́:rniʃ]

v. 갖추다, 비치하다; 공급하다, 제공하다
If you furnish a room or building, you put furniture into it.

**odds and ends**

idiom 잡동사니, 시시한 것
You can refer to a disorganized group of things of various kinds as odds and ends.

**spinning wheel**
[spíniŋ hwí:l]

n. 물레(발로 밟거나 손으로 돌려서 실을 잣는 데 씀)
A spinning wheel is a wooden machine that people used in their homes to make thread from wool, in former times.

84

**rocking chair**
[rákiŋ ʧɛ́ər]

n. 흔들의자
A rocking chair is a chair that is built on two curved pieces of wood so that you can rock yourself backwards and forwards when you are sitting in it.

**sandpaper**
[sǽndpèipər]

n. 사포(砂布)
Sandpaper is strong paper that has a coating of sand on it. It is used for rubbing wood or metal surfaces to make them smoother.

**stuffing**
[stʌ́fiŋ]

n. (쿠션·장난감 등의 안에 넣는) 속, 충전재
Stuffing is material that is used to fill things such as cushions or toys in order to make them firm or solid.

**pod***
[pɑd]

n. (콩이 들어 있는) 꼬투리, 콩과 식물의 깍지
A pod is a seed container that grows on plants such as peas or beans.

**reupholster**
[rí:ʌphóulstər]

v. (소파 등에) 천을 갈다
If you reupholster a furniture, you replace the attached fabric covering on it.

**sand***
[sǽnd]

v. 사포로 닦다; n. 모래
If you sand a wood or metal surface, you rub sandpaper over it in order to make it smooth or clean.

**scrub**<sup>복습</sup>
[skrʌb]

v. 북북 문지르다, 세척하다, 비벼서 씻다
If you scrub something, you rub it hard in order to clean it, using a stiff brush and water.

**peel**<sup>복습</sup>
[pi:l]

v. 껍질을 벗기다; (껍질·피부가) 벗겨지다; n. (과일·채소의 두꺼운) 껍질
When you peel fruit or vegetables, you remove their skins.

**examine**<sup>복습</sup>
[igzǽmin]

v. 조사하다, 검토하다; 검사하다, 진찰하다
If you examine something, you look at it carefully.

**muse****
[mju:z]

vi. 곰곰이 생각하다, 묵상하다
If you muse on something, you think about it, usually saying or writing what you are thinking at the same time.

**rumple**
[rʌ́mpl]

vt. 헝클다
If you rumple someone's hair, you move your hand backwards and forwards through it as your way of showing affection to them.

**chatter****
[ʧǽtər]

v. 수다를 떨다, 재잘거리다; n. 수다, 재잘거림
If you chatter, you talk quickly and continuously, usually about things which are not important.

**tense**<sup>복습</sup>
[tens]

a. 긴장한, 긴박한; 팽팽한; v. 긴장시키다 (tenseness n. 긴장함; 팽팽함)
If you are tense, you are anxious and nervous and cannot relax.

**plaster****
[plǽstər]

n. 회[석고] 반죽; 고약; v. (벽 등에) 회반죽을 바르다
Plaster is a smooth paste made of sand, lime, and water which goes hard when it dries.

**weave**<sup>복습</sup>
[wi:v]

v. (옷감·카펫·바구니 등을) 짜다, 엮다
If you weave cloth or a carpet, you make it by crossing threads over and under each other using a frame or machine.

**exclaim**[***]
[ikskléim]

v. 외치다, 소리[고함]치다
If you exclaim, you say or shout something suddenly because of surprise, fear and pleasure.

**stroke**[**]
[strouk]

① vt. 쓰다듬다, 어루만지다; n. 쓰다듬기, 달램 ② n. 타격, 일격, 치기
If you stroke someone or something, you move your hand slowly and gently over them.

**lag**[**]
[læg]

vi. 뒤에 처지다, 뒤떨어지다
If one thing or person lags behind another thing or person, their progress is slower than that of the other.

**identify**[**]
[aidéntəfài]

v. 식별하다, 확인하다
If you can identify someone or something, you are able to recognize them or distinguish them from others.

## chapter seven

1. How did Molly act?
   A. Giggly and funny
   B. Grouchy and cruel
   C. Quiet and serious
   D. The same way she acted before she got sick

2. What didn't interest Molly?
   A. Talking about the baby
   B. Collecting and categorizing flowers
   C. Making clothing for the baby
   D. Finding wild strawberries

3. Why did Meg think that Molly acted like a baby?
   A. She collected flowers
   B. She sat on Dad's lap
   C. She wasn't taking pills anymore but she still acted sick
   D. She always wanted to play games

4. Who wanted to know about Ben and Maria?
   A. Meg's mother
   B. Will Banks
   C. Clarice Callaway
   D. The mayor of the town

5.  What wasn't true about Ben and Maria?

    A. They walked around nude.

    B. They grew peas and strawberries.

    C. They wanted to have their baby at home.

    D. They are reading books about delivening a baby.

6.  What did Ben and Maria show Meg?

    A. The unfinished cradle they were building

    B. Their wedding pictures

    C. The repairs that they made in the kitchen

    D. The matching chairs that they built for the house

7.  Why was Meg angry at Ben?

    A. He said that there was a serious problem and the baby would die.

    B. He said that he and Maria weren't married.

    C. He said that he and Maria would leave the house before the baby was born.

    D. He showed her where he would bury the baby if it died.

*Check Your Reading Speed*

1분에 몇 단어를 읽는지 리딩 속도를 측정해보세요.

$$\frac{3,418 \text{ words}}{\text{reading time (\quad) sec}} \times 60 = (\quad) \text{ WPM}$$

*Build Your Vocabulary*

**grouch**
[gráutʃ]

n. 불평이 많은 사람; (하찮은 것에 대한) 불평
A grouch is someone who is always complaining in a bad-tempered way.

**gradual**<sup>복습</sup>
[grǽdʒuəl]

a. 점진적인, 단계적인
A gradual change or process occurs in small stages over a long period of time, rather than suddenly.

**giggly**<sup>복습</sup>
[gígli]

a. 낄낄 웃는
Someone who is giggly keeps laughing in a childlike way, because they are amused, nervous, or drunk.

**silly**<sup>복습</sup>
[síli]

a. 익살맞은, 어리석은, 바보 같은; n. 바보, 멍청이
If you say that someone or something is silly, you mean that they are foolish, childish, or ridiculous.

**enthusiasm**<sup>복습</sup>
[inθú:ziæzm]

n. 열정, 열의, 열광
Enthusiasm is great eagerness to be involved in a particular activity which you like and enjoy or which you think is important.

**withdrawn**[*]
[wiðdrɔ́:n]

a. 내성적인, 내향적인
Someone who is withdrawn is very quiet, and does not want to talk to other people.

**polite**[**]
[pəláit]

a. 예의바른, 공손한
Someone who is polite has good manners and behaves in a way that is socially correct and not rude to other people.

**bury**<sup>복습</sup>
[béri]

vt. 묻다; 파묻다, 매장하다
If you bury your head or face in something, you press your head or face against it, often because you are unhappy.

**identify**<sup>복습</sup>
[aidéntəfài]

v. 식별하다, 확인하다
If you can identify someone or something, you are able to recognize them or distinguish them from others.

**classify**[**]
[klǽsəfài]

vt. 분류하다, 등급을 나누다
To classify things means to divide them into groups or types so that things with similar characteristics are in the same group.

**label**[**]
[léibəl]

vt. 라벨을[표를] 붙이다, (표 같은 것에 필요한 정보를) 적다; n. 표, 라벨
If something is labeled, a label is attached to it giving information about it.

90

**put together** 복습  phrasal v. 모으다, 합계하다; 구성하다, 편집하다
If you put together a group of people or things, you form them into a team or collection.

**dare**\*\*\*
[déər]  v. 감히 …하다; 무릅쓰다; 도전하다
If you do not dare to do something, you do not have enough courage to do it, or you do not want to do it because you fear the consequences.

**tease** 복습
[ti:z]  v. 놀리다, 괴롭히다; 졸라대다; n. 곯리기
To tease someone means to laugh at them or make jokes about them in order to embarrass, annoy, or upset them.

**sew**\*\*
[sóu]  v. 바느질하다, 깁다
When you sew something such as clothes, you make them or repair them by joining pieces of cloth together by passing thread through them with a needle.

**smooth** 복습
[smú:ð]  v. 매끄럽게 하다; a. 매끄러운; 유창한
If you smooth something, you move your hands over its surface to make it smooth and flat.

**neat** 복습
[ní:t]  a. 깔끔한, 산뜻한; (구어) 굉장한, 멋진 (neatly ad. 깔끔하게)
A neat place, thing, or person is tidy and smart, and has everything in the correct place.

**drawer** 복습
[drɔ́:ər]  n. 서랍
A drawer is part of a desk, chest, or other piece of furniture that is shaped like a box and is designed for putting things in.

**puzzle** 복습
[pʌzl]  v. 어리둥절하게[이해할 수 없게] 만들다; n. 수수께끼, 어려운 문제
(puzzled a. 어리둥절해하는, 얼떨떨한)
If something puzzles you, you do not understand it and feel confused.

**concern** 복습
[kənsɔ́:rn]  n. 우려, 걱정; v. 영향을 미치다, 관련되다; …를 걱정스럽게[우려하게] 만들다
Someone's concerns are the things that they consider to be important.

**nightgown**\*
[náitgàun]  n. (여자·어린이용) 잠옷
A nightgown is a sort of loose dress that a woman or girl wears in bed.

**pee**
[pí:]  v. 오줌을 누다; n. 오줌, 쉬
When someone pees, they urinate.

**in store for . . .**  idiom …을 위해서 비축하여, 준비하여
If something is in store for someone, it is waiting to happen to them.

**stitch** 복습
[stitʃ]  v. 바느질하다; 꿰매다; n. 한 바늘, 한 땀
If you stitch cloth, you use a needle and thread to join two pieces together or to make a decoration.

**fireplace** 복습
[faiərplèis]  n. (벽)난로
In a room, the fireplace is the place where a fire can be lit and the area on the wall and floor surrounding this place.

**log**\*\*
[lɔ́ːg]

n. 통나무
A log is a piece of a thick branch or of the trunk of a tree that has been cut so that it can be used for fuel or for making things.

**shift**\*\*
[ʃíft]

v. 옮기다, 이동하다; n. (위치 · 입장 · 방향의) 변화; 교대
If you shift something or if it shifts, it moves slightly.

**chimney**<sup>복습</sup>
[tʃímni]

n. 굴뚝
A chimney is a pipe through which smoke goes up into the air, usually through the roof of a building.

**pajamas**\*
[pədʒɑ́ːməz]

n. (바지와 상의로 된) 잠옷
A pair of pajamas consists of loose trousers and a loose jacket that people, especially men, wear in bed.

**lap**\*\*
[læp]

n. 무릎; 한 바퀴; v. 겹치게 하다
If you have something on your lap when you are sitting down, it is on top of your legs and near to your body.

**stroke**<sup>복습</sup>
[strouk]

① vt. 쓰다듬다, 어루만지다; n. 쓰다듬기, 달램 ② n. 타격, 일격, 치기
If you stroke someone or something, you move your hand slowly and gently over them.

**wispy**
[wispi]

a. 숱이 적은, 성긴
If someone has wispy hair, their hair does not grow thickly on their head.

**pill**<sup>복습</sup>
[píl]

n. 알약, 환약
Pills are small solid round masses of medicine or vitamins that you swallow without chewing.

**beauty contest**

n. 미인 대회, 미녀 선발 대회
A beauty contest is a competition in which young women are judged to decide which one is the most beautiful.

**specialist**<sup>복습</sup>
[spéʃəlist]

n. 전문의; 전문가, 전공자
A specialist is a doctor who has special training in and knowledge of a particular area of medicine.

**tolerant**\*
[tɑ́lərənt]

n. 관대한, 아량이 있는
If you describe someone as tolerant, you approve of the fact that they allow other people to say and do as they like, even if they do not agree with or like it.

**adjust**\*\*
[ədʒʌ́st]

v. 적응하다; 조정하다, 조절하다
When you adjust to a new situation, you get used to it by changing your behavior or your ideas.

**experiment**<sup>복습</sup>
[ekspérimənt]

vi. 실험하다; n. 실험
If you experiment with something or experiment on it, you do a scientific test on it in order to discover what happens to it in particular conditions.

**contrast**<sup>복습</sup>
[kɑ́(ɔ́)ntrækt]

n. 콘트라스트(사진 · 그림에서 특수 효과를 위해 색이나 명암 차를 이용하는 것); 대조, 대비
Contrast is the degree of difference between the darker and lighter parts of a photograph, television picture, or painting.

**texture**<sup>*</sup>
[tékstʃər]

n. (직물의) 감촉, 질감
The texture of something is the way that it feels when you touch it, for example how smooth or rough it is.

**stick around**

phrasal v. (구어) 가까이에 있다, 옆에서 떠나지 않고 기다리다
If you stick around, you stay where you are, often because you are waiting for something.

**overdue**<sup>복습</sup>
[òuvərdjú:]

a. (지불 · 반납 등의) 기한이 지난
An overdue library book has not been returned to the library, even though the date on which it should have been returned has passed.

**stickler**
[stíklər]

n. 까다로운 사람
If you are a stickler for something, you always demand or require it.

**achieve**<sup>**</sup>
[ətʃí:v]

v. 이루다, 성취하다, 달성하다
If you achieve a particular aim or effect, you succeed in doing it or causing it to happen, usually after a lot of effort.

**meddle**<sup>**</sup>
[médl]

vi. 쓸데없이 참견하다, 간섭하다
If you say that someone meddles in something, you are criticizing the fact that they try to influence or change it without being asked.

**mean to**<sup>복습</sup>

idiom 계획하다, 의도하다
If you mean to do something, you intend or plan to do it.

**inquisitive**<sup>*</sup>
[inkwízətiv]

a. 꼬치꼬치 캐묻는
An inquisitive person likes finding out about things, especially secret things.

**up in arms**

idiom 들고일어날 태세인, 격분하여, 분개하여
If people are up in arms about something, they are very angry about it and are protesting strongly against it.

**exaggeration**<sup>*</sup>
[igzædʒəréiʃən]

n. 과장
An exaggeration is a statement or description that makes something seem larger, better, worse or more important than it really is.

**frown**<sup>복습</sup>
[fráun]

vi. 눈살을 찌푸리다, 얼굴을 찡그리다; n. 찌푸린 얼굴
When someone frowns, their eyebrows become drawn together, because they are annoyed or puzzled.

**beard**<sup>복습</sup>
[bíərd]

n. (턱)수염
A man's beard is the hair that grows on his chin and cheeks.

**definition**<sup>*</sup>
[defíniʃən]

n. 정의, 말뜻, 의미
A definition is a statement giving the meaning of a word or expression, especially in a dictionary.

**shed light on**

idiom 밝히다, 해명하다; …을 비추다
To shed light on something means to make it easier to understand, because more information is known about it.

**pea**<sup>복습</sup>
[pi:]

n. 완두(콩)
Peas are round green seeds which grow in long thin cases and are eaten as a vegetable.

**squash**
[skwɑʃ]

① n. 호박; ② v. 눌러 찌그러뜨리다; 헤치고[밀치고] 들어가다
A squash is one of a family of vegetables that have thick skin and soft or firm flesh inside.

**variety**\*\*\*
[vəráiəti]

n. 품종, 종류; 여러 가지, 갖가지
A variety of something is a type of it.

**nude**\*
[njúːd]

a. 벌거벗은, 나체의; n. 벌거벗은 사람
A nude person is not wearing any clothes.

**in the middle of nowhere**<sup>복습</sup>

idiom 멀리 인적이 끊긴
If you say that a place is in the middle of nowhere, you mean that it is a long way from other places.

**due**<sup>복습</sup>
[djuː]

a. …하기로 되어 있는, …할 예정인; n. 부과금; 당연히 지불되어야 할 것
If something is due at a particular time, it is expected to happen, be done, or arrive at that time.

**deliver a baby**

idiom (산파 · 간호사 · 의사가) 아기를 받아내다, 아이를 낳다
If you deliver a baby, you help take a baby out of its mother when it is being born.

**exercise**<sup>복습</sup>
[éksərsaiz]

n. 운동, 체조; 연습문제; 활동, 일; v. 운동하다
Exercises are a series of movements or actions which you do in order to get fit, remain healthy, or practice for a particular physical activity.

**impersonal**\*
[impɔ́ːrsənəl]

a. 인간미 없는, 비인격적인
If you describe a place, organization, or activity as impersonal, you mean that it is not very friendly and makes you feel unimportant because it involves or is used by a large number of people.

**convince**\*\*
[kənvíns]

vt. 납득시키다, 확신시키다
If someone or something convinces you of something, they make you believe that it is true or that it exists.

**stir**\*\*\*
[stɔ́ːr]

v. 휘젓다, 움직이다; n. 움직임; 휘젓기
If you stir a liquid or other substance, you move it around or mix it in a container using something such as a spoon.

**soggy**
[sɑ́gi]

a. 질척한, 질척거리는
Something that is soggy is unpleasantly wet.

**rocking chair**<sup>복습</sup>
[rɑ́kiŋ tʃɛ̃ər]

n. 흔들의자
A rocking chair is a chair that is built on two curved pieces of wood so that you can rock yourself backwards and forwards when you are sitting in it.

**porch**<sup>복습</sup>
[pɔːrtʃ]

n. (건물 입구에 지붕이 얹혀 있고 흔히 벽이 둘러진) 현관, 포치
A porch is a sheltered area at the entrance to a building, which has a roof and sometimes has walls.

**pry**
[prai]

① vt. (지레로) 들어 올리다, 비틀어 움직이다; n. 지레
② vi. 엿보다, 동정을 살피다
If you pry something open or pry it away from a surface, you force it open or away from a surface.

**loose**\*\*\*
[lúːs]

a. 풀린, 헐거운; 꽉 죄지 않는
Something that is loose is not firmly held or fixed in place.

**wince**
[wins]

vi. 주춤하다, 움츠리다; n. 위축
If you wince, the muscles of your face tighten suddenly because you have felt a pain or because you have just seen, heard, or remembered something unpleasant.

**might as well**<sup>복습</sup>

idiom …하는 편이 낫다
If you say that you might as well do something, or that you may as well do it, you mean that you will do it although you do not have a strong desire to do it and may even feel slightly unwilling to do it.

**mount**\*\*\*
[maunt]

v. 끼우다, 고정시키다; (자전거 · 말 등에) 올라타다;
n. (사진 등을 붙이는) 대지, 판
If you mount an object on something, you fix it there firmly.

**silhouette**<sup>복습</sup>
[sìluét]

n. 윤곽, 실루엣; vt. …의 그림자를 비추다
A silhouette is the solid dark shape that you see when someone or something has a bright light or pale background behind them.

**bend**\*\*\*
[bend]

v. (bent-bent) 구부리다, 굽히다, 숙이다; n. 커브, 굽음 (bent a. 구부러진)
When you bend, you move the top part of your body downwards and forwards.

**curly**<sup>복습</sup>
[kɔ́ːrli]

a. 곱슬곱슬한
Curly hair is full of curls.

**clothesline**
[klóuzlàin]

n. 빨랫줄
A clothesline is a thin rope on which you hang washing so that it can dry.

**wringer**
[ríŋər]

n. 짜는 기계, 탈수기; 착취자
A wringer is a machine or device for pressing out liquid or moisture.

**garage**\*\*
[gərάːʒ]

n. 차고, 주차장
A garage is a building in which you keep a car.

**squeeze**\*\*
[skwíːz]

vt. 짜내다, 꽉 쥐다, 압착하다; n. 압착, 짜냄; 꽉 끌어안음
If you squeeze something, you press it firmly, usually with your hands.

**lurch**
[ləːrtʃ]

v. (공포 · 흥분으로 가슴이나 속이) 떨리다; (갑자기) 휘청하다;
n. 휘청함, 요동침
To lurch means to make a sudden movement, especially forwards, in an uncontrolled way.

**diaper**<sup>복습</sup>
[dáiəpər]

n. (아기의) 기저귀
A diaper is a piece of soft towel or paper, which you fasten round a baby's bottom in order to soak up its urine and faeces.

**snap**\*\*
[snǽp]

v. 홱 잡다, 잡아채다; 짤깍 소리 내다; 날카롭게[느닷없이] 말하다; n. 짤깍 소리 냄
If you snap something into a particular position, or if it snaps into that position, it moves quickly into that position, with a sharp sound.

| | |
|---|---|
| **wrinkle**<sup>복습</sup><br>[ríŋkl] | n. 주름, 잔주름; v. …에 주름살지게 하다, 구겨지다<br>A wrinkle is a raised fold in a piece of cloth or paper that spoils its appearance. |
| **tray**<sup>복습</sup><br>[tréi] | n. 쟁반, 음식 접시; 서류함<br>A tray is a flat piece of wood, plastic, or metal, which usually has raised edges and which is used for carrying things, especially food and drinks. |
| **recover**<sup>★★</sup><br>[rikʌ́vər] | v. (건강 · 의식 등을) 회복하다; 되찾다<br>If you recover a mental or physical state, it comes back again. |
| **sand**<sup>복습</sup><br>[sǽnd] | v. 사포로 닦다; n. 모래<br>If you sand a wood or metal surface, you rub sandpaper over it in order to make it smooth or clean. |
| **bookcase**<sup>복습</sup><br>[búkkèis] | n. 책장, 책꽂이, 서가<br>A bookcase is a piece of furniture with shelves that you keep books on. |
| **laundry**<sup>★★</sup><br>[lɔ́:ndri] | n. 세탁물, 세탁소<br>Laundry is used to refer to clothes, sheets, and towels that are about to be washed, are being washed, or have just been washed. |
| **absorb**<sup>★★</sup><br>[æbsɔ́:rb] | vt. 열중시키다; 받아들이다, 흡수하다 (absorbed a. 열중한, 몰두한)<br>If something absorbs you, it interests you a great deal and takes up all your attention and energy. |
| **preoccupied**<sup>복습</sup><br>[pri:ʌ́kjupàid] | a. (어떤 생각 · 걱정에) 사로잡힌, 정신이 팔린<br>If you are preoccupied, you are thinking a lot about something or someone, and so you hardly notice other things. |
| **outline**<sup>복습</sup><br>[áutlàin] | n. 윤곽; vt. 윤곽을 보여주다<br>The outline of something is its general shape, especially when it cannot be clearly seen. |
| **cradle**<sup>복습</sup><br>[kréidl] | n. 요람, 아기 침대<br>A cradle is a baby's bed with high sides. |
| **glow**<sup>★★★</sup><br>[glóu] | v. 빛을 내다; n. 빛, 밝음<br>If something glows, it produces a dull, steady light. |
| **crochet**<br>[krouʃéi] | v. 코바늘로 뜨개질하다; v. 코바늘 뜨개질<br>If you crochet, you make cloth by using a needle with a small hook at the end. |
| **hesitant**<br>[hézətənt] | a. 머뭇거리는, 주저하는 (hesitantly ad. 머뭇거리며)<br>If you are hesitant about doing something, you do not do it quickly or immediately, usually because you are uncertain, embarrassed, or worried. |
| **nosebleed**<sup>복습</sup><br>[nóuzblì:d] | n. 코피<br>If someone has a nosebleed, blood comes out from inside their nose. |
| **transfusion**<sup>복습</sup><br>[trænsfjú:ʒən] | n. [의학] 수혈<br>A transfusion is a process in which blood is injected into the body of a person who is badly injured or ill. |

96

**fall out**<sup>복습</sup>

phrasal v. (머리 · 이빨이) 빠지다, 떨어져 나가다
If something such as a person's hair or a tooth falls out, it comes out.

**rough**\*\*\*
[rʌf]

a. 힘든, 골치 아픈; 매끄럽지 않은, 거친
If you say that someone has had a rough time, you mean that they have had some difficult or unpleasant experiences.

**steeple**\*
[stí:pl]

n. (교회의) 첨탑
A steeple is a tall pointed structure on top of the tower of a church.

**grocery**
[gróusəri]

n. (pl.) 식료 잡화류; 식료 잡화점
Groceries are foods you buy at a grocer's or at a supermarket such as flour, sugar, and tinned foods.

**bride**<sup>복습</sup>
[bráid]

n. 신부, 새색시
A bride is a woman who is getting married or who has just got married.

**bouquet**<sup>복습</sup>
[bu:kéi]

n. 부케, 꽃다발
A bouquet is a bunch of flowers which is attractively arranged.

**bridesmaid**
[bráidzmèid]

n. 신부 들러리
A bridesmaid is a woman or a girl who helps and accompanies a bride on her wedding day.

**hesitate**<sup>복습</sup>
[hézətèit]

v. 주저하다, 머뭇거리다, 망설이다
If you hesitate, you do not speak or act for a short time, usually because you are uncertain, embarrassed, or worried about what you are going to say or do.

**make a face**<sup>복습</sup>

idiom 얼굴을 찌푸리다, 침울한 표정을 짓다
If you make a face, you twist your face to indicate a certain mental or emotional state.

**screw**\*\*
[skru:]

v. (입을) 오므리다; 나사로 고정시키다; n. 나사
If you screw your face or your eyes into a particular expression, you tighten the muscles of your face to form that expression, for example because you are in pain or because the light is too bright.

**sideways**<sup>복습</sup>
[sáidwèiz]

ad. (한쪽 부분이 앞을 향하도록) 옆으로 비스듬히
Sideways means from or towards the side of something or someone.

**yuck**
[jʌk]

int. 윽(역겨울 때 내는 소리)
People say 'yuck' to indicate contempt, dislike, or disgust.

**darn**
[dɑ:rn]

① n. (구어, 완곡한 말) damn(제기랄) ② vt. (구멍을) 꿰매다; n. 꿰매기
People sometimes use darn or darned to emphasize what they are saying, often when they are annoyed.

**closet**<sup>복습</sup>
[klázit]

n. 벽장, 찬장
A closet is a piece of furniture with doors at the front and shelves inside, which is used for storing things.

**leer**
[liə:r]

vi. 음흉하게 웃다, 음흉한 시선을 던지다
If someone leers at you, they smile in an unpleasant way.

**diabolical**
[dàiəbálikəl]

a. 사악한, 악마 같은
If you describe something as diabolical, you are emphasizing that it is very bad, extreme, or unpleasant.

**feelthy**
[fíːlθi]

a. (= filthy) 추잡한, 불결한
If you describe something as feelthy, you mean that you think it is morally very unpleasant and disgusting, sometimes in a sexual way.

**technical**<sup>복습</sup>
[téknikəl]

a. 기술적인, 전문의 (technically ad. 기술적으로)
You use technical to describe the practical skills and methods used to do an activity such as an art, a craft, or a sport.

**yucky**<sup>복습</sup>
[jʌ́ki]

a. 역겨운, 구역질나는
Something yucky is disgusting or very unpleasant.

**tuxedo**
[tʌksíːdou]

n. 턱시도
A tuxedo is a black or white jacket worn by men for formal social events.

**tail**\*\*\*
[téil]

n. (pl.) 연미복; (pl.) 여성복의 긴 자락; 꼬리
If a man is wearing tails, he is wearing a formal jacket which has two long pieces hanging down at the back.

**lacy**
[léisi]

a. 레이스로 된, 레이스 같은
Lacy things are made from lace or have pieces of lace attached to them.

**altar**\*\*
[ɔ́ːltər]

n. 제단
An altar is a holy table in a church or temple.

**decorate**\*\*
[dekəréit]

vt. 장식하다, 꾸미다
If you decorate something, you make it more attractive by adding things to it.

**frosting**
[frɔ́ːstiŋ]

n. (케이크에) 설탕을 입힘
Frosting is a sweet substance made from powdered sugar that is used to decorate cakes.

**buck**\*
[bʌk]

n. (미국 · 호주 · 뉴질랜드의) 달러
A buck is a US or Australian dollar.

**cardboard**\*
[káːrdbɔ́ːrd]

n. 마분지, 판지
Cardboard is thick, stiff paper that is used, for example, to make boxes and models.

**stream**<sup>복습</sup>
[stríːm]

n. 흐름, 시내, 개울; v. 흐르다, 흘러나오다
A stream of smoke, air, or liquid is a narrow moving mass of it.

**homemade**\*\*
[hoummèid]

a. 집에서 만든, 손수 만든
Something that is homemade has been made in someone's home, rather than in a shop or factory.

**slam**<sup>복습</sup>
[slǽm]

v. 털썩 내려놓다; (문 따위를) 탕 닫다, 세게 치다; n. 쾅 (하는 소리)
If you slam something down, you put it there quickly and with great force.

**elect**\*\*\*
[ilékt]

vt. (선거로) 선출하다; 선택하다
When people elect someone, they choose that person to represent them, by voting for them.

**carve**<sup>복습</sup>
[kɑ:rv]

vt. 새기다, 조각하다
If you carve writing or a design on an object, you cut it into the surface of the object.

**figure**<sup>복습</sup>
[fígjər]

v. (…일 거라고) 생각[판단]하다; 계산하다; n. 모습, 형태; 계산, 숫자
If you figure that something is the case, you think or guess that it is the case.

**bound**\*\*
[baund]

① v. 뛰어가다; 튀어 오르다; n. 튐, 반동 ② n. 경계, 범위
If a person or animal bounds in a particular direction, they move quickly with large steps or jumps.

**rock**\*\*
[rɑk]

① v. (앞뒤 · 좌우로 살살) 흔들다, 움직이다 ② n. 바위, 암석
When something rocks or when you rock it, it moves slowly and regularly backwards and forwards or from side to side.

**chest**<sup>복습</sup>
[tʃest]

n. 상자, 궤; 가슴, 흉곽
A chest is a large, heavy box used for storing things.

**cup**\*\*\*
[kʌp]

vt. (손 등을) 잔 모양으로 만들다, 손을 모아 쥐다; n. 컵, 잔
If you cup something in your hands, you make your hands into a curved dish-like shape and support it or hold it gently.

**breast**\*\*\*
[brest]

n. 가슴; (옷의) 가슴 부분
A woman's breasts are the two soft, round parts on her chest that can produce milk to feed a baby.

**thrive**\*
[θráiv]

vi. 무성해지다, 번영[번성]하다
If someone or something thrives, they do well and are successful, healthy, or strong.

**feeder**<sup>복습</sup>
[fí:dər]

n. (새 · 동물의) 먹이통
A feeder is a container that you fill with food for birds or animals.

**clump**<sup>복습</sup>
[klʌmp]

n. (촘촘히 붙어 자라는 나무 등의) 무리, 수풀
A clump of things such as trees or plants is a small group of them growing together.

**expose**<sup>복습</sup>
[ikspóuz]

vt. 노출시키다; 드러내다; 폭로하다 (exposed a. (필름 등이) 노출된)
To expose something that is usually hidden means to uncover it so that it can be seen.

**filter**<sup>복습</sup>
[fíltər]

v. 여과하다, 거르다; n. [사진 · 광학] 필터, 여광기; 여과 장치
If light or sound filters into a place, it comes in weakly or slowly, either through a partly covered opening, or from a long distance away.

**seclude**
[siklú:d]

v. 떼어놓다, 격리하다 (secluded a. (장소가) 한적한, 외딴)
If you seclude someone, you keep them away from contact with other people.

**horrible**<sup>복습</sup>
[hɔ́:rəbl]

a. 끔찍한, 소름 끼치게 싫은; 무서운
You can call something horrible when it causes you to feel great shock, fear, and disgust.

**pretend**<sup>복습</sup>
[prit– énd]

v. 가장하다, …인 체하다; a. 가짜의
If you pretend that something is the case, you act in a way that is intended to make people believe that it is the case, although in fact it is not.

**just in case**

idiom 만약을 위해서
If you do something just in case a particular thing happens, you do it because that thing might happen.

**rotten**<sup>복습</sup>
[rátn]

a. 형편없는, 끔찍한; 썩은, 부패한
If you describe someone as rotten, you are insulting them or criticizing them because you think that they are very unpleasant or unkind.

**deserve**<sup>**</sup>
[dizə́ːrv]

vt. (…을) 받을 만하다, 누릴 자격이 있다
If you say that a person or thing deserves something, you mean that they should have it or receive it because of their actions or qualities.

# chapter eight

1. Why was Meg sick of listening to Molly?
   A. Molly only talked about flowers.
   B. Molly was crying about not going back to school.
   C. Molly was complaining about how she looked.
   D. Molly was upset that Tierney started dating another girl.

2. Why did Molly go back to the hospital?
   A. Her legs were dark purple and swollen.
   B. Her nose started to bleed again.
   C. She fell over Meg's shoes.
   D. Her legs had dark red spots.

3. Why did Molly say, "I hate you!" to Meg?
   A. Meg told Molly about Tierney dating another girl.
   B. Meg accidentally stepped on Molly's flower book.
   C. Meg told her parents that there was something wrong with Molly.
   D. Meg told Molly that Ben and Maria had a special place to bury the baby.

4. Molly didn't want _____.
   A. to stay at home
   B. Maria to have the baby before she got home
   C. Meg to show her picture to Ben and Maria
   D. to speak to Meg again

5. Will and Ben liked _____.
   A. the shadows in photographs
   B. the expressions on people's faces
   C. fixing Will's old truck
   D. the technical aspects of photography

6. Ben and Maria wanted _____.
   A. Meg to photograph the birth
   B. Will to deliver the baby
   C. Molly to be in the room when Maria was having the baby
   D. Meg to help deliver the baby

7. What did Meg think when she and her parents danced and wept?
   A. Ben and Maria's baby was going to die.
   B. Molly would come home from the hospital soon.
   C. Will was very sick.
   D. Molly was going to die.

*Check Your Reading Speed*

1분에 몇 단어를 읽는지 리딩 속도를 측정해보세요.

$$\frac{2,654 \text{ words}}{\text{reading time ( ) sec}} \times 60 = (\quad) \text{ WPM}$$

*Build Your Vocabulary*

**regret**[**]
[rigrét]

vt. 후회하다
You can say that you regret something as a polite way of saying that you are sorry about it.

**nerve**[복습]
[nəːrv]

n. 용기; 뻔뻔스러움, 무례; 신경, 신경과민
If you refer to someone's nerves, you mean their ability to cope with problems such as stress, worry, and danger.

**apologize**[복습]
[əpálədʒàiz]

v. 사과하다, 사죄하다
When you apologize to someone, you say that you are sorry that you have hurt them or caused trouble for them.

**blow it**

phrasal v. (구어) 실수하다
If you blow it, you make a mistake which wastes the chance or causes the attempt to fail.

**lying**[복습]
[láiiŋ]

v. LIE(눕다, 누워있다)의 현재분사(ing) 형태; a. 드러누워 있는
lie는 현재분사가 되면서 –ie가 –y로 변한다는 것과, '눕다, 누워있다'와 '거짓말하다'라는 두 가지 의미의 스펠링이 동일하다는 점에 유의하자.

**nightgown**[복습]
[náitgàun]

n. (여자 · 어린이용) 잠옷
A nightgown is a sort of loose dress that a woman or girl wears in bed.

**darn**[복습]
[dɑːrn]

① n. (구어, 완곡한 말) damn(제기랄) ② vt. (구멍을) 꿰매다; n. 꿰매기
People sometimes use darn or darned to emphasize what they are saying, often when they are annoyed.

**to begin with**

idiom 처음에는, 우선, 먼저
People use 'to begin with' to introduce the first point they want to make.

**grouchy**[복습]
[gráutʃi]

a. 불평이 많은, 잘 투덜거리는
If someone is grouchy, they are very bad-tempered and complain a lot.

**senior**[**]
[síːnjər]

n. 마지막 학년[졸업반] 학생; a. (계급 · 지위가) 고위의
Seniors are students in a high school, university, or college who are the oldest and who have reached an advanced level in their studies.

**grumble**[**]
[grʌmbl]

v. 투덜거리다, 불평하다; n. 투덜댐, 불평
If someone grumbles, they complain about something in a bad-tempered way.

104

**be sick of . . .** <sup>복습</sup>

idiom …에 넌더리[신물이] 나다
If you say that you are sick of something or sick and tired of it, you are emphasizing that you are very annoyed by it and want it to stop.

**mess** <sup>복습</sup>
[més]

n. 엉망진창인 상태; (개 · 고양이의) 똥; v. 망쳐놓다, 방해하다
If you say that something is a mess or in a mess, you think that it is in an untidy state.

**billion** <sup>*</sup>
[bíljən]

n. 막대한 수, 엄청난 양; 10억
If you talk about billions of things, you mean that there is a very large number of them but you do not know or do not want to say exactly how many.

**drop dead**

idiom (명령문으로 써서) 꺼져 버려
People say 'drop dead' as a rude way of telling someone to go away.

**sneaker**
[sní:kər]

n. (pl.) 운동화; 살금살금 하는 사람
Sneakers are casual shoes with rubber soles.

**swing** <sup>***</sup>
[swíŋ]

v. (swung–swung) 휙 돌(리)다, 회전시키다; n. 그네; 흔들림
If something swings in a particular direction or if you swing it in that direction, it moves in that direction with a smooth, curving movement.

**criticize** <sup>**</sup>
[krítəsàiz]

v. 비평하다, 비난하다
If you criticize someone or something, you express your disapproval of them by saying what you think is wrong with them.

**spot** <sup>*</sup>
[spɑt]

n. 반점, 얼룩; 장소, 지점; vt. 발견[분별]하다; 더럽히다
Spots on a person's skin are small lumps or marks.

**mosquito** <sup>**</sup>
[məskí:tou]

n. 모기
Mosquitos are small flying insects which bite people and animals in order to suck their blood.

**bite** <sup>복습</sup>
[bait]

n. 물린 상처; 한 입, 물기; v. 물다, 물어뜯다
A bite is an injury or a mark on your body where an animal, snake, or small insect has bitten you.

**swollen** <sup>**</sup>
[swóulən]

a. (몸의 일부가) 부어오른
If a part of your body is swollen, it is larger and rounder than normal, usually as a result of injury or illness.

**puzzle** <sup>복습</sup>
[pʌ́zl]

v. 어리둥절하게[이해할 수 없게] 만들다; n. 수수께끼, 어려운 문제
(puzzled a. 어리둥절해하는, 얼떨떨한)
If something puzzles you, you do not understand it and feel confused.

**weird** <sup>*</sup>
[wiə:rd]

a. 이상한, 기묘한; 수상한
If you describe something or someone as weird, you mean that they are strange.

**dare** <sup>복습</sup>
[déər]

v. 감히 …하다; 무릅쓰다; 도전하다
If you say to someone 'don't you dare (do something)', you are telling them not to do it and letting them know that you are angry.

**frighten** 복습
[fráitn]

v. 놀라게 하다, 섬뜩하게 하다; 기겁하다 (frightened a. 겁먹은, 무서워하는)
If something or someone frightens you, they cause you to suddenly feel afraid, anxious, or nervous.

**yell**\*\*
[jél]

v. 소리치다, 고함치다; n. 고함소리, 부르짖음
If you yell, you shout loudly, usually because you are excited, angry, or in pain.

**drawn**\*\*\*
[drɔ́:n]

a. (사람이나 얼굴이) 핼쑥한
If someone or their face looks drawn, their face is thin and they look very tired, ill, worried, or unhappy.

**abrupt**\*
[əbrʌ́pt]

a. 돌연한, 갑작스런 (abruptly ad. 갑작스럽게)
An abrupt change or action is very sudden, often in a way which is unpleasant.

**bathrobe**
[bǽθròub]

n. 목욕용 가운
A bathrobe is a loose piece of clothing made of the same material as towels.

**sob**\*\*
[sɑ(ɔ)b]

v. 흐느껴 울다; n. 흐느낌, 오열
When someone sobs, they cry in a noisy way, breathing in short breaths.

**screen door**
[skrí:n dɔ́:r]

n. 망(網)을 친 덧문, 망으로 된 문
A screen door is a door made of fine netting which is on the outside of the main door of a house, which is used to keep insects out when the main door is open.

**bang**\*\*
[bæŋ]

v. 탕 치다, 부딪치다, 쾅 닫(히)다; n. 쾅하는 소리
If something bangs, it makes a sudden loud noise, once or several times.

**huddle**\*
[hʌ́dl]

v. 몸을 움츠리다; (떼 지어) 몰리다; n. 군중, 무리
If you huddle somewhere, you sit, stand, or lie there holding your arms and legs close to your body, usually because you are cold or frightened.

**rub** 복습
[rʌ́b]

v. 문지르다, 비비다; 스치다; n. 문지르기
If you rub a part of your body, you move your hand or fingers backwards and forwards over it while pressing firmly.

**choke** 복습
[tʃouk]

v. 숨이 막히다; 질식시키다; n. 질식
When you choke or when something chokes you, you cannot breathe properly or get enough air into your lungs.

**make bed**

idiom (자고 나서) 잠자리를 정돈하다, 이불을 개다; 잠자리를 깔다
When you make the bed, you neatly arrange the sheets and covers of a bed so that it is ready to sleep in.

**chalk** 복습
[tʃɔ́:k]

n. 분필, 초크
Chalk is small white sticks used for writing or drawing with.

**entire** 복습
[intàiər]

a. 전체의; 완전한
You use entire when you want to emphasize that you are referring to the whole of something, for example, the whole of a place, time, or population.

**crop**\*\*\*
[krɔp]

n. 수확, 농작물, 곡물
Crops are plants such as wheat and potatoes that are grown in large quantities for food.

**pea**<sup>복습</sup>
[pi:]

n. 완두(콩)
Peas are round green seeds which grow in long thin cases and are eaten as a vegetable.

**greet**\*\*\*
[gri:t]

vt. …에게 인사하다; 환영하다
When you greet someone, you say 'Hello' or shake hands with them.

**feed**\*\*\*
[fi:d]

vt. (fed–fed) 먹이를 주다, 먹이다; 공급하다
If you feed a person or animal, you give them food to eat and sometimes actually put it in their mouths.

**tender**\*\*\*
[téndər]

a. (tenderer–tenderset) (음식이) 연한, 부드러운; 상냥한, 다정한, 애정 어린
Meat or other food that is tender is easy to cut or chew.

**dumb**<sup>복습</sup>
[dʌm]

a. 멍청한, 바보 같은; 벙어리의, 말을 못 하는
If you call a person dumb, you mean that they are stupid or foolish.

**rock**<sup>복습</sup>
[rɑk]

① v. (앞뒤 · 좌우로 살살) 흔들다, 움직이다 ② n. 바위, 암석
When something rocks or when you rock it, it moves slowly and regularly backwards and forwards or from side to side.

**collar**\*\*
[kálər]

n. (윗옷의) 칼라, 깃
The collar of a shirt or coat is the part which fits round the neck and is usually folded over.

**over and over**

idiom 몇 번이고, 반복해서
If you do something over and over, you do it repeatedly and many times.

**handkerchief**<sup>복습</sup>
[hǽŋkərtʃif]

n. 손수건
A handkerchief is a small square piece of fabric which you use for blowing your nose.

**blame**<sup>복습</sup>
[bleim]

vt. …의 탓으로 돌리다; 비난하다, 나무라다
If you blame a person or thing for something bad, you believe or say that they are responsible for it or that they caused it.

**make sense**

idiom 타당하다, 말이 되다; (표현 · 행동 등이) 이해할 수 있다
If a course of action makes sense, it seems sensible.

**wipe**<sup>복습</sup>
[waip]

vt. 닦다, 닦아 내다; n. 닦음, 닦아 냄
If you wipe something, you rub its surface to remove dirt or liquid from it.

**amaze**<sup>복습</sup>
[əméiz]

vt. 깜짝 놀라게 하다 (amazement n. 놀람)
If something amazes you, it surprises you very much.

**giggle**<sup>복습</sup>
[gígl]

v. 낄낄 웃다; n. 낄낄 웃음
If someone giggles, they laugh in a childlike way, because they are amused, nervous, or embarrassed.

**exhaust**[복습]
[igzɔ́ːst]

vt. 기진맥진하게 만들다; (연구 · 과제 등을) 철저히 규명하다
(exhausted a. 지칠 대로 지친)
If something exhausts you, it makes you so tired, either physically or mentally, that you have no energy left.

**fascinate**[복습]
[fǽsineit]

v. 매혹하다, 황홀케 하다 (fascinated a. 매혹[매료] 된, 마음을 빼앗긴)
If something fascinates you, it interests and delights you so much that your thoughts tend to concentrate on it.

**technical**[복습]
[téknikəl]

a. 기술적인, 전문의
You use technical to describe the practical skills and methods used to do an activity such as an art, a craft, or a sport.

**aspect**＊＊
[ǽspekt]

n. 측면, 양상
An aspect of something is one of the parts of its character or nature.

**contrast**[복습]
[kɑ́(ɔ́)ntrækt]

n. 콘트라스트(사진 · 그림에서 특수 효과를 위해 색이나 명암 차를 이용하는 것); 대조, 대비
Contrast is the degree of difference between the darker and lighter parts of a photograph, television picture, or painting.

**exposure**＊＊
[ikspóuʒər]

n. [사진] 노출 (시간), 노출량; 드러내 놓음, 폭로
In photography, the exposure is the amount of light that is allowed to enter a camera when taking a photograph.

**serene**＊＊
[siríːn]

a. 평온한, 조용한; 고요한, 잔잔한
Someone or something that is serene is calm and quiet.

**floor**＊＊＊
[flɔːr]

v. 어안이 벙벙하게 만들다; n. (방의) 바닥 (floored a. 당황해서 말문이 막힌)
If you are floored by something, you are unable to respond to it because you are so surprised by it.

**golly**
[gɑ́li]

int. 저런, 어머나, 아이고 (놀람 · 감탄)
Some people say golly to indicate that they are very surprised by something.

**occur**[복습]
[əkə́ːr]

vi. 생각이 떠오르다; 일어나다, 생기다
If a thought or idea occurs to you, you suddenly think of it or realize it.

**intrude**＊
[intrúːd]

v. 침범하다, 방해하다, 마음대로 가다
If something intrudes on your mood or your life, it disturbs it or has an unwanted effect on it.

**intrusion**＊
[intrúːʒən]

n. 침범, 침입, 방해
If someone disturbs you when you are in a private place or having a private conversation, you can call this event an intrusion.

**sterile**＊
[stéri]

a. 살균한, 무균의; 불임의, 생산 못하는
Something that is sterile is completely clean and free from germs.

**desperate**＊＊
[déspərit]

a. 간절히 원하는, 필사적인; 절망적인, 자포자기의
(desperately ad. 몹시; 필사적으로)
If you are desperate for something or desperate to do something, you want or need it very much indeed.

**in advance**

idiom (…보다) 미리, 앞서, 사전에
If one thing happens or is done in advance of another, it happens or is done before the other thing.

**cup**<sup>복습</sup>
[kʌp]

vt. (손 등을) 잔 모양으로 만들다, 손을 모아 쥐다; n. 컵, 잔
If you cup something in your hands, you make your hands into a curved dish-like shape and support it or hold it gently.

**megaphone**\*
[mégəfòun]

n. 확성기, 메가폰
A megaphone is a cone-shaped device for making your voice sound louder in the open air.

**instruction**\*\*
[instrʌ́kʃən]

n. (무엇을 하거나 사용하는 데 필요한 자세한) 설명, 지시
An instruction is something that someone tells you to do.

**determined**<sup>복습</sup>
[ditə́:rmind]

a. 굳게 결심한, 결연한
If you are determined to do something, you have made a firm decision to do it and will not let anything stop you.

**obedient**\*\*
[oubí:diənt]

a. 말을 잘 듣는, 순종적인, 복종하는
A person or animal who is obedient does what they are told to do.

**squeeze**<sup>복습</sup>
[skwí:z]

vt. 짜내다, 꽉 쥐다, 압착하다; n. 압착, 짜냄; 꽉 끌어안음
If you squeeze something, you press it firmly, usually with your hands.

**anticipate**\*\*
[æntísipeit]

v. 예상하다, 예측하다
If you anticipate an event, you realize in advance that it may happen and you are prepared for it.

**hang in there**

idiom (역경에도) 굴하지 않다, 꿋꿋이 버티다
If you tell someone to hang in there or to hang on in there, you are encouraging them to keep trying to do something and not to give up even though it might be difficult.

**dislodge**
[dislʌ́dʒ]

v. (억지로 치거나 해서) 제자리를 벗어나게 만들다, 몰아내다
To dislodge something means to remove it from where it was fixed or held.

**toe**<sup>복습</sup>
[tóu]

n. 발가락
Your toes are the five movable parts at the end of each foot.

**sheepish**<sup>복습</sup>
[ʃí:piʃ]

a. 매우 수줍어하는; 양 같은
If you look sheepish, you look slightly embarrassed because you feel foolish or you have done something silly.

**replace**\*\*
[ripléis]

v. 바꾸다, 교체하다; 대신하다, 대체하다
If one thing or person replaces another, the first is used or acts instead of the second.

**bloom**<sup>복습</sup>
[blu:m]

v. 꽃이 피다, 개화하다; 번영시키다; n. 꽃, 개화
(in bloom idiom 꽃이 활짝 핀)
When a plant or tree blooms, it produces flowers. When a flower blooms, it opens.

**grumpy**
[grʌ́mpi]

a. 성격이 나쁜 (grumpily ad. 까다롭게, 언짢게)
If you say that someone is grumpy, you mean that they are bad-tempered and miserable.

**grieve**[*] [gri:v]
v. 비통해 하다, 몹시 슬퍼[슬프게]하다
If you grieve over something, especially someone's death, you feel very sad about it.

**unleave(unleaf)** [ʌnlíːv]
v. 잎이 떨어지다
un (부정·반대의 접두어) + leaf (나뭇잎, 잎이 나다) = 잎이 지다

**poem**[복습] [póuəm]
n. (한 편의) 시; 운문, 시적인 문장
A poem is a piece of writing in which the words are chosen for their beauty and sound and are carefully arranged, often in short lines which rhyme.

**blight**[*] [bláit]
n. 어두운 그림자, 희망을 꺾는 것, 장애; vt. 망치다, 엉망으로 만들다
You can refer to something as a blight when it causes great difficulties, and damages or spoils other things.

**mourn**[**] [mɔːrn]
v. 슬퍼하다, 한탄하다
If you mourn someone who has died or mourn for them, you are very sad that they have died and show your sorrow in the way that you behave.

**arrogant**[*] [ǽrəgənt]
a. 거만한, 오만한 (arrogantly ad. 거만하게)
Someone who is arrogant behaves in a proud, unpleasant way towards other people because they believe that they are more important than others.

**deliver a baby**[복습]
idiom (산파·간호사·의사가) 아기를 받아내다, 아이를 낳다
If you deliver a baby, you help take a baby out of its mother when it is being born.

**preoccupied**[복습] [priːɑ́kjupàid]
a. (어떤 생각·걱정에) 사로잡힌, 정신이 팔린
If you are preoccupied, you are thinking a lot about something or someone, and so you hardly notice other things.

**pipe**[복습] [paip]
n. 담배 파이프; (액체·기체가 흐르는) 관, 파이프
A pipe is an object which is used for smoking tobacco.

**sew**[복습] [sóu]
v. 바느질하다, 꿰매다, 깁다
When you sew something such as clothes, you make them or repair them by joining pieces of cloth together by passing thread through them with a needle.

**hang around**[복습]
idiom 시간을 보내다
If you hang around, you stay in the same place doing nothing, usually because you are waiting for something or someone.

**make up for**[복습]
idiom 뒤진 것을 만회하다, 벌충하다
To make up for something means to do something good for someone because you have treated them badly or because they have done something good for you.

**consume**[**] [kənsúːm]
v. 사로잡다; 소비하다, 소모하다
If a feeling or idea consumes you, it affects you very strongly indeed.

**break up**[복습]
idiom 웃음을 터뜨리다; 부서지다, 끝이 나다
If something breaks someone up, it causes them to lose control and begin to laugh or cry.

**uninhibited**
[ʌninhíbitid]

**a.** (행동 · 의사 표현 등에) 아무 제약을 받지 않는, 거리낌이 없는
If you describe a person or their behavior as uninhibited, you mean that they express their opinions and feelings openly, and behave as they want to, without worrying what other people think.

**sweat**<sup>복습</sup>
[swét]

**v.** 땀 흘리다; **n.** 땀
When you sweat, drops of liquid comes through your skin.

**sigh**<sup>복습</sup>
[sái]

**n.** 한숨, 탄식; **v.** 한숨 쉬다
When you sigh, you let out a deep breath, as a way of expressing feelings such as disappointment, tiredness, or pleasure.

**relief**\*\*\*
[rilí:f]

**n.** 안심, 안도
If you feel a sense of relief, you feel happy because something unpleasant has not happened or is no longer happening.

**tempo**
[témpou]

**n.** 박자, 템포
The tempo of a piece of music is the speed at which it is played.

**hold out**

**phrasal v.** (손 혹은 손에 든 것을) 내밀다, 내뻗다
If you hold out your hand, you move your hand away from your body, for example to shake hands.

**curl up**<sup>복습</sup>

**phrasal v.** (눕거나 앉아서) 몸을 웅크리다
If you curl up, your body forms a curved or round shape.

**waltz**\*
[wɔ:lts]

**v.** 왈츠를 추다; **n.** 왈츠(춤 또는 그 춤곡)
If you waltz with someone, you dance a waltz with them.

**bewilder**\*\*
[biwíldər]

**vt.** 당황하게 하다, 어리둥절하게 하다 (bewilderment **n.** 당황, 어리둥절함)
If something bewilders you, it is so confusing or difficult that you cannot understand it.

**melancholy**\*\*
[mélənkəli]

**a.** 우울한, 슬픈; **n.** 우울, 울적함
You describe something that you see or hear as melancholy when it gives you an intense feeling of sadness.

**blur**<sup>복습</sup>
[blə:r]

**n.** 흐릿한 형체; **v.** 흐릿해지다, 흐릿하게 만들다
A blur is a shape or area which you cannot see clearly because it has no distinct outline or because it is moving very fast.

**enclosure**\*
[enklóuʒər]

**n.** 둘러쌈, 울타리를 친 장소; (편지에) 동봉된 것
An enclosure is an area of land that is surrounded by a wall or fence and that is used for a particular purpose.

**weep**\*\*
[wi:p]

**v.** (wept–wept) 눈물을 흘리다, 울다; 물기를 내뿜다
If someone weeps, they cry.

## chapter nine

1. What was Meg's darker dream about?
   A. Meg couldn't catch up with Molly as they ran.
   B. Molly was stumbling and couldn't catch up to Meg.
   C. Meg saw a baby speak.
   D. Meg was alone in her bedroom but she could hear Molly breathing.

2. What did Meg's dream mean?
   A. Molly would survive.
   B. Meg and Molly would be separated.
   C. Meg wished that she could be like Molly.
   D. Meg's parents lied to her.

3. Why was there no chance for Molly?
   A. Molly refused to take the medicine.
   B. The doctors didn't know what was wrong with Molly.
   C. The medicine Molly took didn't work.
   D. Molly had already died.

4. Why was Meg grateful that her parents didn't bring her to the hospital?
   A. She was afraid to see Molly.
   B. She was too young to go into the hospital.
   C. She didn't want to miss Maria's birth.
   D. She wanted to spend time taking pictures with Will.

5. What did Mom do at home?

    A. She played board games with Meg.

    B. She read a book every night.

    C. She stitched the quilt.

    D. She made large dinners every night.

6. When Meg was a baby, she _____.

    A. looked for things to laugh at

    B. cried and laughed at the same time

    C. cried about everything

    D. was serious and solemn

7. Why was it hard to be like Molly or Mom?

    A. They took life too seriously and didn't laugh a lot.

    B. Times were harder for them when they couldn't laugh.

    C. They weren't successful because they didn't take life seriously.

    D. Times were harder for them when they had to shrug things off.

*Check Your Reading Speed*

1분에 몇 단어를 읽는지 리딩 속도를 측정해보세요.

$$\frac{1{,}463 \text{ words}}{\text{reading time ( ) sec}} \times 60 = ( \quad ) \text{ WPM}$$

*Build Your Vocabulary*

**tan** 복습
[tæn]

a. 황갈색의; n. 햇볕에 그을음; vt. (피부를) 햇볕에 태우다
Something that is tan is a light brown color.

**bare** 복습
[bέər]

a. 발가벗은, 살을 드러낸; 있는 그대로의
If a part of your body is bare, it is not covered by any clothing.

**hold out** 복습
phrasal v. (손 혹은 손에 든 것을) 내밀다, 내뻗다
If you hold out your hand, you move your hand away from your body, for example to shake hands.

**streak** 복습
[striːk]

v. 질주하다; 줄을 긋다; n. 줄 모양의 것; 기미, 경향
If something or someone streaks somewhere, they move there very quickly.

**catch up** 복습
phrasal v. 따라잡다, 따라붙다; 뒤지지 않다
If you catch up with someone who is in front of you, you reach them by walking faster than they are walking.

**misty***
[místi]

a. (엷은) 안개가 낀, 부연, 흐릿한
On a misty day, there is a lot of mist in the air.

**destination****
[dèstənéiʃən]

n. 목적지, 행산지; 목적
The destination of someone or something is the place to which they are going or being sent.

**stumble****
[stʌmbl]

v. 발이 걸리다, 발을 헛디디다
If you stumble, you put your foot down awkwardly while you are walking or running and nearly fall over.

**nightmare** 복습
[náitmɛər]

n. 악몽
A nightmare is a very frightening dream.

**aged****
[éidʒid]

a. 늙은, 고령의, 연로한
Aged means very old.

**shrug** 복습
[ʃrʌg]

v. (양 손바닥을 내보이면서 어깨를) 으쓱하다; n. (어깨를) 으쓱하기
If you shrug, you raise your shoulders to show that you are not interested in something or that you do not know or care about something.

**plead****
[pliːd]

v. 간청하다, 탄원하다; 변론하다, 변호하다
If you plead with someone to do something, you ask them in an intense, emotional way to do it.

114

**terrify** 복습
[térəfài]

vt. 무섭게[겁나게] 하다, 놀래다 (terrified a. 무서워하는, 겁먹은)
If something terrifies you, it makes you feel extremely frightened.

**fuzz**
[fʌz]

n. 솜털, 잔털; v. 보풀이 나다[나게 하다]
Fuzz is a mass of short, curly hairs.

**breeze**\*\*
[briːz]

n. 산들바람, 미풍; vi. 산들산들 불다
A breeze is a gentle wind.

**separate**\*\*\*
[sépəreit]

v. (사람을) 떼어놓다; 가르다, 분리하다 (separated a. 헤어진; 분리된)
If you separate people or things that are together, or if they separate, they move apart.

**crush**\*\*
[krʌʃ]

v. 뭉개다, 짓밟다; 부서지다; (정신·희망을) 꺾다; n. 눌러 터뜨림
To crush something means to press it very hard so that its shape is destroyed or so that it breaks into pieces.

**stem** 복습
[stem]

n. 줄기, 대
The stem of a plant is the thin, upright part on which the flowers and leaves grow.

**blame** 복습
[bleim]

vt. …의 탓으로 돌리다; 비난하다, 나무라다
If you blame a person or thing for something bad, you believe or say that they are responsible for it or that they caused it.

**all along** 복습

idiom 처음부터, 내내, 계속
If something have been there all along, it is there from the very beginning.

**quote**\*\*
[kwout]

vt. 인용하다; n. 인용문, 따옴표
If you quote someone as saying something, you repeat what they have written or said.

**furious**\*\*
[fjúəriəs]

a. 격노한; 맹렬한, 왕성한
Someone who is furious is extremely angry.

**throw up** 복습

phrasal v. 토하다
When someone throws up, they vomit.

**kindergarten** 복습
[kíndərgàːrtn]

n. 유치원
A kindergarten is an informal kind of school for very young children, where they learn things by playing.

**grocery** 복습
[gróusəri]

n. 식료품 잡화점; 식료 잡화류
A grocery or a grocery store is a shop where foods such as flour, sugar, and tinned foods are sold.

**disease** 복습
[dizíːz]

n. 병, 질환
A disease is an illness which affects people, animals, or plants, for example one which is caused by bacteria or infection.

**horrible** 복습
[hɔ́ːrəbl]

a. 끔찍한, 소름 끼치게 싫은; 무서운
You can call something horrible when it causes you to feel great shock, fear, and disgust.

**rotten** 복습
[rɑ́tn]

a. 형편없는, 끔찍한; 썩은, 부패한
You use rotten to emphasize your dislike for something or your anger or annoyance about it.

**enemy** <sup>복습</sup>
[énəmi]

n. 적, 경쟁 상대
If someone is your enemy, they hate you or want to harm you.

**confront** <sup>복습</sup>
[kənfrÁnt]

vt. 직면하다, 마주 대하다; 대조하다
If you confront a difficult situation or issue, you accept the fact that it exists and try to deal with it.

**bitter** <sup>복습</sup>
[bítər]

a. 쓰라린, 쓴, 신랄한; 지독한, 매서운 (bitterly ad. 비통하게, 씁쓸히)
If someone is bitter after a disappointing experience or after being treated unfairly, they continue to feel angry about it.

**muffle** *
[mÁfl]

vt. (소리를) 억제하다, 지우다; 덮다, 목도리로 감싸다
If something muffles a sound, it makes it quieter and more difficult to hear.

**break one's heart**

idiom 비탄에 잠기(게 하)다, (실연 따위로) 몹시 실망시키다
If an event or situation breaks your heart, it makes you feel very sad.

**scare** <sup>복습</sup>
[skɛə:r]

v. 겁주다, 놀라게 하다 (scared a. 무서워하는, 겁먹은)
If something scares you, it frightens or worries you.

**grateful** **
[gréitfəl]

a. 고맙게 여기는, 감사하는
If you are grateful for something that someone has given you or done for you, you have warm, friendly feelings towards them and wish to thank them.

**square** <sup>복습</sup>
[skwɛə:r]

n. 정사각형; 광장 a. 정사각형의; 공명정대한
A square is a shape with four sides that are all the same length and four corners that are all right angles.

**pale** <sup>복습</sup>
[péil]

a. (색깔이) 엷은; 창백한, 핼쑥한; v. 창백해지다
If something is pale, it is very light in color or almost white.

**overall** *
[óuvərɔ̀:l]

n. (pl.) 멜빵바지; 작업용 바지, 작업복; a. 전부의, 전체에 걸친
Overalls are trousers that are attached to a piece of cloth which covers your chest and which has straps going over your shoulders.

**fall down on one's bottom**

idiom 엉덩방아를 찧다
여기서 bottom이 단순히 '바닥, 아래 부분'이라는 의미가 아닌 '엉덩이'라는 의미로 쓰였음에 유의하자.

**on purpose**

idiom 일부러, 고의로
If you do something on purpose, you do it intentionally.

**flowered** <sup>복습</sup>
[fláuərd]

a. 꽃으로 덮인, 꽃무늬로 장식한
Flowered paper or cloth has a pattern of flowers on it.

**impatient** <sup>복습</sup>
[impéiʃənt]

a. 성급한, 조급한, 참을성 없는
If you are impatient, you are easily irritated by things.

**solemn** <sup>복습</sup>
[sá(ɔ́)ləm]

a. 엄숙한, 근엄한
Someone or something that is solemn is very serious rather than cheerful or humorous.

**forehead** <sup>복습</sup>
[fɔ́:rhèd]

n. 이마
Your forehead is the area at the front of your head between your eyebrows and your hair.

116

**figure out** <sup>복습</sup>

phrasal v. …을 생각해내다, 발견하다
If you figure out a solution to a problem or the reason for something, you succeed in solving it or understanding it.

**smooth** <sup>복습</sup>
[smúːð]

v. 매끄럽게 하다; a. 매끄러운; 유창한
If you smooth something, you move your hands over its surface to make it smooth and flat.

**accustom** <sup>**</sup>
[əkʌ́stəm]

vt. 익숙케 하다, 습관을 붙이다 (accustomed a. 익숙한)
If you accustom yourself or another person to something, you make yourself or them become used to it.

**solution** <sup>복습</sup>
[səlúːʃən]

n. 해답, 해결; 용해, 용액
A solution to a problem or difficult situation is a way of dealing with it so that the difficulty is removed.

**helpless** <sup>*</sup>
[hélplis]

a. 무력한, 속수무책의 (helplessness n. 무력감)
If you are helpless, you do not have the strength or power to do anything useful or to control or protect yourself.

**faceless**
[féislis]

a. 얼굴 없는, 정체불명의
If you describe someone or something as faceless, you dislike them because they are uninteresting and have no character.

**prowler**
[práulər]

n. 범행 대상을 찾아[따라] 다니는 자
A prowler is someone who secretly follows people or hides near their houses, especially at night, in order to steal something, frighten them, or perhaps harm them.

**uncertain** <sup>복습</sup>
[ʌnsə́ːrtn]

a. 확신이 없는, 잘 모르는; 불확실한, 불안정한 (uncertainly ad. 확신 없이, 자신 없게)
If you are uncertain about something, you do not know what you should do, what is going to happen, or what the truth is about something.

## chapter ten

1. During the birth, Ben felt in control when _____.
   A. Meg came into the house
   B. he saw the head of the baby
   C. he picked up the stethoscope
   D. Meg picked up her camera

2. What wasn't true as Meg sat in the rocking chair?
   A. The birds were singing.
   B. The baby was crying.
   C. The sun was rising.
   D. Meg was rocking the chair back and forth.

3. How did Ben decide on the baby's name?
   A. Meg said the baby was happy.
   B. He was named after Ben's father.
   C. He was named after Molly's personality.
   D. Ben dreamt of the perfect name.

4. Why did Meg suddenly want to see Molly?
   A. Her dad said that Molly would die.
   B. She wanted to tell Molly about the baby.
   C. She wanted to see what Molly looked like at the hospital.
   D. She wanted to show Molly the pictures of the baby.

5. How did Meg think of Molly?

    A. She thought about how beautiful Molly was.

    B. She thought about how Molly laughed.

    C. She thought about how they fought.

    D. She thought about how Molly made her angry.

6. Dad said that Molly _____.

    A. was in pain

    B. was scared.

    C. couldn't hear or see anymore

    D. was still the same person

7. What did Mom and Dad give Meg back?

    A. Molly's blanket

    B. A new camera

    C. A photograph of Molly

    D. Molly's pussy willows

1분에 몇 단어를 읽는지 리딩 속도를 측정해보세요.

$$\frac{3,036 \text{ words}}{\text{reading time (} \quad \text{) sec}} \times 60 = (\quad) \text{ WPM}$$

*Build Your Vocabulary*

**take turns**

idiom 교대로 하다
If two or more people take turns to do something, they do it one after the other several times, rather than doing it together.

**throw on**

phrasal v. (옷 등을 급히) 걸치다
If you throw on a piece of clothing, you put it on quickly and carelessly.

**sneaker**<sup>복습</sup>
[sníːkər]

n. (pl.) 운동화; 살금살금 하는 사람
Sneakers are casual shoes with rubber soles.

**grab**<sup>복습</sup>
[græb]

v. 잡아채다, 움켜쥐다, 부여잡다; n. 부여잡기
If you grab something, you take it or pick it up suddenly and roughly.

**obey**\*\*\*
[oubéi]

v. … 에 따르다, …에 복종하다
If you obey a person, a command, or an instruction, you do what you are told to do.

**instruction**<sup>복습</sup>
[instrʌ́kʃən]

n. (무엇을 하거나 사용하는 데 필요한 자세한) 설명, 지시
An instruction is something that someone tells you to do.

**elect**<sup>복습</sup>
[ilékt]

vt. 선택하다; (선거로) 선출하다
If you elect to do something, you choose to do it.

**obedient**<sup>복습</sup>
[oubíːdiənt]

a. 말을 잘 듣는, 순종적인, 복종하는
A person or animal who is obedient does what they are told to do.

**sterile**<sup>복습</sup>
[stéri]

a. 살균한, 무균의; 불임의; 생산 못하는
Something that is sterile is completely clean and free from germs.

**sterilize**
[stérəlàiz]

vt. 살균하다, 소독하다
If you sterilize a thing or a place, you make it completely clean and free from germs.

**wrinkle**<sup>복습</sup>
[ríŋkl]

v. 구겨지다, …에 주름살지게 하다; n. 주름, 잔주름 (wrinkled a. 주름이 있는)
If cloth wrinkles, or if someone or something wrinkles it, it gets folds or lines in it.

**apologetic**\*
[əpɑ̀lədʒétik]

a. 미안해하는, 사죄의
If you are apologetic, you show or say that you are sorry for causing trouble for someone, for hurting them, or for disappointing them.

**labor**<sup>복습</sup>
[léibər]

n. 분만, 진통; 노동, 근로, 노력; v. 일하다, 노동하다
Labor is the last stage of pregnancy, in which the baby is gradually pushed out of the womb by the mother.

**hang around** 복습

idiom 시간을 보내다

If you hang around, you stay in the same place doing nothing, usually because you are waiting for something or someone.

**stoplight**
[stáplàit]

n. (교통의) 정지 신호, 빨간불; (자동차 꽁무니의) 정지등

A stoplight is a set of colored lights which controls the flow of traffic on a road.

**helpless** 복습
[hélplis]

a. 무력한, 속수무책의 (helplessness n. 무력감)

If you are helpless, you do not have the strength or power to do anything useful or to control or protect yourself.

**sympathize** **
[símpəθàiz]

vi. 동정하다, 측은히 여기다

If you sympathize with someone's feelings, you understand them and are not critical of them.

**panicky**
[pǽniki]

a. 전전긍긍하는, 공황 상태에 빠진

A panicky feeling or panicky behavior is characterized by a very strong feeling of anxiety or fear, which makes you act without thinking carefully.

**astonishing** *
[əstániʃiŋ]

a. 놀라운, 눈부신 (astonishingly ad. 놀랍게도; 놀랄 만큼, 몹시)

Something that is astonishing is very surprising.

**prop** *
[prɔp]

v. 받치다, 버티다; 기대 세우다; n. 지주, 버팀목

If you prop an object on or against something, you support it by putting something underneath it or by resting it somewhere.

**pillow** 복습
[pílou]

n. 베개

A pillow is a rectangular cushion which you rest your head on when you are in bed.

**naked** **
[néikid]

a. 벌거벗은, 아무것도 걸치지 않은

Someone who is naked is not wearing any clothes.

**bother** 복습
[báðər]

v. 귀찮게 하다, 괴롭히다, 폐 끼치다; 일부러 …하다, 애를 쓰다

If something bothers you, or if you bother about it, it worries, annoys, or upsets you.

**scare** 복습
[skɛə:r]

v. 겁주다, 놀라게 하다 (scared a. 무서워하는, 겁먹은)

If something scares you, it frightens or worries you.

**fall into place**

idiom 딱 맞아떨어지다, 제대로 들어맞다

If things fall into place, events happen naturally to produce a situation you want.

**manipulate** *
[mənípjəlèit]

vt. 조종하다, 조작하다, 교묘하게 다루다

If you manipulate something that requires skill, such as a complicated piece of equipment or a difficult idea, you operate it or process it.

**stethoscope**
[stéθəskòup]

n. 청진기

A stethoscope is an instrument that a doctor uses to listen to your heart and breathing.

**abdomen** *
[ǽbdəmən]

n. 배, 복부

Your abdomen is the part of your body below your chest where your stomach and intestines are.

**instrument**[**] [ínstrəmənt]

n. 기구, 도구; 악기
An instrument is a tool or device that is used to do a particular task, especially a scientific task.

**rapid**[**] [rǽpid]

a. 빠른, 신속한
A rapid movement is one that is very fast.

**lean**[복습] [líːn]

① v. 상체를 굽히다, 기울이다; 기대다, 의지하다 ② a. 야윈, 마른
When you lean in a particular direction, you bend your body in that direction.

**intent**[**] [intént]

① a. 집중된; 열심인, 여념이 없는 (intentness n. 집중됨, 열심임) ② n. 의지, 의향
If you are intent on doing something, you are eager and determined to do it.

**bend**[복습] [bend]

v. (bent-bent) 구부리다, 굽히다, 숙이다; n. 커브, 굽음
When you bend, you move the top part of your body downwards and forwards.

**arch**[**] [áːrtʃ]

v. (몸을) 동그랗게 구부리다, 아치 모양을 그리다; n. 아치
If you arch a part of your body such as your back or if it arches, you bend it so that it forms a curve.

**strain**[*] [strein]

n. 긴장, 팽팽함; v. 잡아당기다, 팽팽하게 하다; 힘껏 작용시키다, 긴장시키다
Strain is a state of worry and tension caused by a difficult situation.

**passage**[***] [pǽsidʒ]

n. (체내의) 관; 통로, 복도; (시간의) 흐름, 경과
A passage is a long narrow hole or tube in your body, which air or liquid can pass along.

**taut** [tɔːt]

a. 팽팽한, 긴장된
Something that is taut is stretched very tight.

**muscle**[**] [mʌsl]

n. 근육
A muscle is a piece of tissue inside your body which connects two bones and which you use when you make a movement.

**withdraw**[**] [wiðdrɔ́ː]

vt. 물러나다, 철회하다, 움츠리다
If you withdraw something from a place, you remove it or take it away.

**mitten**[복습] [mítn]

n. 벙어리장갑
Mittens are gloves which have one section that covers your thumb and another section that covers your four fingers together.

**fist**[**] [fist]

n. (쥔) 주먹
Your hand is referred to as your fist when you have bent your fingers in towards the palm in order to hit someone, to make an angry gesture, or to hold something.

**sleeve**[복습] [sliːv]

n. (옷의) 소맷자락
The sleeves of a coat, shirt, or other item of clothing are the parts that cover your arms.

**poise**[*] [pɔ́iz]

vt. (특정한) 태세를 취하다; n. 균형, 평형
If you poise, you hold something steady in a particular position, especially above something else.

122

**chin**\*\*
[tʃin]

n. 아래턱, 턱 끝
Your chin is the part of your face that is below your mouth and above your neck.

**gasp**\*\*
[gæsp]

v. 헐떡거리다, (놀람 따위로) 숨이 막히다; n. 헐떡거림
When you gasp, you take a short quick breath through your mouth, especially when you are surprised, shocked, or in pain.

**groan**<sup>복습</sup>
[gróun]

v. 신음하다, 끙끙거리다; n. 신음, 끙 하는 소리
If you groan, you make a long, low sound because you are in pain, or because you are upset or unhappy about something.

**take it easy**

idiom 진정해라; 쉬엄쉬엄 해라
When you are saying take it easy to someone, you suggest not to get angry, excited, etc.

**murmur**\*
[mə́:rmə:r]

v. 중얼거리다; 투덜거리다; n. 중얼거림; 사각사각하는 소리
If you murmur something, you say it very quietly, so that not many people can hear what you are saying.

**flat**<sup>복습</sup>
[flæt]

a. 평평한, 균일한, 고른; 바람이 빠진, 구멍 난
Something that is flat is level, smooth, or even, rather than sloping, curved, or uneven.

**hasty**<sup>복습</sup>
[héisti]

a. 급한, 성급한 (hastily ad. 급히, 허둥지둥)
If you describe a person or their behavior as hasty, you mean that they are acting too quickly, without thinking carefully.

**cartoon**\*
[kɑ:rtú:n]

n. 만화
A cartoon is a humorous drawing or series of drawings in a newspaper or magazine.

**slit**\*
[slit]

n. (좁고 기다란) 구멍, 틈; v. 길게 자르다, 구멍을 내다
A slit is a long narrow opening in something.

**swollen**<sup>복습</sup>
[swóulən]

a. (몸의 일부가) 부어오른
If a part of your body is swollen, it is larger and rounder than normal, usually as a result of injury or illness.

**squash**<sup>복습</sup>
[skwɑʃ]

① v. 눌러 찌그러뜨리다; 헤치고[밀치고] 들어가다; ② n. 호박
If someone or something is squashed, they are pressed or crushed with such force that they become injured or lose their shape.

**flatten**\*
[flǽtn]

vt. 평평하게 하다, 납작하게 하다
If you flatten something or if it flattens, it becomes flat or flatter.

**immobile**
[imóubəl]

a. 움직이지 않는, 움직일 수 없는
Someone or something that is immobile is completely still.

**clench**\*
[klentʃ]

v. (이를) 악물다; 단단히 움켜쥐다; n. 이를 악물기; 단단히 쥐기
When your muscle clenches, it squeezed firmly, usually when you are angry or upset.

**slide**<sup>복습</sup>
[sláid]

v. (slid-slidden) 미끄러지다, 미끄러지게 하다
If you slide somewhere, you move there smoothly and quietly.

**shutter**[복습]
[ʃʌtə:r]

n. (카메라의) 셔터; 덧문, 셔터
The shutter in a camera is the part which opens to allow light through the lens when a photograph is taken.

**exhaust**[복습]
[igzɔ́:st]

vt. 기진맥진하게 만들다; (연구 · 과제 등을) 철저히 규명하다
(exhausted a. 지칠 대로 지친!)
If something exhausts you, it makes you so tired, either physically or mentally, that you have no energy left.

**rub**[복습]
[rʌb]

v. 문지르다, 비비다; 스치다; n. 문지르기
If you rub a part of your body, you move your hand or fingers backwards and forwards over it while pressing firmly.

**grayish**
[gréiiʃ]

a. 회색이 도는, 희끄무레한
Grayish means slightly gray in color.

**incredible**[복습]
[inkrédəbl]

a. 믿을 수 없는, 믿기 힘든 (incredibly ad. 믿을 수 없을 정도로)
If you describe something or someone as incredible, you like them very much or are impressed by them, because they are extremely or unusually good.

**startle**[복습]
[stá:rtl]

v. 움찔하다; 깜짝 놀라게 하다; n. 깜짝 놀람
If something sudden and unexpected startles you, it surprises and frightens you slightly.

**wail**[복습]
[weil]

v. 울부짖다, 통곡하다, 흐느끼다; n. 울부짖음, 통곡
If someone wails, they make long, loud, high-pitched cries which express sorrow or pain.

**grin**[복습]
[grín]

v. 이를 드러내고 싱긋 웃다; n. 싱긋 웃음
When you grin, you smile broadly.

**squirm**
[skwə́:rm]

vi. (벌레처럼) 꿈틀거리다, 몸부림치다; 우물쭈물하다
If you squirm, you move your body from side to side, usually because you are nervous or uncomfortable.

**bluish**\*
[blú:iʃ]

a. 푸르스름한, 푸른빛을 띤
Something that is bluish is slightly blue in color.

**sponge**\*\*
[spʌ́ndʒ]

n. (목욕 · 청소 등에 쓰이는) 스펀지, 흡수물; v. (스펀지로 몸 등을) 닦다
Sponge is a very light soft substance with lots of little holes in it, which is used to clean things or as a soft layer.

**dip**\*\*
[díp]

v. 담그다, 적시다; 가라앉다, 내려가다
If you dip something in a liquid, you put it into the liquid for a short time, so that only part of it is covered, and take it out again.

**tongue**[복습]
[tʌ́ŋ]

n. 혀; 말, 말씨
Your tongue is the soft movable part inside your mouth which you use for tasting, eating, and speaking.

**blink**\*
[blíŋk]

v. 눈을 깜박거리다; (등불 · 별 등이) 깜박이다; n. (눈을) 깜박거림
When you blink or when you blink your eyes, you shut your eyes and very quickly open them again.

**squint**
[skwínt]

v. 곁눈질을 하다, 실눈으로 보다
If you squint at something, you look at it with your eyes partly closed.

124

**dew**[**] [dju:]

n. 이슬; v. 이슬로 적시다
Dew is small drops of water that form on the ground and other surfaces outdoors during the night.

**evaporate**[*] [ivǽpərèit]

v. 증발시키다; 사라지다
When a liquid evaporates, or is evaporated, it changes from a liquid state to a gas, because its temperature has increased.

**rocking chair**[복습] [rάkiŋ tʃέər]

n. 흔들의자
A rocking chair is a chair that is built on two curved pieces of wood so that you can rock yourself backwards and forwards when you are sitting in it.

**make up for**[복습]

idiom 뒤진 것을 만회하다, 벌충하다
To make up for something means to do something good for someone because you have treated them badly or because they have done something good for you.

**abrupt**[복습] [əbrʌ́pt]

a. 돌연한, 갑작스런
An abrupt change or action is very sudden, often in a way which is unpleasant.

**agonize**[복습] [ǽgənàiz]

v. 고민하다, 고뇌하다 (agonizing a. 고통스러운)
If you agonize over something, you feel very anxious about it and spend a long time thinking about it.

**overwhelm**[**] [òuvərhwélm]

vt. (격한 감정이) 휩싸다, 압도하다 (overwhelming a. 압도적인, 너무도 강력한)
If something is overwhelming, it affects you very strongly, and you do not know how to deal with it.

**grip**[복습] [grip]

v. 잡다, 움켜잡다; (마음을) 사로잡다, (관심[주의]을) 끌다;
n. 잡음, 붙듦, 움켜쥠; 손잡이
If something grips you, it affects you very strongly.

**being**[***] [bíːiŋ]

n. 존재, 실존; 생명, 인생; a. 존재하는
You can refer to any real or imaginary creature as a being.

**anticipate**[복습] [æntísipeit]

v. 예상하다, 예측하다
If you anticipate an event, you realize in advance that it may happen and you are prepared for it.

**awesome** [ɔ́ːsəm]

a. 경탄할 만한, 어마어마한, 엄청난; 기막히게 좋은, 굉장한
(awesomeness n. 무시무시함)
An awesome person or thing is very impressive and often frightening.

**transition**[*] [trænzíʃən]

n. (다른 상태·조건으로의) 이행
Transition is the process in which something changes from one state to another.

**wipe**[복습] [waip]

vt. 닦다, 닦아 내다; n. 닦음, 닦아 냄
If you wipe something, you rub its surface to remove dirt or liquid from it.

**stain**[복습] [stéin]

v. 더러워지다, 얼룩지게 하다; n. 얼룩, 오점
If a liquid stains something, the thing becomes colored or marked by the liquid.

**delivery**\**
[dilívəri]

n. 분만, 출산; (물품 · 편지 등의) 배달
Delivery is the process of giving birth to a baby.

**jerk**\**
[dʒɔ́:rk]

n. 갑자기 움직임; 바보, 멍청이; v. 갑자기 움직이다
A jerk is a single quick motion of short duration.

**flutter**\*복습
[flʌ́tər]

v. (깃발 등이) 펄럭이다, (새 등이) 날갯짓하다; n. 펄럭임
If something thin or light flutters, or if you flutter it, it moves up and down or from side to side with a lot of quick, light movements.

**momentary**\**
[móuməntèri]

a. 순식간의, 찰나의
Something that is momentary lasts for a very short period of time.

**be through**

phrasal v. 일을 끝마치다
If you are through with something or if it is through, you have finished doing it.

**be taken aback**

idiom 깜짝 놀라다
If you are taken back, you are shocked or surprised by someone or something.

**so long as**

idiom ···하는 한은, ···하는 동안은
If you say that something is the case so long as something else is the case, you mean that it is only the case if the second thing is the case.

**live up to . . .**

idiom ···에 맞는 생활을 하다, 부끄럽지 않게 살다, 기대에 부응하다
If someone or something lives up to what they were expected to be, they are as good as they were expected to be.

**machinery**\*복습
[məʃí:nəri]

n. 기계(류)
You can use machinery to refer to machines in general, or machines that are used in a factory or on a farm.

**separate**\*복습
[sépəreit]

v. (사람을) 떼어놓다; 가르다, 분리하다
If you separate people or things that are together, or if they separate, they move apart.

**throat**\***
[θróut]

n. 목구멍, 숨통
Your throat is the back of your mouth and the top part of the tubes that go down into your stomach and your lungs.

**scary**\*복습
[skéəri]

a. 무서운, 두려운
Something that is scary is rather frightening.

**stuff**\*복습
[stʌ́f]

n. 것(들), 물건, 물질; vt. 채워 넣다, 속을 채우다
You can use stuff to refer to things such as a substance, a collection of things, events, or ideas, or the contents of something in a general way without mentioning the thing itself by name.

**frighten**\*복습
[fráitn]

v. 놀라게 하다, 섬뜩하게 하다; 기겁하다 (frightened a. 겁먹은, 무서워하는)
If something or someone frightens you, they cause you to suddenly feel afraid, anxious, or nervous.

**swallow**\**
[swɑ́lou]

v. 삼키다, 들이켜다; n. 삼킴, 마심
If you swallow something, you cause it to go from your mouth down into your stomach.

126

**solitary** 복습
[sálitèri]

a. 혼자 하는, 홀로 있는
A solitary activity is one that you do alone.

**shift** 복습
[ʃift]

v. 옮기다, 이동하다; n. (위치 · 입장 · 방향의) 변화; 교대
If you shift something or if it shifts, it moves slightly.

**lap** 복습
[læp]

n. 무릎; 한 바퀴; v. 겹치게 하다
If you have something on your lap when you are sitting down, it is on top of your legs and near to your body.

**squeeze** 복습
[skwíːz]

vt. 짜내다, 꽉 쥐다, 압착하다; n. 압착, 짜냄; 꽉 끌어안음
If you squeeze something, you press it firmly, usually with your hands.

**translucent**
[trænslúːsnt]

a. 반투명의
You use translucent to describe something that has a glowing appearance, as if light is passing through it.

**china** **
[tʃáinə]

n. 자기, 도자기
China is a hard white substance made from clay, which is used to make things such as cups, bowls, plates, and ornaments.

**antique** 복습
[æntíːk]

n. (귀중한) 골동품; a. (귀중한) 골동품인
An antique is an old object such as a piece of china or furniture which is valuable because of its beauty or rarity.

**label** 복습
[léibəl]

vt. 라벨을[표를] 붙이다. (표 같은 것에 필요한 정보를) 적다; n. 표, 라벨
If something is labeled, a label is attached to it giving information about it.

**dangle** *
[dǽŋgəl]

v. 매달(리)다; 달랑거리다; n. 매달린 것
If something dangles from somewhere or if you dangle it somewhere, it hangs or swings loosely.

**rack** **
[ræk]

n. 선반, (모자 · 옷 등의) 걸이
A rack is a frame or shelf, usually with bars or hooks, that is used for holding things or for hanging things on.

**vein** **
[vein]

n. 정맥; 광맥
Your veins are the thin tubes in your body through which your blood flows towards your heart.

**solution** 복습
[səlúːʃən]

n. 용액, 용해; 해답, 해결
A solution is a liquid in which a solid substance has been dissolved.

**drip** 복습
[drip]

v. 물방울이 떨어지다; 흠뻑 젖다
When something drips, drops of liquid fall from it.

**adhesive**
[ædhíːsiv]

a. 접착성의, 들러붙는; n. 접착제
An adhesive substance is able to stick firmly to something else.

**knot** **
[nát]

v. (공포심 · 흥분 등으로 근육이) 뻣뻣해지다; 매듭을 묶다; n. 매듭
If your stomach knots or if something knots it, it feels tight because you are afraid or excited.

**lash** **
[læʃ]

n. 속눈썹; 채찍, 끈; v. 부딪히다; 후려치다, 채찍으로 때리다
Your lashes are the hairs that grow on the edge of your upper and lower eyelids.

**outline** <sup>복습</sup>
[áutlàin]

vt. 윤곽을 보여주다; n. 윤곽
You say that an object is outlined when you can see its general
shape because there is light behind it.

**blur** <sup>복습</sup>
[blə:r]

v. 흐릿해지다, 흐릿하게 만들다; n. 흐릿한 형체 (blurred a. 흐릿한)
When a thing blurs or when something blurs it, you cannot see it
clearly because its edges are no longer distinct.

**sweep**<sup>**</sup>
[swí:p]

v. (swept–swept) 휙 지나가다; 쓸어내리다; (감정 등이) 엄습하다; n. 청소
If wind, a stormy sea, or another strong force sweeps someone or
something along, it moves them quickly along.

**curl up** <sup>복습</sup>

phrasal v. (눕거나 앉아서) 몸을 웅크리다
If you curl up, your body forms a curved or round shape.

**doorway** <sup>복습</sup>
[dɔ́:rwèi]

n. 문간, 현관, 출입구
A doorway is a space in a wall where a door opens and closes.

**bouquet** <sup>복습</sup>
[bu:kéi]

n. 꽃다발, 부케
A bouquet is a bunch of flowers which is attractively arranged.

**slip** <sup>복습</sup>
[slip]

① v. 미끄러지다, 미끄러지게 하다; n. 미끄럼, 실수 ② n. (작은 종이) 조각
If something slips, it slides out of place or out of your hand.

**poem** <sup>복습</sup>
[póuəm]

n. (한 편의) 시; 운문, 시적인 문장
A poem is a piece of writing in which the words are chosen for their
beauty and sound and are carefully arranged, often in short lines
which rhyme.

**mourn** <sup>복습</sup>
[mɔ:rn]

v. 슬퍼하다, 한탄하다
If you mourn someone who has died or mourn for them, you are
very sad that they have died and show your sorrow in the way that
you behave.

**off-key** <sup>복습</sup>
[ɔ́:f-kíː]

a. 음정이 맞지 않는
When music is off-key, it is not in tune.

**verse**<sup>**</sup>
[vɔ́:rs]

n. (노래의) 절; (시의) 절; (성서 · 기도서의) 절
A verse is one of the parts into which a poem, a song is divided.

**strike** <sup>복습</sup>
[straik]

v. (struck–struck) (…하다는) 인상[느낌]을 주다; (세게) 치다, 부딪치다;
(시계가) 치다, 알리다
If an idea or thought strikes you, it suddenly comes into your mind.

**dirt road** <sup>복습</sup>
[dɔ́:rt róud]

n. 비포장도로
Dirt road is a rough road in the country that is made from hard
earth.

*chapter eleven*

1. What would Meg have at her house in the city?
   A. A garden
   B. A room to remember Molly
   C. A darkroom
   D. A larger bedroom

2. What hadn't been completed?
   A. Mom's quilt
   B. Dad's book
   C. Meg's darkroom packing
   D. Will's darkroom

3. How did Ben know Mr. Huntington?
   A. Mr. Huntington was his cousin.
   B. Mr. Huntington worked at his father's law firm.
   C. Mr. Huntington was his university professor.
   D. Mr. Huntington was his friend.

4. Ben wanted to _____.
   A. buy the house he was living in
   B. help Will in court
   C. buy all of Will's houses
   D. move to the city permanently

5. What did Meg see in the photograph?
   A. She saw the physical differences between her and Molly.
   B. She saw characteristics of Molly in herself.
   C. She saw a beautiful picture of Molly.
   D. She saw how similar she looked to her parents.

6. Why were purple gentians Will's favorite flower?
   A. Purple was his favorite color
   B. They had the largest petals
   C. They grow all alone at the end of the season
   D. They reminded him of his late wife Margaret

7. What did Meg understand at the end of the book?
   A. She should know and accept that bad things happen.
   B. She should learn about flowers like Molly did.
   C. She should always think that the best things will happen.
   D. She should remember Molly by trying to be like her.

*Check Your Reading Speed*

1분에 몇 단어를 읽는지 리딩 속도를 측정해보세요.

$$\frac{3,260 \text{ words}}{\text{reading time ( \quad ) sec}} \times 60 = ( \quad ) \text{ WPM}$$

*Build Your Vocabulary*

**gradual** <sup>복습</sup>
[grǽdʒuəl]

a. 점진적인, 단계적인 (gradually ad. 점진적으로)
A gradual change or process occurs in small stages over a long period of time, rather than suddenly.

**jagged**[*]
[dʒǽgid]

a. 뾰족뾰족한, 들쭉날쭉한; (목소리 등이) 귀에 거슬리는
Something that is jagged has a rough, uneven shape or edge with lots of sharp points.

**study** <sup>복습</sup>
[stʌ́di]

n. 서재, 집무실; v. 배우다, 공부하다
A study is a room in a house which is used for reading, writing, and studying.

**gloomy**[**]
[glú:mi]

a. 어두운, 우울한 (gloomily ad. 우울하게, 음울하게)
If people are gloomy, they are unhappy and have no hope.

**arrange** <sup>복습</sup>
[əréindʒ]

v. 배열하다, 가지런히 하다; 준비하다
If you arrange things somewhere, you place them in a particular position, usually in order to make them look attractive or tidy.

**sigh** <sup>복습</sup>
[sái]

v. 한숨 쉬다; n. 한숨, 탄식
When you sigh, you let out a deep breath, as a way of expressing feelings such as disappointment, tiredness, or pleasure.

**briefcase**[*]
[brí:fkèis]

n. 서류 가방
A briefcase is a case used for carrying documents in.

**impatient** <sup>복습</sup>
[impéiʃənt]

a. 성급한, 조급한, 참을성 없는
If you are impatient, you are annoyed because you have to wait too long for something.

**annoy**[**]
[ənɔ́i]

v. 성가시게 굴다, 짜증나게 하다 (annoyed a. 짜증나는, 화가 난)
If someone or something annoys you, it makes you fairly angry and impatient.

**shelf** <sup>복습</sup>
[ʃelf]

n. (pl. shelves) 선반
A shelf is a flat piece which is attached to a wall or to the sides of a cupboard for keeping things on.

**plumbing** <sup>복습</sup>
[plʌ́miŋ]

n. (건물의) 배관, 수도 시설
Plumbing is the work of connecting and repairing things such as water and drainage pipes, baths, and toilets.

**wiring** <sup>복습</sup>
[wáiəriŋ]

n. 배선 (장치)
The wiring in a building or machine is the system of wires that supply electricity to the different parts of it.

**maid**\*\*\*
[meid]

n. 하녀, 가정부; 소녀, 아가씨
A maid is a woman who works as a servant in a hotel or private house.

**equip**\*\*
[ikwíp]

vt. 갖추다, 장비하다
If you equip a person or thing with something, you give them the tools or equipment that are needed.

**depress**<sup>복습</sup>
[diprés]

vt. 우울하게 하다, 낙담시키다
If someone or something depresses you, they make you feel sad and disappointed.

**pantry**<sup>복습</sup>
[pǽntri]

n. 식료품 저장실
A pantry is a small room or large cupboard in a house, usually near the kitchen, where food is kept.

**enthusiasm**<sup>복습</sup>
[inθúːziæzm]

n. 열정, 열의, 열광
Enthusiasm is great eagerness to be involved in a particular activity which you like and enjoy or which you think is important.

**chemical**<sup>복습</sup>
[kémikəl]

n. 화학 물질; a. 화학의, 화학적인
Chemicals are substances that are used in a chemical process or made by a chemical process.

**seal**\*\*
[síːl]

v. 봉하다; 굳게 하다; 도장을 찍다; n. 도장, 봉인
When you seal an envelope, you close it by folding part of it over and sticking it down, so that it cannot be opened without being torn.

**utensil**\*\*
[juːténsəl]

n. 기구, 용구
Utensils are tools or objects that you use in order to help you to cook or to do other tasks in your home.

**linen**<sup>복습</sup>
[línin]

n. 리넨 제품(침대 시트, 식탁보, 베갯잇 등); 리넨, 아마 섬유
Linen is tablecloths, sheets, pillowcases, and similar things made of cloth that are used in the home.

**odds and ends**<sup>복습</sup>

idiom 잡동사니, 시시한 것
You can refer to a disorganized group of things of various kinds as odds and ends.

**refrigerator**\*
[rifrídʒərèitəːr]

n. 냉장고
A refrigerator is a large container which is kept cool inside, usually by electricity, so that the food and drink in it stays fresh.

**snap**<sup>복습</sup>
[snæp]

v. 홱 잡다, 잡아채다; 짤깍 소리 내다; 날카롭게[느닷없이] 말하다;
n. 짤깍 소리 냄
If you snap something into a particular position, or if it snaps into that position, it moves quickly into that position, with a sharp sound.

**thread**<sup>복습</sup>
[θred]

n. 실, 바느질 실; vt. 실을 꿰다
Thread or a thread is a long very thin piece of a material such as cotton, nylon, or silk, especially one that is used in sewing.

**spot**<sup>복습</sup>
[spɑt]

n. 장소, 지점; 반점, 얼룩; vt. 발견[분별]하다; 더럽히다
You can refer to a particular place as a spot.

**neat**<sup>복습</sup>
[ní:t]

a. 산뜻한, 깔끔한; (구어) 굉장한, 멋진
A neat place, thing, or person is tidy and smart, and has everything in the correct place.

**stitch**<sup>복습</sup>
[stitʃ]

n. 한 땀, 한 바늘; v. 바느질하다; 꿰매다
Stitches are the short pieces of thread that have been sewn in a piece of cloth.

**laid**<sup>복습</sup>
[leid]

v. LAY(두다, 눕혀놓다; 알을 낳다)의 과거 · 과거분사
lie—lay—lain(눕다, 누워있다)와 의미와 스펠링을 헷갈리지 않도록 주의하자.

**geometric**<sup>*</sup>
[dʒì:əmétrik]

a. 기하학적인, 기하학의
Geometric patterns or shapes consist of regular shapes or lines.

**square**<sup>복습</sup>
[skweər]

n. 정사각형; 광장; a. 정사각형의; 공명정대한
A square is a shape with four sides that are all the same length and four corners that are all right angles.

**pale**<sup>복습</sup>
[péil]

a. (색깔이) 엷은; 창백한, 핼쑥한; v. 창백해지다
If something is pale, it is very light in color or almost white.

**flowery**<sup>*</sup>
[fláuəri]

a. 꽃 모양의; 꽃이 많은
Flowery cloth, paper, or china has a lot of flowers printed or painted on it.

**plaid**<sup>복습</sup>
[plæd]

n. 격자무늬 옷감
Plaid is material with a check design on it.

**subdue**<sup>**</sup>
[səbdjú:]

vt. 억제하다; 정복하다, 진압하다 (subdued a. 억제된, 가라앉은)
If soldiers or the police subdue a group of people, they defeat them or bring them under control by using force.

**fade**<sup>복습</sup>
[feid]

vi. 바래다, 시들다, 희미해지다 (faded a. 시든, 빛깔이 바랜)
When a colored object fades or when the light fades it, it gradually becomes paler.

**argument**<sup>복습</sup>
[á:rgjəmənt]

n. 언쟁, 논의, 말다툼
An argument is a conversation in which people disagree with each other angrily or noisily.

**nephew**<sup>복습</sup>
[néfju:]

n. 조카
Someone's nephew is the son of their sister or brother.

**grin**<sup>복습</sup>
[grín]

v. 이를 드러내고 싱긋 웃다; n. 싱긋 웃음
When you grin, you smile broadly.

**nevertheless**<sup>***</sup>
[nèvərðəlés]

ad. 그럼에도 불구하고, 그렇지마는
You use nevertheless when saying something that contrasts with what has just been said.

**civilized**<sup>**</sup>
[sívəlàizd]

a. 교양이 높은, 품위 있는; 교화된, 문명화한
If you describe a person or their behavior as civilized, you mean that they are polite and reasonable.

**hang up**<sup>복습</sup>

phrasal v. 전화를 끊다, 수화기를 놓다
If you hang up or you hang up the phone, you end a phone call.

134

**inconvenience**[**]
[ìnkənvíːnjəns]

vt. 불편하게 하다, 폐를 끼치다; n. 불편, 애로
If someone inconveniences you, they cause problems or difficulties for you.

**satisfaction**[**]
[sæ̀tisfǽkʃən]

n. 만족(감), 흡족
Satisfaction is the pleasure that you feel when you do something or get something that you wanted or needed to do or get.

**newborn**[*]
[njúːbɔ́ːrn]

a. 갓[방금] 태어난; 부활한
A newborn baby or animal is one that has just been born.

**definite**[*]
[défənit]

a. 명확한; 확정된, 일정한
If something such as a decision or an arrangement is definite, it is firm and clear, and unlikely to be changed.

**personality**[**]
[pə̀ːrsənǽləti]

n. 성격, 개성
Your personality is your whole character and nature.

**screwball**
[skrúːbɔ́ːl]

a. 별난, 엉뚱한; n. 괴짜, 미치광이
Screwball comedy is silly and eccentric in an amusing and harmless way.

**propriety**[*]
[prəpráiəti]

n. (행동의 도덕적·사회적) 적절성
Propriety is the quality of being socially or morally acceptable.

**illogical**
[ilɑ́dʒikəl]

a. 비논리적인, 터무니없는
If you describe an action, feeling, or belief as illogical, you are critical of it because you think that it does not result from a logical and ordered way of thinking.

**assertive**
[əsə́ːrtiv]

a. 독단적인, 자기주장이 강한; 단정적인, 단언적인
Someone who is assertive states their needs and opinions clearly, so that people take notice.

**showoff**
[ʃóuɔ́ːf]

n. 과시적인 사람, 자랑쟁이; 자랑, 과시
If you say that someone is a showoff, you are criticizing them for trying to impress people by showing in a very obvious way what they can do or what they own.

**whack**[*]
[hwæk]

v. 세게 치다, 후려치다; n. 강타, 후려치기; 퍽, 철썩(무엇을 세게 치는 소리)
If you whack someone or something, you hit them hard.

**roar**[***]
[rɔːr]

vi. 고함치다, 으르렁거리다; n. 으르렁거리는 소리
If something, usually a vehicle, roars somewhere, it goes there very fast, making a loud noise.

**closet**[복습]
[klɑ́zit]

n. 벽장, 찬장
A closet is a piece of furniture with doors at the front and shelves inside, which is used for storing things.

**dummy**[*]
[dʌ́mi]

n. (속어) 바보, 멍청이; (의류 제작·전시용) 인체 모형
If you call someone a dummy, you mean that you think they are stupid.

**flip**[*]
[flíp]

v. (책 등의) 페이지를 휙휙 넘기다; 홱 움직이다; 튀기다; n. 공중제비
(flip through idiom 훑어보다, 휙휙 넘기다)
If you flip through the pages of a book, for example, you quickly turn over the pages in order to find a particular one or to get an idea of the contents.

**silly**[복습]
[síli]

a. 익살맞은, 어리석은, 바보 같은; n. 바보, 멍청이
If you say that someone or something is silly, you mean that they are foolish, childish, or ridiculous.

**practically**[***]
[præktikəli]

ad. 거의, …이나 마찬가지; 실지로, 실질상
Practically means almost, but not completely or exactly.

**double up**

phrasal v. (갑자기 통증이 일거나 웃음이 터져 나와) 몸을 웅크리다
If something doubles you up, or if you double up, you bend your body quickly or violently, for example because you are laughing a lot or because you are feeling a lot of pain.

**jerk**[복습]
[dʒə́:rk]

n. 바보, 멍청이; 갑자기 움직임; v. 갑자기 움직이다
If you call someone a jerk, you are insulting them because you think they are stupid or you do not like them.

**lawyer**[**]
[lɔ́:jər]

n. 변호사
A lawyer is a person who is qualified to advise people about the law and represent them in court.

**suit**[***]
[su:t]

n. 정장, …옷; v. (…에게) 편리하다, 어울리다
A particular type of suit is a piece of clothing that you wear for a particular activity.

**beard**[복습]
[bíərd]

n. (턱)수염
A man's beard is the hair that grows on his chin and cheeks.

**infect**[*]
[infékt]

v. 감염시키다, 전염시키다; 감염[오염]되다
To infect people, animals, or plants means to cause them to have a disease or illness.

**disease**[복습]
[dizí:z]

n. 병, 질환
A disease is an illness which affects people, animals, or plants, for example one which is caused by bacteria or infection.

**hold out**[복습]

phrasal v. (손 혹은 손에 든 것을) 내밀다, 내뻗다
If you hold out your hand, you move your hand away from your body, for example to shake hands.

**pompous**[*]
[pámpəs]

a. 젠체하는, 거만한
If you describe someone as pompous, you mean that they behave or speak in a very serious way because they think they are more important than they really are.

**element**[***]
[élimənt]

n. 요소, 원소
A particular element of a situation, activity, or process is an important quality or feature that it has or needs.

**awkward**[복습]
[ɔ́:kwərd]

a. 어색한, 불편한, 곤란한 (awkwardness n. 어색함, 거북함)
Someone who feels awkward behaves in a shy or embarrassed way.

136

| | |
|---|---|
| **proceeding**<sup>**</sup><br>[prousí:diŋ] | n. (pl.) 행사, 일련의 행위들; 소송[법적] 절차<br>The proceedings are an organized series of events that take place in a particular place. |
| **typical**<sup>복습</sup><br>[típikəl] | a. 전형적인, 대표적인<br>If a particular action or feature is typical of someone or something, it shows their usual qualities or characteristics. |
| **shrug**<sup>복습</sup><br>[ʃrʌg] | v. (양 손바닥을 내보이면서 어깨를) 으쓱하다; n. (어깨를) 으쓱하기<br>If you shrug, you raise your shoulders to show that you are not interested in something or that you do not know or care about something. |
| **nurse**<sup>***</sup><br>[nə́:rs] | v. 젖을 먹(이)다; 간호하다; n. 간호사<br>When a baby nurses or when its mother nurses it, it feeds by sucking milk from its mother's breast. |
| **take after** | idiom ····를 닮다<br>If you take after a member of your family, you resemble them in your appearance, your behavior, or your character. |
| **reheat**<br>[ri:hí:t] | vt. (식은 음식을) 다시 데우다<br>If you reheat cooked food, you heat it again after it has been left to go cold. |
| **rug**<sup>복습</sup><br>[rʌg] | n. (방바닥 · 마루에 까는) 깔개, 융단<br>A rug is a piece of thick material that you put on a floor. |
| **terrific**<sup>복습</sup><br>[tərífik] | a. 아주 좋은, 멋진, 훌륭한<br>If you describe something or someone as terrific, you are very pleased with them or very impressed by them. |
| **glum**<br>[glʌm] | a. 시무룩한, 풀죽은, 침울한<br>Someone who is glum is sad and quiet because they are disappointed or unhappy about something. |
| **rent**<sup>복습</sup><br>[rént] | v. 세 놓다, 임대하다; 세내다, 임차하다<br>If you rent something to someone, you let them have it and use it in exchange for a sum of money which they pay you regularly. |
| **staircase**<sup>복습</sup><br>[stéərkèis] | n. (건물 내부에 난간으로 죽 이어져 있는) 계단<br>A staircase is a set of stairs inside a building. |
| **coincidence**<sup>*</sup><br>[kouínsidəns] | n. 우연의 일치; 동시에 일어남<br>A coincidence is when two or more similar or related events occur at the same time by chance and without any planning. |
| **immature**<sup>*</sup><br>[imətjúər] | a. 미숙한, 유치한; 미완성의<br>If you describe someone as immature, you are being critical of them because they do not behave in a sensible or responsible way. |
| **literary**<sup>**</sup><br>[lítərèri] | a. 문학의, 문학적인<br>Literary means concerned with or connected with the writing, study, or appreciation of literature. |
| **device**<sup>**</sup><br>[diváis] | n. 장치, 설비<br>A device is a machine or tool that does a special job. |

**rearrange**[*]
[rìːəréindʒ]

vt. 재배열하다, 재정리하다
If you rearrange things, you change the way in which they are organized or ordered.

**mutter**[복습]
[mʌ́tər]

v. 중얼거리다, 불평하다; n. 중얼거림, 불평
If you mutter, you speak very quietly so that you cannot easily be heard, often because you are complaining about something.

**correspond**[**]
[kɔː(ə)rispáː(ó)nd]

vi. 일치하다, 부합하다; 편지를 주고받다
If one thing corresponds to another, there is a close similarity or connection between them.

**triumphant**[복습]
[traiʌ́mfənt]

a. 의기양양한; 승리를 얻은, 성공한 (triumphantly ad. 의기양양하게)
Someone who is triumphant has gained a victory or succeeded in something and feels very happy about it.

**manuscript**[**]
[mǽnjuskript]

n. (책 · 악보 등의) 원고; 필사본, 사본
A manuscript is a handwritten or typed document, especially a writer's first version of a book before it is published.

**moving van**[복습]
[múːviŋ vǽn]

n. 이삿짐 트럭
A moving van is a vehicle used to transport furniture and other possessions when people move to a new home.

**driveway**[복습]
[dráivwèi]

n. (도로에서 집 · 차고까지의) 진입로
A driveway is a piece of hard ground that leads from the road to the front of a house or other building.

**wave**[복습]
[wéiv]

v. 손을 흔들다, 신호하다; 파도치다; n. 흔들기; 파도, 물결
If you wave or wave your hand, you move your hand from side to side in the air, usually in order to say hello or goodbye to someone.

**comb**[복습]
[kóum]

v. 빗다, 빗질하다; n. 머리빗, 빗
When you comb your hair, you tidy it using a comb.

**someplace**[*]
[sʌ́mplèis]

n. (미 · 구어) 어떤 장소; ad. 어딘가에
You use someplace to refer to a place without saying exactly where you mean.

**sneaker**[복습]
[sníːkər]

n. (pl.) 운동화; 살금살금 하는 사람
Sneakers are casual shoes with rubber soles.

**grab**[복습]
[grǽb]

v. 잡아채다, 움켜쥐다, 부여잡다; n. 부여잡기
If you grab something, you take it or pick it up suddenly and roughly.

**chilly**[**]
[tʃíli]

a. 차가운, 쌀쌀한; (태도 등이) 냉담한
Something that is chilly is unpleasantly cold.

**pumpkin**[복습]
[pʌ́mpkin]

n. 호박
A pumpkin is a large, round, orange vegetable with a thick skin.

**statue**[**]
[stǽtʃuː]

n. 상(像), 조각상
A statue is a large sculpture of a person or an animal, made of stone or metal.

**hush**[**]
[hʌʃ]

v. 쉿, 조용히 해; …을 조용히 시키다; n. 침묵, 고요함
If you hush someone or if they hush, they stop speaking or making a noise.

138

**exhibition**∗∗
[èksəbíʃən]

n. 전시(회)
An exhibition is a public event at which pictures, sculptures, or other objects of interest are displayed, for example at a museum or art gallery.

**wing**∗∗∗
[wíŋ]

n. (건물 본관 한쪽으로 돌출되게 지은) 동(棟), 부속 건물; 날개
A wing of a building is a part of it which sticks out from the main part.

**sink**∗∗∗
[siŋk]

v. 가라앉다, 침몰하다 (sinking a. 가라앉는)
If you have a sinking feeling, you suddenly become depressed or lose hope.

**submit**∗∗
[səbmít]

v. 제출하다; 복종시키다, 굴복하다
If you submit a proposal, report, or request to someone, you formally send it to them so that they can consider it or decide about it.

**permission**복습
[pə:rmíʃən]

n. 허가, 허락, 승인
If someone is given permission to do something, they are allowed to do it.

**frame**복습
[freim]

vt. 틀에 끼우다; …의 뼈대를 만들다, 짜 맞추다; n. 틀, 구조, 골격
When a picture or photograph is framed, it is put in a frame.

**script**∗∗
[skript]

n. 글씨(체); (연극 · 영화 · 방송 · 강연 등의) 대본
You can refer to a particular system of writing as a particular script.

**gaunt**∗
[gɔ:nt]

a. 수척한, 아주 여윈
If someone looks gaunt, they look very thin, usually because they have been very ill or worried.

**weather**복습
[wéðər]

v. (역경 등을) 헤쳐 나가다[견디다]; 풍화되다; n. 날씨, 기상
(weathered a. 풍파를 견뎌낸, 풍화된)
If you weather a difficult time or a difficult situation, you survive it and are able to continue normally after it has passed or ended.

**wrinkle**복습
[ríŋkl]

v. 구겨지다, …에 주름살지게 하다; n. 주름, 잔주름 (wrinkled a. 주름이 있는)
When someone's skin wrinkles or when something wrinkles it, lines start to form in it because the skin is getting old or damaged.

**eager**∗∗
[í:gər]

a. 열망하는, 간절히 하고 싶어 하는
If you are eager to do or have something, you want to do or have it very much.

**speckled**
[spékld]

a. 얼룩덜룩한, 반점이 있는
A speckled surface is covered with small marks, spots, or shapes.

**mount**복습
[maunt]

n. (사진 등을 붙이는) 대지, 판; v. 끼우다, 고정시키다; (자전거 · 말 등에) 올라타다
A mount is the material as cardboard on which a picture is fixed.

**meticulous**
[mətíkjələs]

a. 꼼꼼한, 세심한 (meticulously ad. 꼼꼼하게, 세심하게)
If you describe someone as meticulous, you mean that they do things very carefully and with great attention to detail.

**trim**∗∗
[trím]

v. 다듬다, 손질하다, 정돈하다; n. 다듬기; 장식
If you trim something you cut off small amounts of it in order to make it look neater and tidier.

**rigid** <sup>복습</sup>
[rídʒid]

a. 뻣뻣한, 단단한; 엄격한, 융통성 없는
A rigid substance or object is stiff and does not bend, stretch, or twist easily.

**confine**\*\*
[kənfáin]

n. (pl.) 범위, 영역; vt. 제한하다, 가두다
Something that is within the confines of an area or place is within the boundaries enclosing it.

**chin** <sup>복습</sup>
[tʃin]

n. 아래턱, 턱 끝
Your chin is the part of your face that is below your mouth and above your neck.

**blur** <sup>복습</sup>
[bləːr]

v. 흐릿해지다, 흐릿하게 만들다; n. 흐릿한 형체 (blurred a. 흐릿한)
When a thing blurs or when something blurs it, you cannot see it clearly because its edges are no longer distinct.

**subtle**\*\*
[sʌtl]

a. 미묘한, 감지하기 힘든; 교묘한, 영리한
Something that is subtle is not immediately obvious or noticeable.

**pine** <sup>복습</sup>
[páin]

n. 소나무 (재목)
A pine tree or a pine is a tall tree which has very thin, sharp leaves and a fresh smell. Pine trees have leaves all year round.

**cemetery**\*\*
[sémətèri]

n. 공동묘지
A cemetery is a place where dead people's bodies or their ashes are buried.

**bury** <sup>복습</sup>
[béri]

vt. 매장하다, 파묻다; 묻다
To bury a dead person means to put their body into a grave and cover it with earth.

**heap**\*\*
[híːp]

v. 쌓아올리다, 수북이 담다; n. 더미, 쌓아올린 것
If you heap things somewhere, you arrange them in a large pile.

**startle** <sup>복습</sup>
[stáːrtl]

v. 깜짝 놀라게 하다; 움찔하다; n. 깜짝 놀람
If something sudden and unexpected startles you, it surprises and frightens you slightly.

**define** <sup>복습</sup>
[difáin]

v. 윤곽을 분명히 나타내다; (단어ㆍ구의 뜻을) 정의하다
If you define something, you show, describe, or state clearly what it is and what its limits are, or what it is like.

**separate** <sup>복습</sup>
[sépəreit]

v. 가르다, 분리하다; (사람을) 떼어놓다
If one thing is separate from another, there is a barrier, space, or division between them, so that they are clearly two things.

**forehead** <sup>복습</sup>
[fɔ́ːrhèd]

n. 이마
Your forehead is the area at the front of your head between your eyebrows and your hair.

**identify** <sup>복습</sup>
[aidéntəfài]

v. 식별하다, 확인하다
If you can identify someone or something, you are able to recognize them or distinguish them from others.

**transient**\*
[trǽnʃənt]

a. 순간적인, 깜짝할 사이의; 덧없는, 일시적인
Transient is used to describe a situation that lasts only a short time or is constantly changing.

**shutter**<sup>복습</sup>
[ʃʌ́təːr]

n. (카메라의) 셔터; 덧문, 셔터
The shutter in a camera is the part which opens to allow light through the lens when a photograph is taken.

**permanent**<sup>복습</sup>
[pə́ːrmənənt]

a. 영속하는, 변하지 않는, 영구적인
Something that is permanent lasts for ever.

**grateful**<sup>복습</sup>
[gréitfəl]

a. 고맙게 여기는, 감사하는
If you are grateful for something that someone has given you or done for you, you have warm, friendly feelings towards them and wish to thank them.

**hood**<sup>복습</sup>
[hud]

n. 자동차 보닛, 덮개; 두건
The hood of a car is the metal cover over the engine at the front.

**wipe**<sup>복습</sup>
[waip]

vt. 닦다, 닦아 내다; n. 닦음, 닦아 냄
If you wipe something, you rub its surface to remove dirt or liquid from it.

**chuckle**<sup>복습</sup>
[tʃʌ́kl]

vi. 낄낄 웃다; n. 낄낄 웃음
When you chuckle, you laugh quietly.

**master's degree**

n. 석사 학위
A master's degree is a university degree which is of a higher level than a first degree and usually takes one or two years to complete.

**tidy**<sup>복습</sup>
[táidi]

a. 깔끔한, 단정한, 말쑥한; v. 치우다, 정돈하다
Something that is tidy is neat and is arranged in an organized way.

**weed**<sup>복습</sup>
[wíːd]

v. 잡초를 뽑다; n. 잡초 (weeded a. 풀을 뽑은, 잡초를 없앤)
If you weed an area, you remove the weeds from it.

**brand-new**
[brǽnd-njúː]

a. 아주 새로운, 신상품의
A brand-new object is completely new.

**underbrush**<sup>복습</sup>
[ʌ́ndərbrʌ̀ʃ]

n. (큰 나무 밑에 자라는) 덤불
Underbrush consists of bushes and plants growing close together under trees in a forest.

**moss**<sup>**</sup>
[mɔ́ːs]

n. 이끼
Moss is a very small soft green plant which grows on damp soil, or on wood or stone.

**patch**<sup>복습</sup>
[pætʃ]

n. (채소나 과일을 기르는) 작은 땅; (주변과는 다른 조그만) 부분
A patch of land is a small area of land where a particular plant or crop grows.

**clump**<sup>복습</sup>
[klʌmp]

n. (촘촘히 붙어 자라는 나무 등의) 무리, 수풀
A clump of things such as trees or plants is a small group of them growing together.

**blossom**<sup>복습</sup>
[blásəm]

n. (특히 과수의) 꽃, 개화; vi. (나무 등이) 꽃 피다, 개화하다; 발전하다
Blossom is the flowers that appear on a tree before the fruit.

**stem** 복습
[stem]

n. 줄기, 대
The stem of a plant is the thin, upright part on which the flowers and leaves grow.

**damp**\*\*
[dæmp]

a. 축축한; n. 습기
Something that is damp is slightly wet.

**quote** 복습
[kwout]

vt. 인용하다; n. 인용문, 따옴표
If you quote someone as saying something, you repeat what they have written or said.

**ravish**
[rǽviʃ]

vt. 겁탈하다, 빼앗다, 강탈하다
If a woman is ravished by a man, she is raped by him.

**mockery**\*
[mάkəri]

n. 엉터리, 흉내에 불과한 것, 가짜; 조롱, 놀림
A mockery is an action, a decision, etc. that is a failure and that is not as it is supposed to be.

**poet**\*\*\*
[póuit]

n. 시인
A poet is a person who writes poems.

**mechanic**\*
[məkǽnik]

n. (차량 엔진) 정비공
A mechanic is someone whose job is to repair and maintain machines and engines, especially car engines.

**practical**\*\*\*
[prǽktikəl]

a. 실용적인, 실제적인
The practical aspects of something involve real situations and events, rather than just ideas and theories.

**brownish**
[bráuniʃ]

a. 갈색을 띤
Something that is brownish is slightly brown in color.

**brittle**\*
[brítl]

a. 잘 부러지는
An object or substance that is brittle is hard but easily broken.

**sequence**\*\*
[síːkwəns]

n. (영화에서) 연속된 한 장면, 일련의 화면; 연속적인 사건들, 순서
A film sequence is a part of a film that shows a single set of actions.

**float**\*\*\*
[flóut]

v. 뜨다; 띄우다; n. 뜨는 물건, 부유물
Something that floats in or through the air hangs in it or moves slowly and gently through it.

**pollen**\*
[pάlən]

n. 꽃가루, 화분(花粉)
Pollen is a fine powder produced by flowers, which fertilizes other flowers of the same species so that they produce seeds.

**drift** 복습
[drift]

v. 떠돌다, 표류하다; 전전하다; n. 취지; 경향, 추세; 표류
When something drifts somewhere, it is carried there by the movement of wind or water.

**lean** 복습
[líːn]

① v. 기대다, 의지하다; 상체를 굽히다, 기울이다 ② a. 야윈, 마른
If you lean on or against someone or something, you rest against them so that they partly support your weight.

**rocky** 복습
[rάki]

a. 바위로 된, 바위[돌]투성이의
A rocky place is covered with rocks or consists of large areas of rock and has nothing growing on it.

142

**catch up** <sup>복습</sup>

phrasal v. 따라잡다, 따라붙다; 뒤지지 않다
If you catch up with someone who is in front of you, you reach them by walking faster than they are walking.

**shy** <sup>복습</sup>
[ʃai]

a. 부끄러워하는, 수줍어하는 (shyly ad. 수줍게)
A shy person is nervous and uncomfortable in the company of other people.

**all along** <sup>복습</sup>

idiom 처음부터, 내내, 계속
If something have been there all along, it is there from the very beginning.

## Check Your Reading Speed

1분에 몇 단어를 읽는지 리딩 속도를 측정해보세요.

$$\frac{283 \text{ words}}{\text{reading time ( ) sec}} \times 60 = (\quad) \text{ WPM}$$

## Build Your Vocabulary

**chuckle**<sup>복습</sup>
[tʃʌkl]

vi 낄낄 웃다; n. 낄낄 웃음
When you chuckle, you laugh quietly.

**cancer**<sup>**</sup>
[kǽnsər]

n. 암, 악성 종양
Cancer is a serious disease in which cells in a person's body increase rapidly in an uncontrolled way, producing abnormal growths.

**frequent**<sup>**</sup>
[frí:kwənt]

a. 자주 일어나는, 빈번한 (frequently ad. 종종, 자주)
If something is frequent, it happens often.

**autobiography**<sup>*</sup>
[ɔ̀:toubaiágrəfi]

n. 자서전
Your autobiography is an account of your life, which you write yourself.

**fiction**<sup>**</sup>
[fíkʃən]

n. 소설, 꾸며낸 이야기
Fiction refers to books and stories about imaginary people and events, rather than books about real people or events.

**curable**<sup>*</sup>
[kjúərəbl]

a. 치유 가능한, 고칠 수 있는
If a disease or illness is curable, it can be cured.

**sidekick**
[sàidkìk]

n. 조수, 짝패, 공모자
Someone's sidekick is a person who accompanies them and helps them.

**jealousy**<sup>**</sup>
[dʒéləsi]

n. 질투, 시샘
Jealousy is the feeling of anger or bitterness which someone has when they think that another person is trying to take a lover or friend, or a possession, away from them.

**bicker**
[bíkər]

vi. (사소한 일로) 다투다
When people bicker, they argue or quarrel about unimportant things.

**fierce**<sup>**</sup>
[fiərs]

a. 격렬한, 지독한; 사나운
Fierce feelings or actions are very intense or enthusiastic, or involve great activity.

**helpless**<sup>복습</sup>
[hélplis]

a. 무력한, 속수무책의 (helplessness n. 무력감)
If you are helpless, you do not have the strength or power to do anything useful or to control or protect yourself.

**anguish**<sup>*</sup>
[ǽŋgwiʃ]

n. (극심한) 괴로움, 비통
Anguish is great mental suffering or physical pain.

144

**overcome**[\*\*]
[ouvərkʌ́m]

v. 압도당하다, 무기력하게하다; 극복하다
If you are overcome by a feeling or event, it is so strong or has such a strong effect that you cannot think clearly.

**inescapable**[\*]
[inəskéipəbl]

a. 피할 수 없는, 달아날 수 없는
If you describe a fact, situation, or activity as inescapable, you mean that it is difficult not to notice it or be affected by it.

**giggle**[복습]
[gígl]

v. 낄낄 웃다; n. 낄낄 웃음
If someone giggles, they laugh in a childlike way, because they are amused, nervous, or embarrassed.

**merciful**[\*\*]
[mə́:rsifəl]

a. 자비로운, 다행스러운 (mercifully ad. 다행히도, 친절하게)
If you describe an event or situation as merciful, you mean that it is a good thing, especially because it stops someone's suffering or discomfort.

**absorb**[복습]
[æbsɔ́:rb]

vt. 받아들이다, 흡수하다; 열중시키다
If something absorbs a force or shock, it reduces its effect.

## 수고하셨습니다!

드디어 끝까지 다 읽으셨군요! 축하드립니다! 여러분은 이 책을 통해 총 34,166개의 단어를 읽으셨고, 800개 이상의 어휘와 표현들을 익히셨습니다. 이 책에 나온 어휘는 다른 원서를 읽을 때에도 빈번히 만날 수 있는 필수 어휘들입니다. 이 책을 읽었던 경험은 비슷한 수준의 다른 원서들을 읽을 때 큰 도움이 될 것입니다. 이제 자신의 상황에 맞게 원서를 반복해서 읽거나, 오디오북을 들어 볼 수 있습니다. 혹은 비슷한 수준의 다른 원서를 찾아 읽는 것도 좋습니다. 일단 원서를 완독한 뒤에 어떻게 계속 영어 공부를 이어갈 수 있을지, 아래에 제시되는 도움말을 꼼꼼히 살펴보고 각자 상황에 맞게 적용해 보세요!

## 리딩(Reading)을 확실하게 다지고 싶다면? 반복해서 읽어 보세요!

리딩 실력을 탄탄하게 다지고 싶다면, 같은 원서를 2~3번 반복해서 읽을 것을 권합니다. 같은 책을 여러 번 읽으면 지루할 것 같지만, 꼭 그렇지도 않습니다. 반복해서 읽을 때 처음과 주안점을 다르게 두면, 전혀 다른 느낌으로 재미있게 읽을 수 있습니다.

처음 원서를 읽을 때는 생소한 단어들과 스토리로 인해 읽으면서 곧바로 이해하기가 매우 힘들 수 있습니다. 전체 맥락을 잡고 읽어도 약간 버거운 느낌이지요. 하지만 반복해서 읽기 시작하면 달라집니다. 일단 내용을 파악한 상황이기 때문에 문장 구조나 어휘의 활용에 더 집중하게 되고, 조금 더 깊이 있게 읽을 수 있습니다. 좋은 표현과 문장을 수집하고 메모할 만한 여유도 생기게 되지요. 어휘도 많이 익숙해졌기 때문에 리딩 속도에도 탄력이 붙습니다. 처음 읽을 때는 '내용'에서 재미를 느꼈다면, 반복해서 읽을 때에는 '영어'에서 재미를 느끼게 되는 것입니다. 따라서 리딩 실력을 더욱 확고하게 다지고자 한다면, 같은 책을 2~3회 정도 반복해서 읽을 것을 권해 드립니다.

## 리스닝(Listening) 실력을 늘리고 싶다면?
## 귀를 통해서 읽어 보세요!

많은 영어 학습자들이 '리스닝이 안 돼서 문제'라고 한탄합니다. 그리고 리스닝 실력을 늘리는 방법으로 무슨 뜻인지 몰라도 반복해서 듣는 '무작정 듣기'를 선택합니다. 하지만 뜻도 모르면서 무작정 듣는 일에는 엄청난 인내력이 필요합니다. 그래서 대부분 며칠 시도하다가 포기해 버리고 말지요.

따라서 모르는 내용을 무작정 듣는 것보다는 어느 정도 알고 있는 내용을 반복해서 듣는 것이 더 효과적인 듣기 방법입니다. 그리고 이런 방식의 듣기에 활용할 수 있는 가장 좋은 교재가 오디오북입니다.

리스닝 실력을 향상하고 싶다면, 이 책에서 제공하는 오디오북을 이용해서 듣는 연습을 해 보세요. 활용법은 간단합니다. 일단 책을 한 번 완독했다면, 오디오북을 통해 다시 들어 보는 것입니다. 휴대 기기에 넣어 시간이 날 때 틈틈이 듣는 것도 좋고, 책상에 앉아 눈으로는 텍스트를 보며 귀로 읽는 것도 좋습니다. 이미 읽었던 내용이라 이해하기가 훨씬 수월하고, 애매했던 발음들도 자연스럽게 교정할 수 있습니다. 또 성우의 목소리 연기를 듣다 보면 내용이 더욱 생동감 있게 다가와 이해도가 높아지는 효과도 거둘 수 있습니다.

반대로 듣기에 자신 있는 사람이라면, 책을 읽기 전에 처음부터 오디오북을 먼저 듣는 것도 좋은 방법입니다. 귀를 통해 책을 쭉 읽어 보고, 이후에 다시 눈으로 책을 읽으면서 잘 들리지 않았던 부분을 보충하는 것이지요.

중요한 것은 내용을 따라가면서, 내용에 푹 빠져서 반복해 들어야 한다는 것입니다. 이렇게 연습을 반복해서 눈으로 읽지 않은 책이라도 '귀를 통해' 읽을 수 있을 정도가 되면, 리스닝으로 고생하는 일은 거의 없을 것입니다.

이 책은 미국 현지에서 판매되고 있는 정식 오디오북을 기본 제공하고 있습니다. 오디오북은 MP3 파일로 제공되므로 컴퓨터 또는 휴대 기기에 옮겨서 사용하시면 됩니다. 오디오북에 이상이 있을 경우 help@ltinc.net으로 메일을 주시면 안내를 받으실 수 있습니다.

## 스피킹(Speaking)이 고민이라면? 소리 내어 읽어 보세요!

스피킹 역시 많은 학습자들이 고민하는 부분입니다. 스피킹이 고민이라면, 원서를 큰 소리로 읽는 낭독 훈련(voice reading)을 해 보세요!

'소리 내어 읽는 것이 말하기에 정말로 도움이 될까?'라고 의아한 생각이 들 수도 있습니다. 하지만 인간의 두뇌 입장에서 봤을 때, 성대 구조를 활용해서 '발화'한다는 점에서는 소리 내어 읽기와 말하기에 큰 차이가 없다고 합니다. 소리 내어 읽는 것은 '타인의 생각'을 전달하고, 직접 말하는 것은 '자신의 생각'을 전달한다는 차이가 있을 뿐, 머릿속에서 문장을 처리하고 조음기관(혀와 성대 등)을 움직여 의미를 만든다는 점에서 같은 과정인 것이지요. 따라서 소리 내어 읽는 연습을 꾸준히 하는 것은 스피킹 연습에 큰 도움이 됩니다.

소리 내어 읽기를 하는 방법은 간단합니다. 일단 오디오북을 들으면서 성우의 목소리를 최대한 따라 하며 같이 읽어 보세요. 발음뿐 아니라 억양, 어조, 느낌까지 완벽히 따라 한다고 생각하면서 소리 내어 읽습니다. 따라 읽는 것이 조금 익숙해지면, 옆의 누군가에게 이 책을 읽어 준다는 생각으로 소리 내어 계속 읽어나갑니다. 한 번 눈과 귀로 읽었던 책이기 때문에 보다 수월하게 진행할 수 있고, 자연스럽게 어휘와 표현을 복습하는 효과도 거두게 됩니다. 또 이렇게 소리 내어 읽은 것을 녹음해서 들어 보면 스스로에게도 좋은 피드백이 됩니다.

최근 말하기가 강조되면서 소리 내어 읽기가 크게 각광을 받고 있긴 하지만, 그렇다고 소리 내어 읽기가 무조건 좋은 것만은 아닙니다. 책을 소리 내어 읽다 보면, 무의식적으로 속으로 발음을 하는 습관을 가지게 되어 리딩 속도 자체는 오히려 크게 떨어지는 현상이 발생할 수 있습니다. 따라서 빠른 리딩 속도가 중요한 수험생이나 고학력 학습자들에게는 소리 내어 읽기가 적절하지 않은 방법입니다. 효과가 좋다는 말만 믿고 무턱대고 따라 하기보다는 자신의 필요에 맞게 우선순위를 정하고 원서를 활용하는 것이 좋습니다.

## 라이팅(Writing)까지 욕심이 난다면? 요약하는 연습을 해 보세요!

원서를 라이팅 연습에 직접적으로 활용하는 데에는 한계가 있지만, 적절히 활용하면 원서도 유용한 라이팅 자료가 될 수 있습니다.

특히 책을 읽고 그 내용을 요약하는 연습은 큰 도움이 됩니다. 요약 훈련의 방식도 간단합니다. 원서를 읽고 그날 읽은 분량만큼 혹은 책을 다 읽고 전체 내용을 기반으로, 책 내용을 한번 요약하고 나의 느낌을 영어로 적어 보는 것입니다.

이때 그 책에 나왔던 단어와 표현을 최대한 활용하여 요약하는 것이 중요합니다. 영어 표현력은 결국 얼마나 다양한 어휘로 많은 표현을 해 보았느냐가 좌우하게 됩니다. 이런 면에서 내가 읽은 책을, 그 책에 나온 문장과 어휘로 다시 표현해 보는 것은 매우 효율적인 방법입니다. 책에 나온 어휘와 표현을 단순히 읽고 무슨 말인지 아는 정도가 아니라, 실제로 직접 활용해서 쓸 수 있을 만큼 확실하게 익히게 되는 것이지요. 여기에 첨삭까지 받을 수 있는 방법이 있다면 금상첨화입니다.

이러한 '표현하기' 연습은 스피킹 훈련에도 그대로 적용될 수 있습니다. 책을 읽고 그 내용을 3분 안에 다른 사람에게 영어로 말하는 연습을 해 보세요. 순발력과 표현력을 기르는 좋은 훈련이 될 것입니다.

## 꾸준히 원서를 읽고 싶다면? 뉴베리 수상작을 계속 읽어 보세요!

뉴베리 상이 세계 최고 권위의 아동 문학상인 만큼, 그 수상작들은 확실히 완성도를 검증받은 작품이라고 할 수 있습니다. 특히 '쉬운 어휘로 쓰인 깊이 있는 문장'으로 이루어졌다는 점이 영어 학습자들에게 큰 호응을 얻고 있습니다. 이렇게 '검증된 원서'를 꾸준히 읽는 것은 영어 실력 향상에 큰 도움이 됩니다.

아래에 수준별로 제시된 뉴베리 수상작 목록을 보며 적절한 책들을 찾아 계속 읽어 보세요. 꼭 뉴베리 수상작이 아니더라도 마음에 드는 작가의 다른 책을 읽어 보는 것 또한 아주 좋은 방법입니다.

• 영어 초보자도 쉽게 읽을 만한 아주 쉬운 수준. 소리 내어 읽기에도 아주 적합.
Sarah, Plain and Tall*(Medal, 8,331단어), The Hundred Penny Box (Honor, 5,878단어), The Hundred Dresses*(Honor, 7,329단어), My Father's Dragon (Honor, 7,682단어), 26 Fairmount Avenue (Honor, 6,737단어)

- 중 · 고등학생 정도 영어 학습자라면 쉽게 읽을 수 있는 수준. 소리 내어 읽기에도 비교적 적합한 편.

Because of Winn-Dixie★(Honor, 22,123단어), What Jamie Saw (Honor, 17,203단어), Charlotte's Web (Honor, 31,938단어), Dear Mr. Henshaw (Medal, 18,145단어), Missing May (Medal, 17,509단어)

- 대학생 정도 영어 학습자라면 무난한 수준. 소리 내어 읽기에는 적합하지 않음.

Number The Stars★(Medal, 27,197단어), A Single Shard (Medal, 33,726단어), The Tale of Despereaux★(Medal, 32,375단어), Hatchet★(Medal, 42,328단어), Bridge to Terabithia (Medal, 32,888단어), A Fine White Dust (Honor, 19,022단어), Jennifer, Hecate, Macbeth, William McKinley and Me, Elizabeth (Honor, 23,266단어)

- 원서 완독 경험을 가진 학습자에게 적절한 수준. 소리 내어 읽기에는 적합하지 않음.

The Giver★(Medal, 43,617단어), From the Mixed-Up Files of Mrs. Basil E. Frankweiler (Medal, 30,906단어), The View from Saturday (Medal, 42,685단어), Holes★(Medal, 47,079단어), Criss Cross (Medal, 48,221단어), Walk Two Moons (Medal, 59,400단어), The Graveyard Book (Medal, 67,380단어)

뉴베리 수상작과 뉴베리 수상 작가의 좋은 작품을 엄선한 「뉴베리 컬렉션」에도 위 목록에 있는 도서 중 상당수가 포함될 예정입니다.

★「뉴베리 컬렉션」으로 이미 출간된 도서

어떤 책들이 출간되었는지 확인하려면, 지금 인터넷 서점에서
뉴베리 컬렉션을 검색해 보세요.

## 뉴베리 수상작을 동영상 강의로 만나 보세요!

영어원서 전문 동영상 강의 사이트 영서당(yseodang.com)에서는 뉴베리 컬렉션 『Holes』, 『Because of Winn-Dixie』, 『The Miraculous Journey of Edward Tulane』, 『Wayside School 시리즈』 등의 동영상 강의를 제공하고 있습니다. 뉴베리 수상작이라는 최고의 영어 교재와 EBS 출신 인기 강사가 만난 명강의! 지금 사이트를 방문해서 무료 샘플 강의를 들어 보세요!

## '스피드 리딩 카페'를 통해 원서 읽기 습관을 길러 보세요!

일상에서 영어를 한마디도 쓰지 않는 비영어권 국가에서 살고 있는 우리가 영어 환경에 가장 쉽고, 편하고, 부담 없이 노출되는 방법은 바로 '영어원서 읽기'입니다. 언제 어디서든 원서를 붙잡고 읽기만 하면 곧바로 영어를 접하는 환경이 만들어지기 때문이지요. 하루에 20분씩만 꾸준히 읽는다면, 1년에 무려 120시간 동안 영어에 노출될 수 있습니다. 이러한 이유 때문에 영어 교육 전문가들이 영어원서 읽기를 추천하는 것이지요.
하지만 원서 읽기가 좋다는 것을 알아도 막상 꾸준히 읽는 것은 쉽지 않습니다. 그럴 때에는 13만 명 이상의 회원을 보유한 국내 최대 원서 읽기 동호회 <스피드 리딩 카페> (cafe.naver. com/readingtc)를 방문해 보세요.
원서별로 정리된 무료 PDF 단어장과 수준별 추천 원서 목록 등 유용한 자료는 물론, 뉴베리 수상작을 포함한 다양한 원서의 리뷰를 무료로 확인할 수 있습니다. 특히 함께 모여서 원서를 읽는 '북클럽'은 중간에 포기하지 않고 원서를 끝까지 읽는 습관을 기르는 데 큰 도움이 될 것입니다.

chapter one

1. D    It was Molly who drew the line. She did it with chalk—a fat piece of white chalk left over from when we lived in town. … She took the chalk and drew a line right on the rug. … she kept right on drawing the line up the wall, across the wallpaper with its blue flowers. She stood on her desk and drew the line up to the ceiling, and then she went back to the other side of the room and stood on her bed and drew the line right up to the ceiling on that wall, too.

2. A    I want with my whole being to *be* something someday; I like to think that someday, when I'm grown up, people everywhere will know who I am, because I will have accomplished something important.

3. C    She's content, waiting for that; I'm restless, and so impatient. She's sure, absolutely sure, that what she's waiting for will happen, just the way she wants it to; and I'm so uncertain, so fearful my dreams will end up forgotten somewhere, someday, like a piece of string and a paper clip lying in a dish.

4. C    The quiet is why we came. The university has given my dad just this year to finish his book.

5. B    Molly is fifteen, which means that she puts on eyeshadow when Mom doesn't catch her at it, and she spends hours in front of the mirror arranging her hair different ways. … Me, I'm only two years younger, and that seems to make such a difference, though I haven't figured out why.

6. B    I did all my packing alone that week. I cried when I fitted my new, unused box of oil paints—a gift for my thirteenth birthday the month before—into a box, and I cried again when I packed my camera. But at least those things, the things I cared about most, were going with me. Molly had to give her blue and white cheerleading outfit to one of the substitute cheerleaders, a girl named Lisa Halstead, who pretended to be sad and sympathetic, but you could tell it was phony; she couldn't wait to get home and try on that pleated skirt.

7. D     But I was talking about the age of houses. As my mother had said, this house was built in 1840. That makes it almost one hundred and forty years old. Our house in town was fifty years old.


chapter two

1. B     Molly has a boyfriend. Boys have *always* liked Molly.

2. B     How could boys *not* like a girl who looks the way she does? I've gotten used to Molly's looks because I've lived with her for thirteen years. But every now and then I glance at her and see her as if she were a stranger. ... I held my breath when I looked at her for that moment, because she looked so beautiful.

3. A     And beside the truck—no, actually in the truck, or at least with his head inside it, under the hood, was a man. ... "Forgive me. My hands are very dirty. My battery dies in this cold weather."

4. C     "You lived in my house?" I asked in surprise. He laughed again. "My dear Meg," he said, "*you* live in *my* house. My grandfather built that house. Actually, he built the one across the field, first. Then he built the other one, where you live."

5. C     "How did I know Meg for Margaret? Because Margaret was my wife's name; therefore, one of my favorite names, of course. And I called her Meg at times, though no one else did." ... I've rented the family houses whenever I come across someone who has reason to want to live in this wilderness. ... There were times, when I was young, when Margaret was with me, when I was tempted to leave, to take a job in a city, to make a lot of money, but—"... "Well, it was my grandfather's land, and my father's, before it was mine. ... I couldn't leave them behind." ... "The little room was mine," he said, "when I was a small boy. Sometime when your father isn't working there, go in and look in the closet. On the closet floor you'll find my name carved, if no one's refinished the floor.

6. B     "Will, then. Would you mind if I took your picture?" "My dear," he said, straightening his shoulders and buttoning the top button of his plaid shirt. "I would be honored." ... He sat right there, smoked his pipe, and talked, and I finished the whole roll of film, just shooting quickly as he gestured and smiled.

7. D     And deep, way deep inside me somewhere was something else that kept me warm on the walk home, even though the sun was going down and the wind was coming over the piles of snow on either side of the road, blowing stinging powder into my eyes. It was the fact that Will Banks had called me beautiful.

chapter three

1. A   "Well, he's happy there, Meg, and you can't argue with happiness. Problem is, there's a nephew in Boston who's going to make trouble for Will, I'm afraid." ... Will owns all this land, and the houses—they were left to him—but when he dies, they'll go to this nephew, his sister's son. It's valuable property. ... If he could do that, he'd have control over the property. He'd like to sell it to some people who want to build cottages for tourists, and to turn the big house into an inn."

2. D   Mom was in the kitchen, sitting by the fireplace stitching on her quilt. She was so excited about that quilt, and it *was* pretty, what she had done so far.

3. C   My father sat up straight in his chair very suddenly. "Meg," he said, "I have a *great* idea!"... "Let's build a darkroom!" he said.

4. C   In a way, it's fun having Molly sick, because she's home all the time, instead of off with her friends after school and on weekends. We've been doing things we hadn't done since we were little, like playing Monopoly.

5. A   It's also a nuisance, Molly being sick. She's grouchy, which isn't like her, because she's missing school.

6. B   Molly's flu consists mainly of nosebleeds. Mom says that's because she's an adolescent; Mom says that about almost everything.

7. C   Molly grabbed a piece of Kleenex and clutched her nose. From behind her Kleenex she said haughtily, "I don'd know what anyone is talking about either. Bud I'm going to camp, whether Meg does or nod."


chapter four

1. D   I know how Molly must have felt when Tierney McGoldrick asked her to go steady, which is what happened two weeks ago. ... Molly's nose had finally stopped bleeding at the beginning of March. ... The first pictures I developed were the ones of Will Banks.

2. C   I've hardly seen the sun at all because I've been in my darkroom. My darkroom! It's finished; it's all finished, and perfect.

3. A   He had bought it in Germany, he said, after the Second World War, when he was stationed there with the army. That surprised me.

4. A   She was on her bed, drawing pictures in her school notebook, when I went in and put the pictures on the wall. ... "Hey," said Molly suddenly, sitting up and looking

154

over at the wall. "Those are really *good*"

5. B    "Wouldn't it be great," she said slowly, "to be married to someone who felt that way about you, so that he smiled like that whenever he thought of you?"... To be honest, I find the whole idea of marriage intensely boring. But right at that moment I knew what Molly meant, and I could feel how important it was to her.

6. B    I could see the whiteness of it as I looked out the window. Beyond the corner of the barn, far across, beyond the pine trees, there was a light in the window of the empty house.

7. D    Molly was covered with blood. Her pillow, her hair, her face were all wet with it. ... "Meg," said my mother again. I nodded. "We have to take Molly to the hospital. Don't be scared. It's just another of those nosebleeds, but it's a bad one, as you can see."

## chapter five

1. D    I made two Easter eggs, one for Will and one for Molly.

2. C    And my parents were very strange about the whole thing. They were just like the doctors; they didn't even think of Molly as a person anymore. They talked about her as if she were a clinical specimen. ..."Stop it!" I said angrily. "Stop talking about it! If you want to talk about *Molly*, then talk about Molly, not her stupid medicine!

3. C    Why did I want to cry when he finished talking? I don't even know what ephemeral means. But something inside me welled up like hot fudge sauce—sweet, and warm, and so rich that you can't bear to have very much. It was because someone who was a real friend was having the exact same feelings I was having, about something that was more important to me than anything else.

4. B    "But I'm going to get it out of the attic. The camera, and four lenses, and a set of filters that go with it. I want you to use it."

5. C    "In return, I want you to teach me to use the darkroom. Let me borrow your little camera while you're using mine, and we'll set up a regular schedule for lessons."

6. A    "But I forgot to ask them something," he confessed. "What?" He looked in several other directions before he answered. He was embarrassed. Finally he explained, "I forgot to ask them if they're married."

7. D    "Would you take my picture when I get home? I want a really good one, to give Tierney for his birthday this summer." "Molly, I'll make you look like a movie star," I told her, and she giggled before she hung up.

chapter six

1. C    Will Banks is learning to use the darkroom, and he's fantastic. Ben and Maria have moved into the house, and they're terrific. Molly is home, and she's being thoroughly unbearable. … My parents don't say a word. That's different, too. … Dad doesn't lay down the law. … Dad gets tense and silent and goes off to his study without saying anything.

2. D    Worst of all, for Molly, her hair is falling out. That's because of the pills she has to take, my parents said. One of the side effects is that your hair falls out!

3. A    One night he brought a handful of pussy willows that he had found behind his house: the first ones of spring, and Molly was thrilled. It was the first time I'd seen her really happy about something for a long time.

4. B    It's not surprising that Will knows so much about so many things, because he has an incredible memory.

5. A    She was so interested in the baby. "When is the baby due?" asked Molly. "Do you mind my asking? I just love babies."

6. C    "You know," I said slowly to Will, as we walked back through the field together, "I wish I were more like Molly. I mean, I wish I knew the right things to say to people. Sometimes I seem to just *sit* there."

7. B    "I've never seen a fringed gentian." "It will be after you've moved back to town," he said. "It won't bloom until the end of September, maybe even October. But I want you to come back, so I can show it to you." … "It's important, Meg," Will said. "You promise?" Well, if it was important to him, all right. I would want to come back, anyway, and I didn't mind looking at his flower. Maybe he wanted to photograph it or something.


chapter seven

1. C    Finally Molly has stopped being a grouch. It was gradual, and I'm not even sure the change is a good one. She hasn't gone back to being the old Molly she was before she was sick. She isn't giggly, funny Molly anymore, full of smiles and ideas and silly enthusiasms … She's quieter, more serious, almost withdrawn.

2. D    Only a few things interest her now. She spends a lot of time with the flowers. … The other thing that still interests her is the baby. … She visits Maria often, and they talk and talk about the baby. Molly is helping Maria to make clothes for it.

156

3. B    Suddenly, very quietly, Molly got up, went over to Dad, and climbed onto his lap. He didn't say anything. He just put his book down, put his arms around her, held her, and watched the fire. She put her head on his shoulder like a sleepy two-year-old, and with one hand he stroked the fine, wispy, babylike hair she has left.

4. C    "I just got a phone call," he said, "from Clarice Callaway." ... "Right. And that means she means to be inquisitive. I can see you have Clarice figured out, Meg. Well, this time she's upset about Will renting the house. She says the whole village is up in arms which I assume is a Callaway exaggeration because there are hippies living in Will's house."

5. A    "Is it true that they walk around nude?" "Good grief, Dad. No, it isn't true, but even if it were, whose business would it be? ... I started to laugh. "Dad, of course not. They've put in peas and strawberries so far. ... "Is it true that they're planning to have that baby by themselves, in the house?" "Yes. But they've both been reading everything they can find about delivering a baby."

6. B    Ben went into the living room and took a box out of the closet. He brought it back to the kitchen table and set it down. ... And they were of Ben and Maria's wedding, for pete's sake. They were in a thick white leather album that said *Our Wedding* on the cover in gold letters.

7. D    He put his arm over my shoulders and said, "This is where we'll bury the baby, if it doesn't live." I couldn't believe it. I pushed his arm off me and said, "*What?*" ... "It's not going to die! What a horrible thing to say!"


chapter eight


1. C    But there she was, lying on her bed, grumbling about how awful she looks. I am so sick of hearing Molly talk about how she looks. Her face is too fat. Her hair is too thin. To hear her talk, you'd think she was really a mess, when the truth is that she's still a billion times prettier than I am, which is why I'm sick of listening to her.

2. D    Both of her legs were covered with dark red spots. It looked like a lot of mosquito bites, except that they weren't swollen. ... Things quieted after a few minutes, and then my father came down. His face was very drawn, very tired. "We have to take Molly back to the hospital," he told me abruptly.

3. C    "I will, too. I'm telling Mom." I started out of the room. "Don't you *dare*," Molly ordered. ... I went downstairs and told Mom that there was something wrong with Molly's legs. ... I heard Mom and Molly arguing. I heard my mother get my father

from the study. Then more arguing with Molly. … She was in her bathrobe and slippers, and she was sobbing. When they were by the front door, Molly saw me standing all alone in the living room. She turned to me, still crying, and said, "I hate you! I hate you!"

4. B    Molly was in the back seat, huddled in the corner, rubbing her eyes with the back of her hand. "Meg," she said, choking a little because she was trying to stop crying, "tell Ben and Maria not to have the baby until I get home!"

5. D    I took out the photographs of Maria. Will had seen them, of course, because we'd worked on them together. … He is fascinated by the technical aspects of photography: by the chemicals, and the inner workings of cameras. I don't care so much about those things. I care about the expressions on people's faces, the way the light falls onto them, and the way the shadows are in soft patterns and contrast. … Ben was much like Will, interested in the problems of exposure and film latitude.

6. A    "Meg," she said, "Ben and I were talking about something the other night, and we want you to think it over and talk about it with your parents. If you want to, and if they don't mind, we'd like you to photograph the birth of the baby."

7. D    I knew then what they hadn't wanted to tell me, and they knew that I knew, that Molly wouldn't be coming home again, that Molly was going to die.


chapter nine

1. B    Sometimes they are darker dreams of the same field. I am the one, in this darker dream, who has run faster; I have reached some misty destination, a dark and empty house, where I stand waiting for her, watching her from a window as she runs. But the flowers in the field have begun to turn brown, as if summer is ending too soon, and Molly is stumbling; it is she who is calling to me, "Meg, wait! Wait! I can't make it, Meg!" And there is no way I can help her.

2. B    "Your dreams come out of what is real, you know. It helps, some, to think about what they mean. That you and Molly are going to be separated, even though you don't want to be. That you want to know why, why life sometimes ends too soon, but no one can answer that."

3. C    "Then isn't there *still* a chance?" He shook his head slowly. "Meg, we can hope for it. We *do* hope for it. Bur the doctors say there isn't, now. The medicines aren't working for Molly now."

4. A    I'm afraid to see my own sister, and grateful that they don't ask me to come.

5. C    When she's at home, my mother stitches on the quilt and talks about the past.

158

6. D    "… You were very serious and solemn, pulling yourself to your feet, trying to walk across the grass alone."

7. B    "But you know, Meg," Mom said, smoothing the quilt with her fingers, "when the big, difficult things come, people like Molly and me aren't ready for them. We're so accustomed to laughing. It's harder for us when the time comes that we can't laugh."

chapter ten

1. C    Ben had a stethoscope, and he listened through Maria's abdomen to the baby. I could see that he experienced the same thing; when he picked up the simple instrument, he felt in control of things again.

2. B    I held him for a moment in the open front doorway of the house. The sun was golden now, and the dew was already evaporating from the tall grass and flowers in the field. The birds were awake. "Listen," I whispered to the baby, "the birds are singing to you." But he was asleep, his fingers relaxed and warm against my chest. I sat in the rocking chair and moved slowly back and forth, trying with the soft, steady rhythm of the chair to make up for the abrupt and agonizing journey he had just had.

3. A    "Yes? Everything okay? I'm almost through." "Everything's fine. He says to tell you he's happy." Ben came out of the room where Maria was, wiping his hands on a towel. He leaned over me, looked down at the baby, and grinned. "He says he's happy? I *told* you he'd tell us his name." … And they did name him Happy. Happy William Abbott-Brady.

4. B    Suddenly I wanted to be the one to tell Molly. I had been afraid to see Molly, and now I wasn't. There isn't any way to explain that. The only thing that had happened was that I had watched Maria give birth to Happy, and for some reason that made a difference.

5. B    Dad sighed. "Well, I'm not sure I do either. But listen, Meg—when you think of Molly, how do you think of her?" I was quiet for a minute, thinking. "I guess mostly I think of how she used to laugh."

6. D    "She'll look like a stranger to you, at first. And it'll be scary. But she can hear you, Meg. Talk to her. And you'll realize that underneath all that stuff, the tubes and needles and medicines, our Molly is still there. You have to remember that. It makes it easier. … "One more thing. Remember, too, that Molly's not in any pain, and she's not scared. It's only you and I and Mom, now, who are hurting and frightened."

7. D    Two weeks later she was gone. She just closed her eyes one afternoon and

didn't ever open them again. Mom and Dad brought the pussy willows back for me to keep.

## chapter eleven

1. C    I went back to the darkroom where I was trying to pack. I was going to have a darkroom in town; Dad had already hired a couple of his students to build the shelves and do the plumbing and wiring in what had been a maid's room, many years ago, on the third floor of the house there.

2. D    There was a box marked "Quilt." Two nights before, my mother had snapped off a thread, looked at the quilt in surprise, and said, "I think it's finished. How can it be finished?" … "Lydia! Meg! The book is *finished!* It only needs rearranging! I didn't realize it until now!" … I sealed the packing boxes with tape, wrote "Darkroom" on them, and carried them to a corner of the kitchen. … And Will Banks had almost completed work on the darkroom that he was building for himself, in what had been a pantry of his little house.

3. B    "It's Martin Huntington!" Ben was practically doubled up, laughing. … "How do you know *him?*" I asked. "He's been a junior partner in my father's law firm for years," laughed Ben.

4. A    "I'd like to buy this house from Will, if my dad will lend me the money for a down payment."

5. B    There was something of Molly in my face. It startled me, seeing it. The line that defined my face, the line that separated the darkness of the trees from the light that curved into my forehead and cheek was the same line that had once identified Molly by its shape. The way I held my shoulders was the way she had held hers.

6. C    "They're my favorite flower," he told me, "I suppose because they're the last of the season. And because they grow here all alone, not caring whether anyone sees them or not."

7. A    I understood then what Ben had told me once, about knowing and accepting that bad things will happen, because I understood, watching him, that someday Will would be gone from me too.

160